GREAT GROUND-BEEF RECIPES

BY FAMILY CIRCLE FOOD STAFF

WITH ANNE M. FLETCHER

DRAWINGS BY GRAMBS MILLER

A New York Times Company Publication NYT

CONTENTS

DEAR HOMEMAKER:

A meat-counter bargain-best—that's ground beef. And for many reasons: It's all meat with no waste, so you can depend on getting your money's worth from what you buy. It's a versatile meat, as much at home on a party table as on a back-yard grill. And what's best, it's all beef, and just about everybody likes it.

Proudly we present this cookbook of ground-beef favorites—from hamburgers in a bun to gourmet treasures—all carefully tested by FAMILY CIRCLE'S Food Staff. We hope you will keep this book in a handy spot in your kitchen and use it whenever you're thinking, "How about hamburger!"

1 REGULAR GROUND BEEF

2 GROUND CHUCK

3 GROUND ROUND

4 MEAT-LOAF MIXTURES

Ground beef and pork

Ground beef, pork, and veal

Meat loaf

CHAPTER 1

WHAT WOULD WE DO WITHOUT

GROUND BEEF!

Many a supermarket builds its reputation around ground beef, for it is one of its most popular meats. It is always ground fresh each day—often several times, when stores are busiest—so whether you pick up a package labeled ground regular, chuck, round, or meat-loaf mixture, all pictured here, you can be sure it is a today's pack of quality meat your supermarket is proud to offer. The next pages describe each of these good meat buys.

HOW TO BUY GROUND BEEF

Your supermarket displays are bountiful, and, depending on the cut of beef used, the cost will vary. Here are descriptions of the choices pictured on page 6, with reasons why their price tags vary.

1

REGULAR GROUND BEEF—Freshly ground beef made from lean meat and fat as cut from a whole side of beef. You can recognize it by its speckled pink and white color, and its good beef flavor makes it an all-round favorite for hamburger patties, casseroles, meat loaves, and sauces. To speed shopping, this popular budget-tagged grind is wrapped in 1-, 2-, and 3-pound packs, often with a "special" price on the 3-pounders.

2

GROUND CHUCK—Its name describes it, for only flavorful chuck is used. Its pink meatiness has just enough fat to give it juicy goodness. Sold mostly in about-1-pound packages, this grind, too, is a perfect choice for all-round hamburger needs.

3

GROUND ROUND—This is de luxe "hamburger" with a price tag to match its quality. Your supermarket grinds it from lean beef round, which gives it its rich red color. Like ground chuck, it is sold mostly in about-1-pound packs, or you can ask your meatman to grind any amount you want to your order.

4

MEAT-LOAF MIXTURES—Most meat-loaf recipes in this book call for plain ground beef, so choose regular, chuck, or round. When a recipe suggests a mixture such as ground beef and pork or ground beef, pork, and veal, ask your meatman to grind it to your order, or pick up a package packed in any of these ways: (1) Each meat ground separately and displayed in a single package as ground beef and pork, or ground beef, pork, and veal; (2) Ground meats already blended and labeled MEAT-LOAF.

The most-popular-weight package is about 2 pounds—1½

pounds ground beef to ½ pound ground pork for beef-pork mix and 1¼ pounds ground beef to 6 ounces each ground pork and veal for the three-meat combination. Either choice is enough to make a 6-to-8-serving meat loaf.

ODD WEIGHTS NEEDN'T CONFUSE YOU

In this book all recipes call for an even weight of 1 pound or more of ground beef or meat-loaf mixture. In shopping for the meat you need, you are likely to find packages labeled slightly under or over these even weights. And for a very good reason. Meatmen are good guessers of the weights needed, so they watch the meat as it comes from the grinder, and divide it into mounds. With no further handling, each mound is weighed automatically and marked with its exact ounce weight. Buy the weight nearest to the amount you need for your recipe, for any slightly over or under ounces will make no difference.

YOUR MEATMAN EXPLAINS "BLOOM"

If you open a package of rich red ground beef only to find the meat darker on the inside, you needn't be concerned about its freshness. This change in color—"bloom" your meatman calls it—is natural because much of the air has been closed out of the package. Leave the meat unwrapped in the refrigerator for a short time and its bright color will "bloom" again.

STORE GROUND BEEF THESE WAYS

To use the same day or the next: Tear off a corner of the transparent covering to expose the meat to the air, or remove wrapper entirely and rewrap meat loosely in waxed paper or foil. Store in the meat-keeper or coldest part of your refrigerator.

To freeze ground beef for patties: Shape meat lightly into patties, preferably plain, as seasoning flavors tend to build up during freezing. Wrap patties in freezer paper, foil, or transparent wrap or bags and seal tightly. For single servings, wrap each patty separately. For family serving, stack three, four, or more patties with double-thick waxed paper or foil between, then wrap and seal. Come cooking time patties are easy to separate.

Want a bagful for a cookout or party? Arrange patties, without touching, on a cooky sheet, then fast-freeze in the coldest part of the freezer. When frozen, pile into a transparent bag and seal. You can take out as many as you need at a time, reseal the bag, and return the rest to the freezer. Be sure to label all packages with the contents and the date, and plan to use within four months.

YOUR EASY STEPS TO PERFECT HAMBURGERS

☐ Follow a tip your supermarket uses and handle ground beef as little as possible, for the gentler your touch, the juicier and tenderer the burger.

☐ Season each 1 pound of ground beef with 1 teaspoon salt and ⅛ teaspoon pepper. Nothing more is really needed but for variety, you may want to add other seasonings as many of our recipes suggest.

☐ Use a mixing fork to blend in seasonings. Even an egg will mix in quickly without beating first.

☐ Making four or six patties? Pat out seasoned meat about 1 inch thick, cut into even mounds, and shape lightly with your hands. For small appetites, or for children, you may prefer to divide each mound again, then shape it into a thinner patty.

HOW TO COOK BURGERS JUST RIGHT

☐ To pan-fry: Heat a heavy frying pan until sizzling hot. (A few drops of water sprinkled into the pan should bounce about.) For plain burgers, there's no need to add any fat,

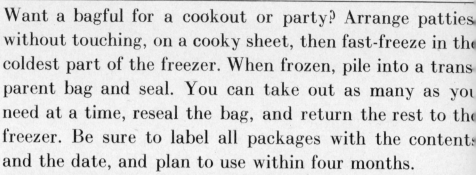

but you can sprinkle the pan lightly with salt, if you wish, to prevent sticking. For burgers seasoned with extras such as egg, bread crumbs, or rolled oats, you may need to add a little butter or margarine or salad oil. Lay patties in hot pan and lower heat to medium. Cook 1-inch-thick patties 8 minutes on each side for medium. For ½-inch-thick patties, allow 4 minutes on each side for medium.

□ To broil: Remove broiler pan, then turn heat to BROIL. Lay patties, without touching, on rack in pan, then slide back into broiler about 4 inches from heat. Broil 1-inch-thick patties 6 minutes on each side for medium. Since thin patties—those ½ inch thick—will cook through before they brown on the outside, it is better, if your choice is medium-rare, to pan-fry them.

□ Turn the meat just once, for flipping it over and over tends to dry it. Juices oozing out around edges are your clue for turning.

□ Undercook a hamburger if it has to stand. Each patty has enough heat in it to continue some cooking, and you can reheat it without overcooking.

IF PATTIES HAVE BEEN FROZEN

Cooking patties while frozen is all right, but it takes slightly longer and the meat is likely to turn out well-done. As all recipes here are based on freshly ground beef, we prefer to thaw the meat first this way: Remove patties from the freezer a day ahead and store in their sealed wrapper in the refrigerator. If time is short and you must cook them frozen, follow these tips:

□ To pan-fry: Brown each side quickly in a hot frying pan, then lower heat and cook, turning two or three times, until meat is done as you like it.

□ To broil: Set the broiler pan farther from the heat than when cooking fresh patties and turn several times.

Ground beef moves right into the company spot when turned into Burger-tomato Towers *(recipe on page 19)*. Meat patties, tomatoes, and mushrooms are all skillet-grilled, then stacked to make this inviting platter

CHAPTER 2
ALL THE WORLD LOVES A
HAMBURGER

And what homemaker isn't happy about that? It's a burger-in-a-bun piled high with trimmings when hungry teens get together. It's a quick "steak" meat when dinner must be ready fast. It's hearty family fare when your budget's in a squeeze, and an easy-to-dress-up star when company comes.

The recipes in this chapter provide dozens of ways to fix sandwich patties—from those that are just plain good to others fancied up with all kinds of extras. . . . Looking for a dinner idea? Stop here, too, for there are ever so many suggestions for varying the seasoning, shape, or topping; serving them stuffed or sauced, broiled or skillet-cooked, as miniatures or jumbos.

Yes, the whole world loves a hamburger—just about any time, any way—and is it any wonder?

Meat patties...
the quick
"steak" meal

DILL ROLLS WITH MUSHROOM SAUCE

Makes 6 servings

1½ pounds ground beef
  1 egg
  1 cup soft bread crumbs (2 slices)
  ½ cup water
  1 teaspoon dry mustard
1½ teaspoons salt
  2 dill pickles
  1 tablespoon salad oil
  1 can condensed cream of mushroom soup
  ¼ cup dill-pickle juice

1. Mix ground beef lightly with egg, bread crumbs, water, mustard, and salt until well-blended; divide into 12 equal portions.
2. Cut each dill pickle into 6 strips; shape a portion of meat around each strip to cover completely.
3. Pan-fry over medium heat in salad oil just until brown; pour off all drippings. Blend mushroom soup and pickle juice; pour over rolls; cover.
4. Simmer, basting several times, 20 minutes.

COUNTRY BURGERS

Makes 4 servings

  1 pound ground beef
  1 teaspoon dry mustard
  ½ teaspoon salt
  ⅛ teaspoon pepper
  2 tablespoons finely chopped green pepper
  ½ cup milk
  1 tablespoon butter or margarine
  1 can condensed cream of mushroom soup

1. Mix ground beef lightly with mustard, salt, pepper, green pepper, and milk; shape into 4 patties about 1 inch thick.
2. Pan-fry over medium heat in butter or margarine just until brown on both sides. Spoon soup over; stir lightly to blend with drippings, being careful not to break patties; cover.
3. Simmer, basting patties often, 10 to 15 minutes.

DINNER BEEF PATTIES
(Pictured at right)

Makes 4 servings

  1 large Bermuda onion
  2 tablespoons butter or margarine
  ¼ cup water
  3 tablespoons brown sugar
    Paprika
  2 pounds ground beef
  2 teaspoons salt
    Chili Glaze (*recipe follows*)

1. Peel onion and cut crosswise into 4 thick slices. Saute in butter or margarine until lightly browned on bottom; turn carefully; add water and brown sugar; cover. Simmer 10 minutes, or just until tender; sprinkle with paprika. Keep hot while fixing and cooking meat.
2. Mix ground beef lightly with salt; shape into 4 large and 4 medium-size patties about 1 inch thick.
3. Pan-fry over medium heat 8 minutes; turn; cook 5 minutes longer. Spoon CHILI GLAZE over; continue cooking, basting with glaze in pan, 3 minutes longer for medium, or until meat is done as you like it.
4. Put one each large and medium-size patty together with a Bermuda-onion slice between, as pictured, on a serving plate. Top with any remaining sauce from pan.
CHILI GLAZE—Combine ½ cup chili sauce with ½ cup water, 1 tablespoon corn syrup, and 1 tablespoon Worcestershire sauce in a 2-cup measure. Makes about 1 cup.

Dinner Beef Patties *(recipe at left)* look fancy for so little effort. To make, glaze large and small burgers, sandwich with a paprika-onion slice, and serve with a baked potato, steamed broccoli, and a pickled pepper

15

PEPPER STEAKETTES

Makes 6 servings

- 1 envelope instant beef broth
  OR: 1 beef-flavor bouillon cube
- ¼ cup boiling water
- 2 pounds ground beef
- 1 tablespoon Worcestershire sauce
- 2 teaspoons soy sauce
- ¼ teaspoon salt
  Freshly ground black pepper

1. Dissolve instant beef broth or bouillon cube in boiling water; stir lightly into ground beef with Worcestershire sauce, soy sauce, and salt. Shape into 6 patties about 1 inch thick.
2. Sprinkle each side generously with pepper, pressing it into meat lightly with hands.
3. Pan-fry over medium heat 8 minutes on each side for medium, or until meat is done as you like it.

BEEF-VEGETABLE PATTIES

Makes 6 servings

- 1½ pounds ground beef
- 1 small onion, grated
- 1 cup finely chopped peeled cooked potatoes
- ½ cup finely chopped peeled cooked beets
- 2 tablespoons bottled hamburger relish
- 1 egg
- ⅓ cup evaporated milk
- 1½ teaspoons salt
- ⅛ teaspoon pepper
- 3 tablespoons butter or margarine

1. Mix ground beef lightly with onion, potatoes, beets, relish, egg, evaporated milk, salt, and pepper until well-blended; shape into 6 patties about 1 inch thick.
2. Pan-fry over medium heat in butter or margarine 8 minutes on each side for medium, or until meat is done as you like it.

Cooksaver tip:

When company's coming, dress up burger plates these simple ways: Stuffed olives and pickled onions on wooden picks, pepper relish in cucumber cups, cherry tomatoes sauteed in butter

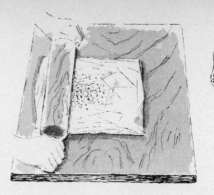

Cooksaver tip:

No pepper grinder? Crush peppercorns like this: Place them in a transparent bag and pound with a rolling pin just enough to crack the little balls

RANCH BREAKFAST BURGERS

Makes 6 servings

- 2 pounds ground beef
- 2 teaspoons salt
- 1 teaspoon monosodium glutamate (MSG)
- ⅛ teaspoon pepper
- 2½ cups prepared instant mashed potatoes
- 6 tablespoons catsup

1. Mix ground beef lightly with salt, MSG, and pepper; shape into 12 patties about ½ inch thick.
2. Pan-fry over medium heat 4 minutes on each side for medium, or until meat is done as you like it.
3. Spoon potatoes onto 6 heated serving plates; top each with 2 meat patties put together, sandwich style, with a dollup of catsup.

BACON-CHEESE SURPRISES

Makes 4 servings

- 1½ pounds ground beef
- 4 slices crisp diced bacon
- ½ cup grated Cheddar cheese
- 1 teaspoon salt
- ⅛ teaspoon pepper
  Bacon drippings

1. Mix ground beef lightly with bacon, cheese, salt, and pepper; shape into 4 patties about 1 inch thick.
2. Pan-fry over medium heat in bacon drippings 8 minutes on each side for medium, or until meat is done as you like it.

STUFFED BURGERS

Makes 4 servings

    ½ cup grated Cheddar cheese
    ½ cup soft bread crumbs (1 slice)
    2 tablespoons chopped parsley
    2 tablespoons milk
    1½ pounds ground beef
    1 small onion, grated
    2 teaspoons Worcestershire sauce
    1½ teaspoons salt

1. Combine cheese, bread crumbs, parsley, and milk; form lightly into 4 balls.
2. Mix ground beef lightly with onion, Worcestershire sauce, and salt; divide into quarters and shape each around a stuffing ball, then flatten lightly with palm of hand to make a patty about 1 inch thick.
3. Pan-fry over medium heat 8 minutes on each side for medium, or until meat is done as you like it.

BARBECUED SKILLET BURGERS

Makes 4 servings

Hamburgers
    1 pound ground beef
    1 teaspoon salt
    ½ teaspoon chili powder
    ⅛ teaspoon pepper
    1 small onion, grated
    1 tablespoon butter or margarine
Barbecue Sauce
    ½ cup catsup
    ½ cup water
    ¼ cup chili sauce
    1 tablespoon brown sugar
    1 tablespoon Worcestershire sauce
    1 teaspoon lemon juice
    ¼ teaspoon chili powder
    ¼ teaspoon salt

1. Make hamburgers: Mix ground beef lightly with salt, chili powder, pepper, and onion. Shape into 4 patties about 1 inch thick.
2. Pan-fry over medium heat in butter or margarine just until brown on both sides; remove; pour off all drippings.
3. Make barbecue sauce: Combine all ingredients in same frying pan; heat to boiling, then simmer 3 minutes to blend flavors.
4. Return hamburgers to sauce; cover. Simmer 5 to 10 minutes.

DIXIE HAMBURGERS

Makes 4 servings

    3 medium-size onions, peeled and sliced
    1 large green pepper, halved, seeded, and sliced
    3 tablespoons salad oil
    1 pound ground beef
    1½ teaspoons salt
    ¼ teaspoon pepper
    1 can (8 ounces) tomato sauce with mushrooms
    ⅛ teaspoon thyme

1. Saute onions and green pepper in salad oil just until soft; remove.
2. Mix ground beef lightly with ½ teaspoon of the salt and pepper; shape into 4 patties about 1 inch thick.
3. Pan-fry over medium heat just until brown on both sides; return onions and green pepper to pan.
4. Pour tomato sauce over; stir in thyme and remaining 1 teaspoon salt; cover.
5. Simmer, basting several times, 15 minutes.

BEEF-AND-GRAVY BURGERS

Makes 4 servings

    1½ pounds ground beef
    1 egg
    ½ cup soft bread crumbs (1 slice)
    ⅓ cup evaporated milk
    2 tablespoons minced onion
    1½ teaspoons salt
    ¼ teaspoon pepper
    1 tablespoon salad oil
    1 can condensed cream of chicken soup
    ½ cup apple juice
    2 teaspoons paprika
    ½ cup dairy sour cream
    2 teaspoons flour

1. Mix ground beef lightly with egg, bread crumbs, evaporated milk, onion, salt, and pepper until well-blended; shape into 8 patties about ¾ inch thick.
2. Pan-fry over medium heat in salad oil until brown on both sides; remove, then pour off all drippings. Stir soup, apple juice, and paprika into pan; return patties; cover.
3. Simmer, basting often, 20 minutes. Mix sour cream with flour; stir in a few tablespoons of the hot sauce, then blend all back into pan. Heat, stirring constantly, 1 minute.

SOUR-CREAM BURGERS

Makes 4 servings

1 pound ground beef
1 can (8 ounces) tomato sauce
½ cup soft bread crumbs (1 slice)
1 egg
1 tablespoon Worcestershire sauce
1 small onion, grated
½ teaspoon salt
1 tablespoon butter or margarine
1 envelope sour-cream sauce mix
  Milk

1. Mix ground beef lightly with ¼ cup of the tomato sauce, bread crumbs, egg, Worcestershire sauce, onion, and salt until well-blended; shape into 4 patties about 1 inch thick.
2. Pan-fry over medium heat in butter or margarine just until brown on both sides.
3. Blend sour-cream sauce mix with milk, following label directions; stir in remaining tomato sauce; pour over patties; cover.
4. Simmer, basting several times, 25 minutes.

BEEF BAVARIAN

Makes 6 servings

1½ pounds ground beef
2 eggs
1 teaspoon salt
½ teaspoon onion salt
1 teaspoon grated lemon rind
¼ cup nonfat dry milk powder
¼ cup water
¼ cup fine dry bread crumbs
1 tablespoon butter or margarine
1 envelope brown gravy mix
3 tablespoons lemon juice
¼ cup firmly packed brown sugar
¼ teaspoon ginger
3 whole cloves

1. Mix ground beef lightly with eggs, plain and onion salts, lemon rind, dry milk, water, and bread crumbs until well-blended; shape into 6 patties about 1 inch thick.
2. Pan-fry over medium heat in butter or margarine just until brown on both sides.
3. Prepare gravy mix, following label directions; stir in lemon juice, brown sugar, and spices. Pour over patties; cover.
4. Simmer, basting several times, 30 minutes. Remove cloves before serving.

JUMBOS

Makes 4 servings

1½ pounds ground beef
¼ cup quick-cooking rolled oats
⅓ cup evaporated milk
1 teaspoon salt
⅛ teaspoon pepper
2 teaspoons Worcestershire sauce
1 teaspoon prepared mustard
½ medium-size green pepper, sliced
1 can condensed onion soup
½ cup chili sauce

1. Mix ground beef lightly with rolled oats, evaporated milk, salt, pepper, and Worcestershire sauce until well-blended; shape into 4 patties about 1 inch thick.
2. Pan-fry over medium heat just until brown on both sides; spread each with mustard. Stir in green pepper, soup, and chili sauce; cover.
3. Simmer, basting patties often, 20 minutes.

Hot sandwiches... all ways, always a hit

CITY BURGERS

Makes 4 servings

1 pound ground beef
1 medium-size onion, grated
1 teaspoon salt
½ teaspoon marjoram
⅛ teaspoon pepper
8 slices toast, buttered
2 tablespoons butter or margarine
1 tablespoon bottled steak sauce

1. Mix ground beef lightly with onion, salt, marjoram, and pepper; spread evenly on toast slices to edges.
2. Broil, 4 inches from heat, 3 to 5 minutes, or until meat is done as you like it. Heat butter or margarine with steak sauce until butter melts; spoon over meat.

18

BURGER-TOMATO TOWERS

(Pictured on page 12)

Makes 6 servings

2 pounds ground beef
1 teaspoon seasoned salt
2 large tomatoes
1 can (3 or 4 ounces) mushroom caps
3 tablespoons butter or margarine
3 split hamburger buns, toasted

1. Mix ground beef lightly with seasoned salt; shape into 6 patties about 1 inch thick.
2. Pan-fry over medium heat 8 minutes on each side for medium, or until meat is done as you like it.
3. While meat cooks, remove stem ends from tomatoes; cut each tomato crosswise into 3 thick slices. Drain mushrooms, saving liquid for next step. Saute tomato slices and mushroom caps in butter or margarine in a second large frying pan, turning tomatoes once, just until heated through.
4. Place a meat patty on each bun half on a heated serving platter. Heat liquid from mushrooms in same frying pan; spoon over patties. Top each with a tomato slice; garnish with mushroom caps and parsley, if you wish. (Our picture shows mushroom caps threaded on wooden picks, kebab style.)

TEXAS TOMATO BURGERS

Makes 4 servings

1 pound ground beef
½ cup coarsely chopped pecans
1 teaspoon salt
  Dash of ground allspice
4 split hamburger buns, toasted and buttered
2 tablespoons chopped parsley
4 thick slices tomato
4 small sweet pickles

1. Mix ground beef lightly with pecans, salt, and allspice; shape into 4 patties about 1 inch thick.
2. Pan-fry over medium heat 8 minutes on each side for medium, or until meat is done as you like it.
3. Sprinkle buttered rolls with parsley; place a meat patty and tomato slice in each. Hold together with a wooden pick topped with a pickle.

Cooksaver tip:

Another idea: Omit tomato in sandwich; top with a gay kebab of cherry tomatoes

JUST-PLAIN-GOOD BURGERS

Makes 4 servings

1 pound ground beef
1 small onion, grated
1 teaspoon salt
½ teaspoon monosodium glutamate (MSG)
⅛ teaspoon pepper
4 split hamburger buns, buttered and toasted

1. Mix ground beef lightly with seasonings; shape into 4 patties about 1 inch thick.
2. Pan-fry over medium heat 8 minutes on each side for medium, or broil, 4 inches from heat, 6 minutes on each side for medium, or until meat is done as you like it.
3. Put together, sandwich style, with toasted buns.

Variations:

TIVOLI BURGERS—Prepare mixture for JUST-PLAIN-GOOD BURGERS; broil, following directions above. Mix ¼ cup mashed blue cheese, 1 tablespoon mayonnaise or salad dressing, and ½ teaspoon soy sauce; spread on patties. Return to broiler until cheese is bubbly. Serve, sandwich style, in toasted buns.
HERBED BURGERS—Prepare mixture for JUST-PLAIN-GOOD BURGERS, adding ½ teaspoon mixed salad herbs. Pan-fry or broil, following directions above. Cream 1 tablespoon butter or margarine with 1 teaspoon finely cut chives; spread over hot patties. Serve, sandwich style, in toasted buns.
CHILI-CHEESE BURGERS—Prepare mixture for JUST-PLAIN-GOOD BURGERS, adding ½ cup diced Muenster cheese and ½ teaspoon chili powder. Pan-fry or broil, following directions above. Serve, sandwich style, in toasted buns.

CRUNCHY CHEESEBURGERS

Makes 6 servings

1 pound ground beef
½ cup wheat-flakes cereal
1 cup grated sharp Cheddar cheese (4 ounces)
½ cup chopped walnuts
½ teaspoon seasoned salt
½ cup water
12 slices rye bread, toasted and buttered

1. Mix ground beef lightly with wheat-flakes cereal, cheese, walnuts, seasoned salt, and water; shape into 6 patties about ½ inch thick.
2. Broil, 3 inches from heat, 4 minutes on each side for medium, or until meat is done as you like it. Put together, sandwich style, with toasted bread.

BRONCOS

Makes 6 servings

- 1 pound ground beef
- 1 teaspoon salt
- ⅛ teaspoon pepper
- Bacon drippings
- ⅔ cup bottled barbecue sauce
- 6 split frankfurter rolls, toasted and buttered

1. Mix ground beef lightly with salt and pepper; shape into 6 sausagelike rolls.
2. Pan-fry over medium heat in bacon drippings, turning often, 10 minutes; pour barbecue sauce over.
3. Simmer, basting meat once or twice, 5 minutes, or until lightly glazed.
4. Serve in toasted frankfurter rolls; spoon any remaining sauce over.

LUNCHEON CHEESE DREAMS

Makes 6 servings

- 1½ pounds ground beef
- 1½ teaspoons salt
- ⅛ teaspoon pepper
- 6 tomato slices
- 3 slices bacon, halved
- 6 slices French bread
- 6 slices process American cheese, halved diagonally
- Oregano

1. Mix ground beef lightly with salt and pepper; shape into 6 patties about 1 inch thick.
2. Broil, 4 inches from heat, 6 minutes; turn; broil 3 minutes. Top each with a tomato and bacon slice; broil 3 minutes longer for medium, or until meat is done as you like it and bacon is crisp.
3. Place bread slices on broiler rack with patties; toast; turn. Top each with 2 cheese triangles; sprinkle with oregano. Toast just until cheese melts slightly. Top each with a tomato-bacon patty.

HAMBURGER CLUBS

(Pictured at right)

Makes 6 servings

- 2 pounds ground beef
- 2 teaspoons bottled steak sauce
- 2 packages (9 ounces each) frozen cut green beans
- 1 can condensed cream of mushroom soup
- 12 slices bacon (about ½ pound)
- 6 split hamburger buns, buttered
- 3 slices mozzarella or pizza cheese, cut into 12 strips
- 1 can (about 3 ounces) French-fried onion rings

1. Mix ground beef lightly with steak sauce; shape into 6 patties about 1 inch thick.
2. Cook green beans, following label directions; drain. Stir in soup; heat, stirring carefully so as not to break beans, just until bubbly.
3. While beans cook, place meat patties on one side of rack in broiler pan and bacon on the other. Broil, 4 inches from heat and without turning bacon, 5 minutes, or just until bacon starts to crisp; remove. Continue broiling patties 1 minute; turn; broil 5 minutes longer for medium, or until meat is done as you like it.
4. Place each patty on a buttered bun half; arrange cheese strips over each to form an X. Spoon hot green-bean mixture onto remaining bun halves, dividing evenly; crisscross bacon, uncrisped side up, over top.
5. Broil 1 minute longer, or just until cheese melts and bacon is crisp. Garnish meat patties with French-fried onion rings. (To crisp, heat in shallow pan in oven.)

Cooksaver tip:

To chop parsley fast, place it in a cup and snip away with scissors, or bunch a handful of tufts on a board and use a French knife. Same tricks work equally well with water cress or fresh herbs

Dinner patties... each with a company twist

ENGLISH PUB BEEF WITH MUSTARD SAUCE

Makes 4 servings

1½ pounds ground beef
1½ teaspoons salt
⅛ teaspoon pepper
¼ cup dry mustard
¼ cup milk
1½ teaspoons bottled steak sauce
1 tablespoon chili sauce

1. Mix ground beef lightly with salt and pepper; shape into 4 patties about 1 inch thick.
2. Broil, 4 inches from heat, 6 minutes on each side for medium, or until meat is done as you like it.
3. While meat cooks, blend mustard with milk to make a paste; stir in steak and chili sauces. Cook, stirring constantly, just until sauce thickens.
4. Serve sauce warm as a dip with meat. It's **hot,** so dip sparingly.

LITTLE "STEAKS" ORIENTAL

Makes 4 servings

1 pound ground beef
1 teaspoon salt
4 teaspoons soy sauce
1 teaspoon grated lemon rind
¼ teaspoon ground ginger
1 tablespoon lemon juice

1. Mix ground beef lightly with salt, 1 teaspoon of the soy sauce, lemon rind, and ginger; shape into 4 patties about 1 inch thick.
2. Mix remaining 3 teaspoons soy sauce with lemon juice; brush part over patties.
3. Broil, 4 inches from heat, basting with remaining soy mixture, 6 minutes on each side for medium, or until meat is done as you like it.

KING BURGERS

Makes 4 servings

1½ pounds ground beef
1½ teaspoons salt
¼ teaspoon pepper
    Instant mashed potatoes
1 egg
1 can (1 pound) cling peach halves, drained
2 tablespoons melted butter or margarine
¼ cup pickle relish

1. Mix ground beef lightly with salt and pepper; shape into 4 patties about 1 inch thick.
2. Prepare 4 servings of instant mashed potatoes, following label directions; beat in egg until well-blended.
3. Spoon into 4 mounds in one end of a greased shallow baking pan; place drained peach halves, cut sides up, at other end. Brush all with melted butter or margarine. Set aside for Step 5.
4. Broil patties, 4 inches from heat, 6 minutes on each side for medium, or until meat is done as you like it.
5. Broil potatoes and peaches along with meat, 3 to 5 minutes, or until tips of potatoes turn golden.
6. Top each burger with a mashed-potato mound; garnish plate with a peach half filled with pickle relish.

POCKET BEEFBURGERS

Makes 4 servings

1 pound ground beef
1 tablespoon Worcestershire sauce
½ teaspoon salt
⅛ teaspoon pepper
    Cheddar Filling *(recipe follows)*
    Scotch Filling *(recipe follows)*

1. Mix ground beef lightly with Worcestershire sauce, salt, and pepper. Pat into a square, 8x8, on a sheet of waxed paper; cut in half lengthwise, then crosswise to make 4 even-size blocks.
2. Spoon your choice of filling, dividing evenly, on each block; fold over, pressing edges together.
3. Broil, 4 inches from heat, 6 minutes on each side for medium, or until meat is done as you like it.

CHEDDAR FILLING: Mix 1 cup grated Cheddar cheese (4 ounces) with ¼ cup chili sauce.

SCOTCH FILLING: Mix ½ cup diced fresh tomato with 1 tablespoon minced onion and ½ teaspoon salt.

BELMONT PATTY-STEAKS

Makes 4 servings

1½ pounds ground beef
2 tablespoons finely chopped green pepper
2 tablespoons finely cut chives
2 tablespoons finely chopped parsley
1 teaspoon salt
½ teaspoon paprika
⅛ teaspoon pepper
2 tablespoons flour
Salad oil
4 tablespoons (½ stick) butter or margarine
½ cup chili sauce
¼ cup orange juice
1 teaspoon sugar
1 tablespoon lemon juice
1 teaspoon prepared mustard
5 drops red-pepper seasoning

1. Mix ground beef lightly with green pepper, chives, parsley, salt, paprika, and pepper until well-blended; shape into 4 patties about 1 inch thick. Dust with flour, then brush each with salad oil.
2. Broil, 4 inches from heat, 6 minutes on each side for medium, or until meat is done as you like it.
3. While meat cooks, melt butter or margarine in a small saucepan; stir in remaining ingredients; heat just to boiling.
4. Place meat patties on a heated serving platter; pour hot sauce over.

GOOBER BURGERS

Makes 4 servings

1 pound ground beef
1 small onion, grated
¼ cup crunchy-style peanut butter
½ teaspoon seasoned salt
⅛ teaspoon seasoned pepper

1. Mix ground beef lightly with onion, peanut butter, and seasoned salt and pepper until well-blended; shape into 4 patties about 1 inch thick.
2. Pan-fry over medium heat 8 minutes on each side for medium, or until meat is done as you like it.
3. Serve with mashed sweet potatoes, buttered rice, or paprika-topped hominy grits, and watermelon pickle or sweet-pepper relish, if you wish.

YANKEE HAMBURGERS

Makes 4 servings

¼ cup milk
½ cup soft bread crumbs (1 slice)
1 pound ground beef
1 teaspoon salt
⅛ teaspoon pepper
½ teaspoon prepared mustard
¼ teaspoon ground sage

1. Stir milk into bread, then lightly mix in ground beef, salt, pepper, mustard, and sage; shape into 4 patties about 1 inch thick.
2. Broil, 4 inches from heat, 6 minutes on each side for medium, or until meat is done as you like it.

BURGER BUILDUPS

Makes 4 servings

1 pound ground beef
1 teaspoon salt
⅛ teaspoon pepper
4 thick slices tomato
2 tablespoons crumbled blue cheese

1. Mix ground beef lightly with salt and pepper; shape into 4 patties about 1 inch thick.
2. Broil, 4 inches from heat, 6 minutes on each side for medium, or until meat is done as you like it.
3. While meat cooks, top each tomato slice with blue cheese. About 2 minutes before meat is done, place a tomato slice on top of each patty to heat and melt cheese.

MEAT-AND-POTATO CAKES

Makes 4 servings

1½ pounds ground beef
3 tablespoons bottled barbecue sauce
1 small onion, grated
1 teaspoon salt
Seasoned hot mashed potatoes
4 tablespoons grated Cheddar cheese

1. Mix ground beef lightly with barbecue sauce, onion, and salt; shape into 4 patties about 1 inch thick.
2. Broil, 4 inches from heat, 6 minutes on each side for medium, or until meat is done as you like it.
3. Top each patty with a mound of hot mashed potatoes; sprinkle cheese over. Broil 1 minute longer, or just until cheese starts to melt.

GEORGIA BURGERS

Makes 4 servings

1 pound ground beef
¼ cup chopped pecans
1 small onion, grated
1 teaspoon salt
⅛ teaspoon ground cloves
1 jar (about 5 ounces) baby-pack strained
   peaches
1 tablespoon brown sugar
2 teaspoons cider vinegar
⅛ teaspoon ground ginger

1. Mix ground beef lightly with pecans, onion, salt, cloves, and 3 tablespoons of the peaches. (Set remaining aside for glaze.) Shape meat into 4 patties about 1 inch thick.
2. Broil, 4 inches from heat, 6 minutes.
3. While meat cooks, season remaining peaches with brown sugar, vinegar, and ginger. Brush on hot patties; turn; brush again. Broil 6 minutes longer for medium, or until meat is done as you like it.

TREASURE BURGERS

Makes 6 servings

2 pounds ground beef
1 teaspoon salt
½ teaspoon celery salt
⅛ teaspoon pepper
1 egg
½ cup mixed vegetable juices
½ cup chopped stuffed green olives
2 tablespoons chopped parsley
1 tablespoon chopped onion
1 package cheese sauce mix

1. Mix ground beef lightly with salt, celery salt, pepper, egg, and mixed vegetable juices until well-blended; shape into 12 patties about ¼ inch thick.
2. Mix olives, parsley, and onion; spread on 6 patties, dividing evenly; top with remaining patties, pressing edges together.
3. Broil, 4 inches from heat, 4 minutes on each side for medium, or until meat is done as you like it. While meat cooks, prepare cheese sauce mix, following label directions; spoon over hot patties.

Cooksaver tip:

If you're broiling only one or two meat patties, save dishwashing by using a disposable foil pie plate or cake pan

DOUBLE ONION BURGERS

Bake at 350° for 50 minutes.
Makes 6 servings

1 large Bermuda onion, peeled
¼ cup salad oil
1½ pounds ground beef
1 small onion, chopped (¼ cup)
2 tablespoons chopped parsley
¾ cup soft bread crumbs (1½ slices)
1 egg
1½ teaspoons salt
⅛ teaspoon pepper
¼ cup catsup
6 slices bacon, halved

1. Cut Bermuda onion into 6 slices; arrange in a single layer in a shallow baking pan; pour salad oil over top. Bake in moderate oven (350°) 20 minutes.
2. While onion cooks, mix ground beef lightly with chopped onion, parsley, bread crumbs, egg, salt, and pepper until well-blended; shape into 6 patties about 1 inch thick.
3. Place one each on a baked onion slice; spread with catsup; top each with 2 half slices of bacon.
4. Bake 30 minutes longer, or until bacon is crisp and meat is done as you like it.

BONUS BURGERS

Makes 4 servings

1 small onion, chopped (¼ cup)
1 tablespoon salad oil
¼ cup ready-mix bread stuffing
3 tablespoons water
1½ pounds ground beef
1 tablespoon bottled steak sauce
1 teaspoon salt
1 tablespoon crumbled blue cheese

1. Saute onion lightly in salad oil; stir in bread stuffing and water; remove from heat.
2. Mix ground beef lightly with steak sauce and salt; shape into 4 patties about 1 inch thick. Make a slight hollow in top of each to hold stuffing.
3. Broil, top side down, 5 to 6 inches from heat, 6 minutes; turn. Fill centers with stuffing mixture; top with blue cheese. Broil 6 minutes* longer for medium, or until meat is done as you like it.

*If broiling closer to heat than 5 to 6 inches, add stuffing and cheese about 3 minutes before meat is done to keep stuffing from burning.

BURGER STEAKS DIABLE

Makes 4 servings

1½ pounds ground beef
1½ teaspoons salt
¾ teaspoon monosodium glutamate (MSG)
¼ cup chili sauce
2 tablespoons brown sugar
1 tablespoon cider vinegar
1 tablespoon prepared mustard
4 drops red-pepper seasoning

1. Mix ground beef lightly with salt and MSG; shape into 4 "steaks" about 1 inch thick.
2. Broil, 4 inches from heat, 6 minutes on each side for medium, or until meat is done as you like it.
3. While "steaks" broil, mix chili sauce, brown sugar, vinegar, mustard, and red-pepper seasoning; heat just until blended. Spoon sparingly over meat, for this sauce is **hot.**

Special burgers... from round the world

BURGERS ROMA

Makes 4 servings

1 pound ground beef
1 teaspoon salt
½ teaspoon basil
¼ teaspoon oregano
⅛ teaspoon pepper
¼ cup tomato sauce (from an 8-ounce can)
2 slices mozzarella or pizza cheese, halved
4 split hard rolls, toasted and buttered

1. Mix ground beef lightly with salt, herbs, and pepper; shape into 4 patties about 1 inch thick.
2. Pan-fry over medium heat 8 minutes; turn; cook 5 minutes. Top each with 1 tablespoon tomato sauce and ½ slice cheese; cook about 3 minutes longer, or until cheese melts and meat is done as you like it.
3. Put together, sandwich style, with buttered rolls.

ALL-AMERICAN CHEESEBURGERS

Makes 4 servings

1 pound ground beef
1 teaspoon salt
⅛ teaspoon pepper
2 teaspoons catsup
4 slices (half an 8-ounce package) process sharp American cheese
4 slices tomato
4 slices Bermuda onion
4 split hamburger buns, toasted and buttered

1. Mix ground beef lightly with salt and pepper; shape into 4 patties about 1 inch thick.
2. Pan-fry over medium heat 8 minutes on each side for medium, or until meat is done as you like it. Brush tops lightly with catsup; cover with cheese slices. (Heat from meat will melt cheese slightly.)
3. Top each with a tomato and onion slice; put together, sandwich style, with buttered buns.

DANISH BURGERS

Makes 4 servings

1½ pounds ground beef
1 teaspoon seasoned salt
1 tablespoon Worcestershire sauce
4 slices Bermuda onion
4 tablespoons (½ stick) butter or margarine
4 eggs
1 large tomato, cut in 4 slices
2 split hamburger buns, toasted and buttered

1. Mix ground beef lightly with seasoned salt and Worcestershire sauce; shape into 4 patties about 1 inch thick.
2. Saute onion slices, turning once, in 2 tablespoons of the butter or margarine, 4 minutes, or just until lightly golden. Remove and keep warm.
3. Pan-fry patties over medium heat 8 minutes on each side for medium, or until meat is done as you like it.
4. While meat cooks, melt remaining 2 tablespoons butter or margarine in a medium-size frying pan; break eggs into pan; cover. Cook slowly 3 to 4 minutes, or just until yolks set. Cut around whites to separate eggs neatly.
5. Place a tomato slice on each bun half; top with an onion slice, meat patty, and a fried egg.

BEEF TACOS

Makes 6 servings

1 pound ground beef
1 teaspoon salt
1 teaspoon chili powder
⅛ teaspoon pepper
1 can (about 8 ounces) baked beans
¼ cup chopped stuffed green olives
1 cup grated Cheddar cheese (4 ounces)
1 can (8 ounces) tortillas
2 cups shredded lettuce

1. Mix ground beef lightly with salt, chili powder, and pepper; shape into a large patty. Brown 5 minutes on each side, then break up into chunks.
2. Stir in baked beans, mashing them slightly, then olives. Cook, stirring often, 3 minutes, or just until heated through. Stir in cheese; keep hot.
3. Prepare tortillas, following label directions for tacos. Place a spoonful of the hot beef mixture in center of each; top with some shredded lettuce, then fold over.

HAWAIIAN BURGERS

Makes 4 servings

1 pound ground beef
1 teaspoon salt
⅛ teaspoon pepper
1 can (8 ounces) pineapple tidbits
1 tablespoon prepared mustard
1 teaspoon brown sugar
¼ teaspoon ground ginger
4 flat corn-meal cakes, toasted and buttered
   Flaked coconut

1. Mix ground beef lightly with salt and pepper; shape into 4 patties about 1 inch thick.
2. Drain syrup from pineapple; combine with mustard, brown sugar, and ginger.
3. Pan-fry patties over medium heat, brushing several times with sauce, 8 minutes; turn. Brush with more sauce; cook 4 minutes longer. Stir in pineapple and any remaining sauce; cook 4 minutes longer, or until meat is done as you like it.
4. Place a patty on each corn-meal cake; top with pineapple and sauce from pan; sprinkle with coconut.

Cooksaver tip:

For a different Islands dress-up, top burgers with chopped macadamia nuts

HONG KONG BURGERS

Makes 4 servings

1 pound ground beef
2 tablespoons drained chopped mushrooms (from a 3- or 4-ounce can)
1 teaspoon salt
⅛ teaspoon pepper
1 tablespoon soy sauce
4 split sesame-seed buns, toasted

1. Mix ground beef lightly with mushrooms, salt, and pepper; shape into 4 patties about 1 inch thick. Brush both sides with soy sauce.
2. Broil, 4 inches from heat, 6 minutes on each side for medium, or until meat is done as you like it. Put together, sandwich style, with toasted buns.

PARISIAN BURGERS

Makes 4 servings

1 pound ground beef
1 teaspoon salt
1 teaspoon sherry flavoring or extract
½ teaspoon herb seasoning
⅛ teaspoon pepper
8 slices French bread, toasted and buttered
8 radishes, grated

1. Mix ground beef lightly with salt, sherry flavoring or extract, herb seasoning, and pepper; shape into 8 patties about ½ inch thick.
2. Pan-fry over medium heat 4 minutes on each side for medium, or until meat is done as you like it.
3. Top each slice of French bread with a patty; sprinkle with grated radishes.

BANGKOK BURGERS

Makes 4 servings

1½ pounds ground beef
2 tablespoons brewed coffee
1 teaspoon salt
2 tablespoons soy sauce
1 tablespoon butter or margarine
4 poppy-seed rolls, split and buttered

1. Mix ground beef lightly with coffee and salt; shape into 4 patties about 1 inch thick; brush with part of the soy sauce.
2. Pan-fry over medium heat in butter or margarine 8 minutes; turn. Brush again with more soy sauce; cook 8 minutes longer for medium, or until meat is done as you like it. Put together, sandwich style, with rolls.

RHINE BURGER STACKS

Makes 4 servings

- 1 pound ground beef
- 1 teaspoon salt
- ¼ teaspoon caraway seeds
- ⅛ teaspoon pepper
- ½ cup well-drained sauerkraut (from an about-1-pound can)
- 8 slices bacon
- 8 slices square pumpernickel bread, buttered

1. Mix ground beef lightly with salt, caraway seeds, and pepper; shape into 8 patties about ½ inch thick.
2. Place 2 tablespoonfuls of sauerkraut on each of 4 patties; top with remaining patties. Wrap 2 slices bacon around each; fasten with moistened wooden picks.
3. Broil, 4 inches from heat, 6 minutes on each side for medium, or until bacon is crisp and meat is done as you like it.
4. Put together, sandwich style, with pumpernickel bread.

MIDNIGHT SUN BURGERS

Makes 4 servings

- 1 pound ground beef
- 1 egg
- ½ cup soft bread crumbs (1 slice)
- 2 tablespoons milk
- 1 teaspoon salt
- ¼ teaspoon nutmeg
- ⅛ teaspoon pepper
- 2 slices caraway cheese, halved
- 8 slices square rye bread, buttered

1. Mix ground beef lightly with egg, bread crumbs, milk, salt, nutmeg, and pepper until well-blended; shape into 4 patties about 1 inch thick.
2. Pan-fry over medium heat 8 minutes on each side for medium, or until meat is done as you like it.
3. Lay cheese slices on top of patties. (Heat from meat will melt cheese slightly.) Put together, sandwich style, with buttered bread. Serve with pickled beets, if you wish.

EAST INDIAN BURGERS

Makes 4 servings

- 1 pound ground beef
- 1 teaspoon salt
- ½ teaspoon curry powder
- ⅛ teaspoon pepper
- 4 split hamburger buns, toasted and buttered
- 2 bananas, peeled and sliced
  Bottled chutney
- 2 tablespoons flaked coconut

1. Mix ground beef lightly with salt, curry powder, and pepper; shape into 4 patties about 1 inch thick.
2. Pan-fry over medium heat 8 minutes on each side for medium, or until meat is done as you like it.
3. Place a patty on the bottom half of each bun. Arrange banana slices in a ring on top; spoon chutney in the center; sprinkle coconut over all. Top with remaining bun halves.

GREEK BURGERS

Makes 4 servings

- 1 pound ground beef
- 1 small onion, grated
- ¼ cup chopped parsley
- 1 teaspoon salt
- ¼ teaspoon ground coriander
- 4 large sesame-seed wafers
- ½ cup cottage cheese or ricotta cheese
- 4 lemon wedges

1. Mix ground beef lightly with onion, parsley, salt, and coriander; shape into 4 patties about 1 inch thick.
2. Pan-fry over medium heat 8 minutes on each side for medium, or until meat is done as you like it.
3. Place each patty on a sesame-seed wafer; top with cottage cheese or ricotta cheese. (For an authentic Greek touch, use sliced *Feta* cheese.) Serve with lemon to squeeze over.

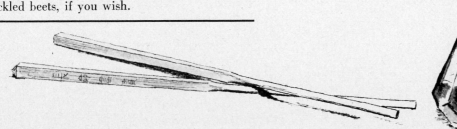

Deviled Meat Loaf (*recipe on page 30*) framed with snowy cauliflowerets and sauteed cherry tomatoes makes this colorful platter for a family meal. Loaf owes its mellow flavor to a surprise ingredient

CHAPTER 3

GOOD COOKS COUNT ON

MEAT LOAVES

And with good reason! They please beef-eating families, are quick to put together, take easily to all sorts of platter dress-ups, hold well if dinner is delayed, slice neatly for serving hot or turning into cold sandwiches, and—a big, big plus—are good to your food budget.

In this chapter we have included more than 50 recipes for meat loaves, all with their own special seasoning and shaping twists, and all starting with either plain ground beef or a mixture of ground beef and pork or ground beef, pork, and veal.

Some are quickies for days when mealtime comes fast; others are stuffed and rolled, baked in layers, sauced simply, or served with perky toppers. Whatever your choices may be, all of them are wonderful eating.

Fix these easy stand-bys on busy days

CARAWAY LOAF

Bake at 375° for 50 minutes.
Makes 6 servings

  1 tablespoon instant minced onion
  2 tablespoons lemon juice
1½ cups caraway-rye bread crumbs
      (3 slices)
  ¾ cup milk
  1 pound ground beef
  ½ pound ground pork
  1 egg
  ¼ cup chopped parsley
1½ teaspoons salt
  ⅛ teaspoon pepper

1. Combine onion, lemon juice, bread crumbs, and milk; let stand until milk is absorbed. Mix lightly with ground beef and pork, egg, parsley, salt, and pepper until well-blended; press into a baking pan, 8x8x2.
2. Bake in moderate oven (375°) 50 minutes, or until brown.
3. Cut into oblongs; remove with a wide spatula or pancake turner.

BAKED FRENCH MEAT LOAF

Bake at 350° for 1 hour.
Makes 8 servings

  5 slices French bread, cut in cubes (about 1½ cups)
  1 cup milk
  2 pounds ground beef
  ½ cup chopped celery
  ½ cup grated pared raw carrot
  1 small onion, grated
  1 egg
  1 tablespoon prepared horseradish
  2 teaspoons salt
  ¼ teaspoon pepper

1. Combine bread cubes and milk; let stand 5 minutes, or until milk is absorbed.
2. Mix lightly with ground beef, celery, carrot, onion, egg, horseradish, salt, and pepper until well-blended. Shape into a loaf in a shallow baking pan; make deep cuts in top to mark into 8 even portions.
3. Bake in moderate oven (350°) 1 hour, or until brown.

DEVILED MEAT LOAF
(Pictured on page 28)

Bake at 350° for 1 hour.
Makes 8 servings

  2 pounds ground beef
  1 can (4½ ounces) deviled ham
  ¾ cup chopped parsley
  ½ cup fine dry bread crumbs
  1 egg
  1 small onion, grated
  2 teaspoons salt
  2 teaspoons basil
  ⅛ teaspoon pepper
  1 cup tomato juice

1. Mix ground beef and deviled ham lightly with remaining ingredients until well-blended; shape into a loaf in a shallow baking pan.
2. Bake in moderate oven (350°) 1 hour, or until brown. To serve as pictured, place loaf on a serving platter; frame with mounds of cooked cauliflowerets and sauteed cherry-tomato halves, and garnish with a kebab of two onion rings centered with a whole cherry tomato and parsley.

OLD-FASHIONED SAGE LOAF

Bake at 350° for 1 hour and 15 minutes.
Makes 8 servings

    2 pounds meat-loaf mixture (ground beef
          and pork)
    2 eggs
    1 cup quick-cooking rolled oats
    1 medium-size onion, grated
    1 cup canned applesauce
    2 teaspoons salt
   ¼ teaspoon pepper
   ½ teaspoon crumbled leaf sage
    1 tablespoon bottled steak sauce

1. Mix meat-loaf mixture lightly with eggs, rolled oats, onion, applesauce, salt, pepper, and sage until well-blended.
2. Pack firmly into a loaf pan, 9x5x3; unmold into a shallow baking pan. Score top in crisscross pattern; brush with steak sauce.
3. Bake in moderate oven (350°) 1 hour and 15 minutes, or until brown.

Variation:

PICNIC SQUARES—Prepare and bake OLD-FASHIONED SAGE LOAF, following directions above, then chill. (A day ahead is best.) Cut lengthwise into 2 long blocks, then crosswise into ½-inch-thick slices; wrap each block tightly in foil to carry to your picnic spot. Just before serving, spread split soft rolls generously with bottled mustard-dressing sauce; put together, sandwich style, with sliced meat loaf. Each block of meat loaf will cut into about 16 slices.

FAMILY-BEST BEEF LOAF

Bake at 350° for 1 hour.
Makes 8 servings

    2 pounds ground beef
    1 cup soft bread crumbs (2 slices)
    1 medium-size onion, chopped (½ cup)
    1 egg
   ¼ cup chili sauce
    1 teaspoon salt
   ⅛ teaspoon pepper
    2 small bay leaves

1. Mix ground beef lightly with bread crumbs, onion, egg, chili sauce, salt, and pepper until well-blended.
2. Shape into a loaf in a shallow baking pan; tuck a bay leaf under each end of loaf.
3. Bake in moderate oven (350°) 1 hour, or until brown. Discard bay leaves before serving.

BUSY-DAY BEEF ROUND

Bake at 350° for 1 hour.
Makes 6 servings

  1½ pounds ground beef
    1 cup grated pared raw carrots
    1 cup grated pared raw potatoes
    1 small onion, grated
    1 can (3 or 4 ounces) chopped
          mushrooms
   ½ cup fine dry bread crumbs
    1 teaspoon salt
   ¼ teaspoon pepper
    1 cup (8-ounce carton) dairy sour cream

1. Mix ground beef lightly with carrots, potatoes, onion, mushrooms and liquid, bread crumbs, salt, pepper, and sour cream until well-blended; shape into a round about 1 inch thick in a shallow baking pan. Mark top into 6 wedges.
2. Bake in moderate oven (350°) 1 hour, or until brown. Cut at marks into wedges.

DOUBLE-RICH MEAT LOAF

Bake at 350° for 1 hour.
Makes 8 servings

    2 pounds meat-loaf mixture (ground beef,
          pork, and veal)
   ¾ cup wheat germ (from a 12-ounce jar)
    2 eggs
   ½ cup milk
    1 medium-size onion, chopped (½ cup)
    1 can (3 or 4 ounces) chopped mushrooms
    2 teaspoons salt
   ¼ teaspoon pepper
    1 tablespoon Worcestershire sauce
  1½ teaspoons prepared horseradish
          Quick Bordelaise Sauce (*recipe follows*)

1. Mix meat-loaf mixture lightly with wheat germ, eggs, milk, onion, mushrooms and liquid, and seasonings until well-blended.
2. Pack into a loaf pan, 9x5x3; unmold into a shallow baking pan.
3. Bake in moderate oven (350°) 1 hour, or until brown. Slice and serve with QUICK BORDELAISE SAUCE.

QUICK BORDELAISE SAUCE — Combine 1 can (about 11 ounces) mushroom gravy, 1 can (3 or 4 ounces) chopped mushrooms and liquid, 1 tablespoon grated onion, 2 tablespoons butter or margarine, 1 teaspoon cider vinegar, and ¼ teaspoon thyme. Simmer about 15 minutes to blend flavors. Stir in ¼ cup chopped parsley. Makes about 2 cups.

MOCK POT ROAST WITH VEGETABLES
(Pictured on page 49)

Bake at 375° for 1 hour and 15 minutes.
Makes 8 servings

    2   pounds meat-loaf mixture (ground beef,
          pork, and veal)
 ½   cup quick-cooking rolled oats
    2   eggs
 ½   cup catsup
    1   tablespoon prepared horseradish
    1   teaspoon dry mustard
    3   teaspoons salt
 ¼   teaspoon pepper
    1   teaspoon bottled gravy coloring
    8   small carrots, pared
    8   small potatoes, pared
  16   small white onions, peeled
    1   package (10 ounces) frozen peas

1. Mix meat-loaf mixture lightly with rolled oats, eggs, catsup, horseradish, mustard, 2 teaspoons of the salt, and pepper until well-blended. Shape into a loaf in a shallow baking pan; brush with gravy coloring.
2. Halve carrots lengthwise; arrange with potatoes and onions around meat; sprinkle with the remaining 1 teaspoon salt. Cover pan with foil.
3. Bake in moderate oven (375°) 40 minutes; uncover; add peas. Cover again; bake 30 minutes. Uncover; baste meat and vegetables with pan juices; bake 5 minutes longer, or until vegetables are tender.

EARLY HARVEST MEAT LOAF

Bake at 350° for 50 minutes.
Makes 6 servings

 1½   pounds ground beef
 ¾   cup fine dry bread crumbs
 ¾   cup canned applesauce
    6   tablespoons catsup
 ¾   teaspoon salt
 ¼   teaspoon ground sage

1. Mix ground beef lightly with remaining ingredients until well-blended; shape into a 6-inch square in a shallow baking pan.
2. Bake in moderate oven (350°) 50 minutes, or until brown.
3. Cut into oblongs; remove with a wide spatula or pancake turner. Garnish each with a spiced apple ring (from a 12-ounce jar), if you wish.

CHEESE-AND-CRACKER MEAT LOAF

Bake at 350° for 1 hour.
Makes 6 to 8 servings

    1   large sweet red pepper
    1   large onion, chopped (1 cup)
    2   tablespoons shortening
 1½   pounds ground beef
    2   cups coarsely crumbled saltines
          (¼ pound)
    1   teaspoon salt
 ½   teaspoon celery salt
 ½   teaspoon paprika
 ¼   teaspoon pepper
    2   eggs
    1   cup milk
 ½   pound Cheddar cheese, cut in ½-inch
          cubes
    1   tablespoon butter or margarine

1. Cut stem end from red pepper, then remove seeds. Slice 8 thin rings from center and set aside for topping; chop remaining. (There should be about ½ cup.)
2. Saute chopped pepper and onion in shortening just until soft.
3. Mix ground beef lightly with saltines, salt, celery salt, paprika, pepper, eggs, and milk until well-blended; stir in pepper-onion mixture, then fold in cheese cubes.
4. Pack lightly into a 6-cup oval or round baking dish; unmold into a shallow baking pan; score top in crisscross pattern.
5. Bake in moderate oven (350°) 1 hour, or until brown.
6. Saute red-pepper rings in butter or margarine, turning once, just until slightly wilted; arrange on top of loaf.

PATTYCAKE LOAF

Bake at 350° for 45 minutes.
Makes 6 servings

 1½   pounds ground beef
 ¾   cup fine dry bread crumbs
    1   jar (8 ounces) junior apples and
          pineapple
 ⅓   cup catsup
    1   teaspoon salt
 ¼   teaspoon ground sage

1. Mix ground beef lightly with remaining ingredients until well-blended; shape into a big patty in a shallow baking pan; score top in crisscross design with knife.
2. Bake in moderate oven (350°) 45 minutes, or until brown.

EASY MEAT LOAF

Bake at 350° for 1 hour.
Makes 6 servings

1½ pounds ground beef
1 cup coarsely crushed shredded wheat cereal
1 small onion, chopped (¼ cup)
1¼ cups milk
1 egg
1½ teaspoons salt
¼ teaspoon pepper
¼ teaspoon poultry seasoning

1. Mix ground beef lightly with remaining ingredients until well-blended; shape into a loaf in a shallow baking pan.
2. Bake in moderate oven (350°) 1 hour, or until brown.

Cooksaver tip:

It's a good idea to remove the hot meat juices and drippings from the baking pan before unmolding meat loaf. A baster does a fast neat job, or you can use a small spoon. Make the drippings into gravy or save to use as a base for soup another day. And for easier unmolding — dishwashing, too — line the bottom and ends of the baking pan with a strip of foil

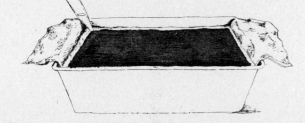

Season these loaves with a savory sauce

PIQUANT RING WITH GREEN RICE
(Pictured on page 42)

Bake at 350° for 1 hour.
Makes 10 to 12 servings

3 pounds meat-loaf mixture (ground beef, pork, and veal)
2 cups soft bread crumbs (4 slices)
3 eggs
1 medium-size onion, grated
½ cup milk
¼ cup prepared mustard
2 teaspoons salt
½ teaspoon ground cloves
½ cup firmly packed brown sugar
⅓ cup cider vinegar
¼ cup orange juice
¼ cup molasses
Green Rice *(recipe follows)*

1. Mix meat-loaf mixture lightly with bread crumbs, eggs, onion, milk, mustard, salt, and cloves until well-blended. Pack into an 8-cup ring mold; unmold into a shallow baking pan.
2. Bake in moderate oven (350°) 30 minutes.
3. While ring bakes, combine brown sugar, vinegar, orange juice, and molasses; cook, stirring often, 10 minutes, or until slightly thick. Spoon part over meat.
4. Continue baking, basting often with remaining glaze, 30 minutes longer, or until richly browned.
5. To serve as pictured, place loaf on a heated serving platter; spoon GREEN RICE in center. Garnish with pitted ripe olives stuffed with thin slices of carrot and celery "plumes."

GREEN RICE—Combine 1 cup uncooked rice, 2½ cups water, 2 tablespoons butter or margarine, and 1 teaspoon salt in a 6-cup baking dish; cover. Bake along with meat ring in moderate oven (350°) 1 hour, or until rice is tender and liquid is absorbed. Stir in ½ cup finely chopped celery and ¼ cup chopped parsley. Makes 4 cups.

TWIN PARTY LOAVES

Bake at 375° for 1 hour.
Makes 16 servings

 3 eggs
 1 cup evaporated milk (from a tall can)
 2 cups soft bread crumbs (4 slices)
 4 pounds meat-loaf mixture (ground beef and pork)
 1 medium-size onion, chopped (½ cup)
 3 teaspoons salt
 2 teaspoons sugar
 ½ teaspoon ground allspice
 ½ teaspoon nutmeg
 ½ teaspoon thyme
 ¼ teaspoon pepper
 Parsley Sauce (recipe follows)

1. Beat eggs with evaporated milk; stir in bread crumbs; let stand a few minutes. Mix lightly with meat-loaf mixture, onion, and seasonings until well-blended.
2. Press half into a loaf pan, 9x5x3; unmold at one end of a large shallow baking pan. Repeat with remaining meat mixture.
3. Bake in moderate oven (375°) 1 hour, or until richly browned. Lift out with 2 wide spatulas onto a heated serving platter.
4. Spoon a ribbon of PARSLEY SAUCE down middle of each; serve remaining sauce separately.

PARSLEY SAUCE—Blend 1 envelope Strogonoff-sauce mix with 1½ cups water. Heat to boiling; lower heat and simmer 10 minutes. Stir a few tablespoons hot mixture into ½ cup dairy sour cream, then blend back into remaining in pan; heat just to boiling. Stir in ¼ cup chopped parsley. Makes 2 cups.

SAUCY CHEESEBURGER LOAVES

Bake at 350° for 1 hour.
Makes 6 servings

 2 pounds ground beef
 1 cup crushed corn flakes
 ¼ cup bottled hot-dog relish
 1 small onion, grated
 1 can condensed cheese soup
 ¼ cup milk

1. Mix ground beef lightly with corn flakes, hot-dog relish, and onion.
2. Divide into 6 even-size portions; shape each into a small loaf; place in a shallow baking dish.
3. Blend cheese soup with milk, then spoon over loaves.
4. Bake in moderate oven (350°), basting several times with sauce in dish, 1 hour, or until browned.

GLAZED DINNER RING

Bake at 375° for 1 hour and 15 minutes.
Makes 8 servings

 2 pounds meat-loaf mixture (ground beef, pork, and veal)
 1 medium-size onion, chopped (½ cup)
 1 cup grated pared raw carrots
 2 cups soft bread crumbs (4 slices)
 2 eggs
 1 small can evaporated milk (⅔ cup)
 2 teaspoons salt
 ¼ teaspoon pepper
 ¾ cup chili sauce
 2 tablespoons corn syrup
 1 teaspoon Worcestershire sauce
 2 teaspoons horseradish-mustard

1. Mix meat-loaf mixture lightly with onion, carrots, bread crumbs, eggs, evaporated milk, salt, and pepper until well-blended.
2. Pack into a 5-cup ring mold; unmold into a shallow baking pan.
3. Bake in moderate oven (375°) 1 hour. Mix chili sauce, corn syrup, Worcestershire sauce, and horseradish-mustard; spoon over ring. Bake 15 minutes longer, or until top is glazed. Fill center with fluffy hot mashed potatoes, if you wish.

Cooksaver tip:

To give meat loaf a fancy shape, pack mixture into a ring mold, then invert into baking pan. When baked, fill center of loaf with mashed potatoes or a vegetable. No ring mold? Make your own by molding loaf around a custard cup

DUXBURY LOAF

Bake at 375° for 1 hour.
Makes 6 servings

1 pound ground beef
½ pound pork sausage meat
1 egg
1 small onion, chopped (¼ cup)
½ cup chopped celery
½ cup soft bread crumbs (1 slice)
¼ cup milk
1 teaspoon salt
¼ teaspoon poultry seasoning
1 can (7 ounces) whole-fruit cranberry
    sauce

1. Mix ground beef and sausage meat lightly with egg, onion, celery, bread crumbs, milk, and seasonings until well-blended.
2. Shape into a loaf in a shallow baking pan; spoon cranberry sauce over.
3. Bake in moderate oven (375°) 1 hour, or until glazed.

SKILLET SAUERBRATEN

Makes 8 servings

2 pounds ground beef
2 teaspoons salt
¼ teaspoon pepper
¼ teaspoon ground cloves
¾ cup cider vinegar
1 carrot, pared and sliced
1 medium-size onion, peeled and sliced
1 stalk celery, sliced
1 bay leaf
¾ cup water
2 tablespoons brown sugar
3 gingersnaps
½ cup hot water

1. Mix ground beef lightly with salt, pepper, cloves, and ¼ cup of the vinegar; shape into a big patty in a frying pan.
2. Place carrot, onion, celery, and bay leaf around meat. Mix water, remaining ½ cup vinegar, and brown sugar; pour over meat; cover.
3. Simmer, basting often, 1 hour. Remove meat to a heated platter; discard bay leaf.
4. Soften gingersnaps in hot water; stir into drippings in pan. Heat, stirring constantly, just until gravy thickens. Pour over meat or serve separately to spoon over.

BEEF-VEGETABLE LOAF
(Pictured on pages 36-37)

Bake at 350° for 1 hour.
Makes 6 servings

1½ pounds ground beef
1 egg
1 cup cooked rice (¼ cup uncooked)
1 small onion, chopped (¼ cup)
1 small carrot, pared and grated
5 tablespoons chopped parsley
1 teaspoon salt
⅛ teaspoon pepper
½ cup milk
2 tablespoons bottled steak sauce
1 medium-size onion, peeled, sliced, and
    separated into rings
1 tablespoon butter or margarine

1. Mix ground beef lightly with egg, rice, chopped onion, carrot, 4 tablespoons of the parsley, salt, pepper, and milk until well-blended.
2. Pat into a bowl-shape loaf in a greased shallow baking pan; mark top deeply into quarters.
3. Bake in moderate oven (350°) 45 minutes; brush with steak sauce. Bake 15 minutes longer, or until richly browned.
4. While loaf bakes, saute onion rings in butter or margarine just until soft; sprinkle with remaining 1 tablespoon parsley; toss lightly to mix.
5. Spoon onions in a mound on top of loaf. Cut loaf into quarters at marks, then slice.

MEAT LOAF AU GRATIN

Bake at 350° for 1½ hours.
Makes 8 servings

2 pounds ground beef
1 cup grated Cheddar cheese (4 ounces)
1 egg
2 cups soft bread crumbs (4 slices)
1 small onion, grated
1 tablespoon Worcestershire sauce
1 tablespoon prepared mustard
1 teaspoon salt
1 can (8 ounces) tomato sauce

1. Mix ground beef lightly with ¾ cup of cheese, egg, bread crumbs, onion, and seasonings until well-blended. Shape into a loaf in a shallow baking pan.
2. Bake in moderate oven (350°) 1 hour. Pour off drippings.
3. Pour tomato sauce over loaf; sprinkle with remaining ¼ cup cheese. Bake 30 minutes longer.

For extra flavor, extra moistness, snowy rice and shreds of golden carrots go into this easy-fix Beef-vegetable Loaf *(recipe on page 35)*. Good menu mates: Oven-steamed zucchini sticks, corn on the cob, muffins, and rosy baked apples to top with cream

DILL-SAUCED MEAT LOAF

(Pictured on page 42)

Bake at 350° for 1 hour and 15 minutes.
Makes 6 servings

1½ pounds meat-loaf mixture (ground beef and pork)
1 medium-size onion, chopped (½ cup)
½ cup soft bread crumbs (1 slice)
½ cup bottled dill-pickle juice
1 egg
1½ teaspoons salt
¼ teaspoon pepper
½ cup chopped dill pickle
½ cup catsup
¼ cup water
2 tablespoons sugar
1 teaspoon Worcestershire sauce

1. Mix meat-loaf mixture lightly with onion, bread crumbs, dill-pickle juice, egg, salt, and pepper until well-blended. Shape into a loaf in a shallow baking pan.
2. Combine dill pickle, catsup, water, sugar, and Worcestershire sauce; pour over loaf.
3. Bake in moderate oven (350°), basting twice with sauce in pan, 40 minutes. Continue baking, without basting, 35 minutes longer, or until richly glazed. To serve as pictured, place loaf on a heated serving platter; garnish with a dill-pickle fan and frame with buttered Brussels sprouts and tiny whole carrots.

DINNER LOAF

Bake at 350° for 1½ hours.
Makes 6 servings

1½ pounds ground beef
2 eggs
1 cup ready-mix bread stuffing
1 can (8 ounces) tomato sauce
1 medium-size onion, chopped (½ cup)
1½ teaspoons salt
⅛ teaspoon thyme
⅛ teaspoon marjoram
¼ cup chili sauce
1 bay leaf

1. Mix ground beef lightly with eggs, bread stuffing, tomato sauce, onion, salt, thyme, and marjoram until well-blended.
2. Shape into a loaf in a shallow baking pan; score top. Spread with chili sauce; lay bay leaf on top.
3. Bake in moderate oven (350°) 1½ hours, or until richly browned. Remove bay leaf.

HERB SQUARE

Bake at 350° for 1 hour and 15 minutes.
Makes 8 servings

2 pounds meat-loaf mixture (ground beef and pork)
1 egg
1 can condensed cream of celery soup
1 cup soft bread crumbs (2 slices)
1 medium-size onion, chopped (½ cup)
1 teaspoon paprika
½ teaspoon basil
½ teaspoon ground sage
½ teaspoon salt
¼ teaspoon pepper
¼ cup chili sauce
¼ cup shredded process American cheese
1 teaspoon prepared mustard

1. Mix meat-loaf mixture lightly with egg, soup, bread crumbs, onion, and seasonings until well-blended. Pack into a baking pan, 9x9x2.
2. Mix chili sauce, cheese, and mustard; spread on top of loaf.
3. Bake in moderate oven (350°) 45 minutes; pour off all drippings. Bake 30 minutes longer. or until browned.

TOMATO MEAT LOAF

Bake at 375° for 45 minutes.
Makes 6 servings

1 medium-size onion, peeled and sliced
1½ pounds ground beef
½ teaspoon salt
½ teaspoon basil
¼ teaspoon oregano
1 can condensed tomato soup

1. Place half the onion slices in the bottom of a baking pan, 8x8x2; cover with ground beef, breaking it up lightly with a fork, but do not pack down. Sprinkle with salt, basil, and oregano; top with remaining onion slices; pour tomato soup over.
2. Bake in moderate oven (375°) 45 minutes, or until brown.

Variation:

DOUBLE CHEESE LOAF—Place onion and ground beef in baking pan, following directions above; spoon 1 cup (8-ounce carton) cream-style cottage cheese on top, then add seasonings and soup. Bake as above 30 minutes. Sprinkle with ¼ cup grated Parmesan cheese; bake 15 minutes longer.

TEXAS MEAT LOAF

Bake at 350° for 1 hour.
Makes 8 servings

1¾ pounds ground beef
¼ pound pork sausage meat
1 cup soft bread crumbs (2 slices)
1 cup catsup
1 large onion, chopped (1 cup)
1 egg
2 teaspoons Worcestershire sauce
1½ teaspoons salt
1 tablespoon brown sugar
¼ teaspoon dry mustard

1. Mix ground beef and sausage meat lightly with bread crumbs, ½ cup of the catsup, onion, egg, Worcestershire sauce, and salt until well-blended; shape into a loaf in a shallow baking pan.
2. Bake in moderate oven (350°) 45 minutes; remove from oven. Mix the remaining ½ cup catsup, brown sugar, and mustard; spread on top of loaf.
3. Bake, basting once or twice, 15 minutes, or until top is bubbly brown.

Shape miniatures to step up cooking time

BARBECUED BEEF CAKES

Bake at 350° for 40 minutes.
Makes 6 servings

1½ pounds ground beef
1 egg
½ cup bottled smoky-flavor barbecue sauce
½ teaspoon salt

1. Mix ground beef lightly with egg, 6 tablespoons of the barbecue sauce, and salt; spoon into 6 large muffin-pan cups or 6-ounce custard cups.
2. Bake in moderate oven (350°), brushing once or twice with remaining 2 tablespoons barbecue sauce, 40 minutes, or until tops are glazed.

MEAT LAYER LOAVES

Bake at 350° for 30 minutes.
Makes 4 servings

1 pound ground beef
2 cups soft bread crumbs (4 slices)
1 egg
1 small onion, chopped (¼ cup)
⅓ cup instant nonfat dry milk powder
1 teaspoon salt
¼ teaspoon pepper
½ cup water
Milk Gravy (recipe follows)
Hot mashed potatoes

1. Mix ground beef lightly with bread crumbs, egg, onion, dry milk, salt, pepper, and water until well-blended.
2. Spread in an even layer in a greased jelly-roll pan, 15x10x1, spreading to within 1 inch of edges.
3. Bake in moderate oven (350°) 30 minutes. Cut into 8 serving-size pieces; remove to a heated platter; keep warm while making MILK GRAVY.
4. To serve, put each 2 pieces of meat loaf together with mashed potatoes between and on top; spoon hot gravy over all.

MILK GRAVY—Stir 1 cup hot water into drippings in jelly-roll pan. Mix 3 tablespoons instant nonfat dry milk powder, 2 tablespoons flour, and 1 teaspoon salt with ½ cup cold water until smooth in a small saucepan; stir in drippings mixture. Cook, stirring constantly, until gravy thickens and boils 1 minute. Season to taste with salt and pepper. Strain, if you wish. Makes 1½ cups.

GLAZED BROILED LOAVES

Makes 6 servings

1½ pounds ground beef
1 small onion, grated
1½ teaspoons salt
⅛ teaspoon pepper
¾ cup chili sauce
2 tablespoons brown sugar
1 teaspoon dry mustard
1 tablespoon cider vinegar
2 drops red-pepper seasoning

1. Mix ground beef lightly with onion, salt, and pepper; shape into 6 small loaves about 1¼ inches thick; place on rack in broiler pan.
2. Combine chili sauce with remaining ingredients.
3. Broil loaves, 4 inches from heat, 7 minutes; turn. Spoon sauce over tops; broil 8 minutes longer, or until glazed.

QUICK GOURMET ROUNDS

Bake at 350° for 30 minutes.
Makes 6 servings

1½ pounds ground beef
 1 cup grated American cheese (4 ounces)
 ¼ cup finely crushed saltines (about 4 crackers)
 1 small onion, grated
 1 can (about 11 ounces) mushroom gravy
 1 teaspoon salt
 ⅛ teaspoon pepper
 Seasoned hot mashed potatoes

1. Mix ground beef lightly with cheese, saltines, onion, ½ cup of the mushroom gravy, salt, and pepper until well-blended; shape into 6 even-size thick rounds. Place, without touching, in a shallow baking pan.
2. Bake in moderate oven (350°) 30 minutes, or until richly browned.
3. Heat remaining mushroom gravy to boiling. Spoon mashed potatoes into mounds on serving plates; make a well in the center of each; fill with mushroom gravy. Top each with a meat round.

DUCHESS MEAT LOAF

Makes 6 servings

 1 envelope onion-soup mix
1½ cups water
 2 pounds ground beef
 Seasoned hot mashed potatoes

1. Stir soup mix into water in a 2-cup measure. Measure out ½ cup and blend into ground beef.
2. Shape mixture into a thick 8-inch round in a large frying pan; cut into 6 wedges but leave in patty shape. Pour remaining soup mixture over; cover.
3. Cook over medium heat 25 minutes, or until richly browned.
4. Spoon hot mashed potatoes into a mound on top of meat; dip gravy from bottom of pan and drizzle over.

Cooksaver tip:

Dinnertime delayed? Wrap meat loaf in its baking pan with foil and slide back into the oven with the heat off. It will wait well for about an hour

CREOLE SKILLET LOAVES

Makes 4 servings

 1 can (3 or 4 ounces) chopped mushrooms
1½ pounds ground beef
 1 can condensed tomato-rice soup
 ⅓ cup fine dry bread crumbs
 1 egg
 ¼ cup chopped green pepper
 1 teaspoon salt
 ⅛ teaspoon pepper
 ⅛ teaspoon thyme
 1 tablespoon salad oil

1. Drain mushrooms, saving liquid for sauce-gravy in Step 4.
2. Mix ground beef lightly with mushrooms, ½ can of the soup, bread crumbs, egg, green pepper, and seasonings until well-blended; shape into 4 small loaves.
3. Brown on all sides in salad oil; cover. Cook over low heat 20 minutes; pour off drippings.
4. Mix remaining soup with mushroom liquid; pour over loaves.
5. Simmer, basting loaves several times, 15 minutes.

DANISH BEEF LOAVES

Bake at 350° for 40 minutes.
Makes 6 servings

 2 pounds ground beef
 1 can (about 1 pound) tomatoes, well-drained
 1 cup soft bread crumbs (2 slices)
 1 egg
1½ teaspoons salt
 ¼ teaspoon pepper
 1 teaspoon Worcestershire sauce
 2 tablespoons crumbled blue cheese

1. Mix ground beef lightly with tomatoes (break up with a fork, if needed), bread crumbs, egg, salt, pepper, and Worcestershire sauce until well-blended.
2. Shape into 6 individual loaves; make a small hollow in top of each.
3. Bake in moderate oven (350°) 30 minutes; spoon 1 teaspoon blue cheese into hollow in each. Bake 10 minutes longer, or until cheese is melty and loaves are richly browned.

MIDGET MEAT LOAVES

Bake at 350° for 35 minutes.
Makes 4 servings

- 1 pound ground beef
- 1 cup soft bread crumbs (2 slices)
- ½ cup chopped walnuts
- ¼ cup chili sauce
- 1 teaspoon seasoned salt
- ½ cup milk

1. Mix ground beef lightly with remaining ingredients. Shape into 4 small loaves.
2. Bake in moderate oven (350°) 35 minutes, or until richly browned.

Cooksaver tip:

When making individual loaves, try one of these easy shaping tricks:

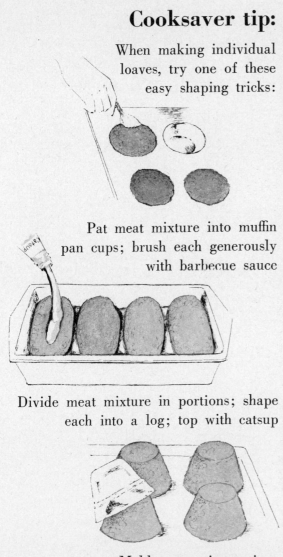

Pat meat mixture into muffin pan cups; brush each generously with barbecue sauce

Divide meat mixture in portions; shape each into a log; top with catsup

Mold meat mixture in a custard cup, then turn out into a shallow baking pan

Serve these rolls for partytime

APRICOT-BEEF ROLLUP

Bake at 350° for 1 hour.
Makes 8 servings

- ½ cup chopped dried apricots
- ½ cup water
- 2 pounds meat-loaf mixture (ground beef, pork, and veal)
- 2 tablespoons chopped parsley
- 1 egg
- ¼ cup dairy sour cream
- 1¼ teaspoons salt
- ⅛ teaspoon pepper
- 2 cups ready-mix bread stuffing (half an 8-ounce package)
- ¼ cup chopped celery
- 2 tablespoons melted butter or margarine
  Dash of cayenne
- 4 slices bacon

1. Simmer apricots in water 1 minute; remove from heat.
2. Mix meat-loaf mixture lightly with parsley, egg, sour cream, 1 teaspoon of the salt, and pepper until well-blended; pat into a rectangle, 16x10, on waxed paper or foil. (For easy handling, paper should be a few inches longer than meat layer.)
3. Stir bread stuffing, celery, melted butter or margarine, remaining ¼ teaspoon salt, and cayenne into apricots. Spread evenly over meat to within 1 inch of edges. Roll up, jelly-roll fashion, using waxed paper or foil as a guide. Pinch together at ends to seal.
4. Place roll, seam side down, in a greased large shallow baking pan; top with bacon slices.
5. Bake in moderate oven (350°) 1 hour, or until richly browned.

Just look at this inviting array of meat loaves, perfect for any occasion. Left to right: Perky Dill-sauced Meat Loaf *(recipe on page 38)*, double-good Piquant Ring with Green Rice *(recipe on page 33)*, and colorful Beef-macaroni Loaf *(recipe on page 48)*

PINWHEEL MEAT LOAF

Bake at 375° for 1 hour.
Makes 8 servings

    Raisin Filling (*recipe follows*)
    OR: Cheese Filling (*recipe follows*)
2 pounds meat-loaf mixture (ground beef, pork, and veal)
1 egg
1 small onion, chopped (¼ cup)
1 teaspoon salt
⅛ teaspoon pepper
1 tablespoon Worcestershire sauce
4 slices bacon, halved

1. Make your choice of RAISIN or CHEESE FILLING.
2. Mix meat-loaf mixture with egg, onion, and seasonings. Pat into a thin rectangle, 16x10, on waxed paper or foil. (For easy handling, paper should be a few inches longer than meat layer.)
3. Spread filling evenly over meat to within 1 inch of edges; roll up, jelly-roll fashion, using waxed paper or foil as a guide.
4. Place, seam side down, in a greased large shallow baking pan; top with bacon.
5. Bake in moderate oven (375°) 1 hour, or until bacon is crisp.

RAISIN FILLING—Combine 4 cups small bread cubes (about 8 slices), ¼ cup seedless raisins, ¼ cup chopped celery, ½ teaspoon poultry seasoning, ½ teaspoon salt, ⅛ teaspoon pepper, and 2 tablespoons butter or margarine. Pour ½ cup boiling water over; toss to mix well.

CHEESE FILLING—Pour ½ cup boiling water over 2 cups ready-mix bread stuffing; toss to mix well. Stir in 1 cup grated Cheddar cheese (4 ounces), 1 egg, and ¼ cup catsup.

VEGETABLE-STUFFED BEEF ROLL

Bake at 375° for 1 hour.
Makes 8 servings

1 medium-size onion, chopped (½ cup)
2 tablespoons butter or margarine
1 package (10 ounces) frozen mixed vegetables
2 pounds ground beef
1 egg
1 tablespoon prepared mustard
2 teaspoons Worcestershire sauce
1 teaspoon salt
¼ teaspoon pepper
1 cup grated process American cheese (4 ounces)
3 slices bacon, halved

1. Saute onion in butter or margarine just until soft; stir in frozen mixed vegetables. Heat over low heat, breaking up vegetables with a fork; cover, then cook 10 minutes, or until almost tender. Drain well; cool while preparing meat.
2. Mix ground beef lightly with egg, mustard, Worcestershire sauce, salt, and pepper until well-blended; pat into a rectangle, 16x10, on waxed paper or foil. (For easy handling, paper should be a few inches longer than meat layer.)
3. Spread cooled vegetable mixture evenly over meat to within 1 inch of edges; sprinkle with cheese. Roll up, jelly-roll fashion, using waxed paper or foil as a guide. Pinch together at ends to seal.
4. Place roll, seam side down, in a greased large shallow baking pan; top with bacon slices.
5. Bake in moderate oven (375°) 1 hour, or until richly browned.

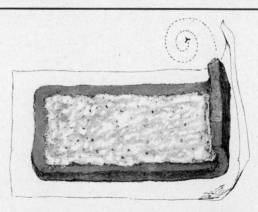

Cooksaver tip:

A few slices of bacon arranged over meat loaf will help to keep it moist during baking and give it extra flavor as well as a pretty top. Another idea: Brush with barbecue sauce

Cooksaver tip:

When making a stuffed rolled loaf, keep filling in from the edges so it doesn't squeeze out as meat is rolled. Paper serves as your rolling guide, and if the meat should stick a bit, just loosen it with a spatula as you go along

BEEF IN A BLANKET

Bake at 475° for 15 minutes,
then at 325° for 45 minutes.
Makes 8 servings

2 pounds meat-loaf mixture (ground beef
    and pork)
1 cup ready-mix bread stuffing
1 small onion, grated
1 teaspoon salt
⅛ teaspoon pepper
1 egg
2 cans (about 11 ounces each) mushroom
    gravy
½ package piecrust mix

1. Mix meat-loaf mixture lightly with bread stuffing, onion, salt, pepper, egg, and ¾ cup of the mushroom gravy until well-blended. Shape into a roll about 9 inches long.
2. Prepare piecrust mix, following label directions. Roll out on a lightly floured pastry cloth or board to a rectangle, 12x9. Place meat loaf in center; fold pastry up over loaf; seal edges, but leave ends open. Place, seam side down, in an ungreased large shallow baking pan; cut several slits in top of pastry.
3. Bake in very hot oven (475°) 15 minutes; lower heat to slow (325°). Bake 45 minutes longer, or until pastry is golden-brown.
4. Heat remaining mushroom gravy to boiling; serve separately to spoon over loaf when sliced.

SOUTHERN BEEF ROLL

Bake at 375° for 1 hour.
Makes 8 servings

1 can (8 ounces) tomato sauce
1½ cups soft bread crumbs (3 slices)
2 pounds meat-loaf mixture (ground beef
    and pork)
1 egg
1 small onion, chopped (¼ cup)
½ cup chopped celery
¼ cup chopped green pepper
1 envelope French salad-dressing mix
1 teaspoon prepared mustard
4 slices bacon, halved

1. Pour tomato sauce over bread crumbs; let stand a few minutes. Mix lightly with meat-loaf mixture, egg, onion, celery, green pepper, salad-dressing mix, and mustard until well-blended.
2. Shape into a long roll in a shallow baking pan. Lay bacon slices across top.
3. Bake in moderate oven (375°) 1 hour, or until bacon is crisp.

WINTER GARDEN MEAT ROLLS

Bake at 350° for 35 minutes.
Makes 6 servings

1½ pounds ground lean beef round
1 jar (about 5 ounces) baby-pack strained
    carrots
½ cup tomato juice
¼ cup chopped parsley
1 small onion, chopped (¼ cup)
1½ teaspoons salt
½ teaspoon Italian seasoning
⅛ teaspoon pepper

1. Mix ground beef lightly with carrots, tomato juice, parsley, onion, and seasonings until well-blended.
2. Shape into 6 even-size rolls about 1 inch thick; place on rack in broiler pan or set on a wire rack in a shallow baking pan.
3. Bake in moderate oven (350°) 35 minutes, or until richly browned.

CONFETTI ROLLS

Bake at 400° for 30 minutes.
Makes 4 servings

2 cups biscuit mix
1 teaspoon paprika
1 cup (8-ounce carton) dairy sour cream
1 pound ground beef
1 egg
1 small onion, grated
¼ cup chopped parsley
1 tablespoon horseradish-mustard
1 teaspoon seasoned salt
¼ teaspoon seasoned pepper
1 package frozen creamed mixed vegetables

1. Combine biscuit mix and paprika; stir in sour cream just until dough holds together. Knead about 8 times on a lightly floured pastry cloth or board; pat into a thin rectangle, 14x12, on waxed paper or foil. (For easy handling, paper should be a few inches longer than biscuit layer.)
2. Mix ground beef lightly with egg, onion, parsley, and seasonings; spread evenly over dough. Roll up, jelly-roll fashion, using waxed paper or foil as a guide.
3. Cut into 8 slices; place, without touching, in an ungreased large shallow baking pan.
4. Bake in hot oven (400°) 30 minutes, or until rolls are crusty-brown.
5. While rolls bake, heat creamed vegetables, following label directions; spoon over hot meat rolls.

Make these fancies in layers

RIBBON MEAT LOAF

Bake at 350° for 1 hour.
Makes 6 servings

1½ pounds ground beef
  1 egg
  2 tablespoons chili sauce
  2 teaspoons salt
  1 teaspoon dry mustard
    Dash of pepper
  1 small onion, chopped (¼ cup)
  2 tablespoons butter or margarine
  ½ teaspoon lemon juice
  1 can (3 or 4 ounces) sliced mushrooms, drained
  2 tablespoons chopped parsley
  2 tablespoons chopped pimiento
  ¼ teaspoon thyme
  2 cups soft bread crumbs (4 slices)

1. Grease a loaf pan, 9x5x3; line bottom and ends with a double-thick strip of foil, leaving a 1-inch overhang; grease foil.
2. Mix ground beef lightly with egg, chili sauce, 1½ teaspoons of the salt, mustard, and pepper until well-blended.
3. Sauté onion in butter or margarine just until soft; remove from heat. Stir in lemon juice, drained mushrooms, parsley, pimiento, remaining ½ teaspoon salt, and thyme. Pour over bread crumbs; toss lightly to mix.
4. Spoon half of the meat mixture in an even layer in prepared pan; top with all of the stuffing mixture; pat remaining meat mixture over stuffing to cover completely.
5. Bake in moderate oven (350°) 1 hour, or until richly browned.
6. Cool loaf in pan 5 minutes; loosen from sides with knife, then lift up ends of foil and set loaf on a heated serving platter; slide out foil.

MEXICALI BEEF WHEEL

Bake at 375° for 50 minutes.
Makes 6 servings

  1 can (12 ounces) Mexican-style whole-kernel corn
  1 can (about 2 ounces) chopped ripe olives, drained
  ½ cup fine dry bread crumbs
  ¼ teaspoon poultry seasoning
1½ pounds ground beef
  1 egg
  ½ cup catsup
  1 teaspoon prepared mustard
1½ teaspoons salt
  ⅛ teaspoon pepper

1. Combine corn and liquid, olives, bread crumbs, and poultry seasoning.
2. Mix ground beef lightly with egg, ¼ cup of the catsup, mustard, salt, and pepper. Press half into a shallow 9-inch round baking dish; spread with corn mixture, then with remaining meat mixture.
3. Mark top deeply into 6 wedges with a knife; spoon remaining ¼ cup catsup along marks to resemble spokes.
4. Bake in moderate oven (375°) 50 minutes, or until browned. Garnish with a "hub" of sliced stuffed olives, if you wish.

SPAGHETTI-CHEESE LOAF

Bake at 350° for 1 hour.
Makes 6 servings

1½ pounds ground beef
  1 can (about 1 pound) spaghetti in tomato sauce
  1 egg
  1 teaspoon salt
  ¼ teaspoon oregano
  ⅛ teaspoon garlic powder
  1 small onion, peeled and sliced thin
  4 slices (half an 8-ounce package) process American cheese

1. Mix ground beef lightly with spaghetti, egg, salt, oregano, and garlic powder until well-blended.
2. Press half into a baking pan, 8x8x2; top with onion and cheese slices, then remaining meat mixture.
3. Bake in moderate oven (350°) 1 hour, or until browned.

SNOWCAP MEAT LOAF

Bake at 375° for 50 minutes.
Makes 8 servings

- 2 pounds meat-loaf mixture (ground beef, pork, and veal)
- 1 small onion, grated
- 1 cup soft whole-wheat bread crumbs
- ½ cup chopped celery
- 1 tablespoon chopped parsley
- 1 egg
- ½ cup apple juice
- 2 teaspoons salt
- ¼ teaspoon ground cloves
- Snowcap Potatoes (recipe follows)

1. Mix meat-loaf mixture lightly with onion, bread crumbs, celery, parsley, egg, apple juice, salt, and cloves until well-blended.
2. Pat into a square pan, 8x8x2; unmold into a shallow baking pan.
3. Bake in moderate oven (375°) 30 minutes; spoon SNOWCAP POTATOES in small mounds on top. Bake 20 minutes longer, or until brown.

SNOWCAP POTATOES—Pare 4 large potatoes and cut up; cook, covered, in a small amount of boiling salted water 15 minutes, or until tender; drain. Mash, then beat in 4 tablespoons (½ stick) butter or margarine, 1 egg, 2 tablespoons milk, 1 teaspoon salt and a dash of pepper until light and fluffy. Makes about 4 cups.

BEEF-ONION LOAF

Bake at 350° for 1 hour.
Makes 8 servings

- 2 pounds ground beef
- 1 egg
- ½ cup soft bread crumbs (1 slice)
- ¼ cup milk
- 1 teaspoon salt
- 4 large onions, peeled and sliced thin
- 4 tablespoons (½ stick) butter or margarine
- 1 tablespoon brown sugar
- ¼ teaspoon cracked pepper

1. Mix ground beef lightly with egg, bread crumbs, milk, and salt until well-blended.
2. Saute onions until soft in butter or margarine; stir in brown sugar.
3. Pat half of the meat mixture into a loaf pan, 9x5x3; top with all of the onion mixture, then remaining meat mixture. Unmold into a shallow baking pan; sprinkle loaf with pepper.
4. Bake in moderate oven (350°) 1 hour, or until richly browned.

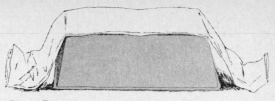

Cooksaver tip:

To line a loaf pan: Fold a double sheet of foil to fit across bottom and up ends of pan with an inch overhang. Flip pan right side up and grease; press the strip inside and grease again

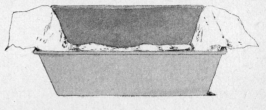

QUICK BEEF SHORTCAKE

Bake at 425° for 30 minutes.
Makes 6 servings

- 1½ pounds ground beef
- 1 egg
- 1 envelope onion-soup mix
- 1 cup soft bread crumbs (2 slices)
- ½ cup milk (for meat mixture)
- 2 cups biscuit mix
- 2 tablespoons chopped parsley
- ⅔ cup milk (for biscuit topping)
- 3 tablespoons salad oil
- Vegetable Sauce (recipe follows)

1. Mix ground beef lightly with egg, onion-soup mix, bread crumbs, and the ½ cup milk until well-blended; pack into a 9-inch layer-cake pan; unmold into a jelly-roll pan, 15x10x1.
2. Bake in hot oven (425°) 30 minutes, or until richly browned.
3. While loaf bakes, combine biscuit mix and parsley; stir in the ⅔ cup milk and salad oil all at once, stirring lightly with a fork just until blended. Pat mixture on the back of a greased 9-inch layer-cake pan.
4. Bake in same oven with meat 15 minutes, or until golden-brown.
5. Lift meat onto a heated serving plate and top with biscuit; cut into wedges. Serve with VEGETABLE SAUCE.

VEGETABLE SAUCE—Heat 1 can condensed cream of mushroom soup with ⅓ cup milk and a few drops red-pepper seasoning just until bubbly. Makes about 1½ cups.

STUFFED BEEF LOAF

Bake at 350° for 1 hour.
Makes 6 servings

1½ pounds ground beef
1 medium-size onion, chopped (½ cup)
¼ cup chili sauce
1 egg
1½ teaspoons salt
Dash of pepper
2 tablespoons chopped parsley
2 tablespoons butter or margarine
1½ cups ready-mix bread stuffing
¼ cup water

1. Grease a loaf pan, 9x5x3; line bottom and ends with a double-thick strip of foil, leaving a 1-inch overhang; grease foil.
2. Mix ground beef lightly with ¼ cup of the onion, chili sauce, egg, salt, and pepper until well-blended.
3. Saute remaining ¼ cup onion and parsley in butter or margarine just until onion is soft; stir in bread stuffing and water until well-blended. (Stuffing will be crumbly, but will absorb moisture from meat as loaf bakes.)
4. Pat half of the meat mixture in an even layer in prepared pan; top with all of the stuffing mixture, then with remaining meat mixture.
5. Bake in moderate oven (350°) 1 hour, or until richly browned.
6. Cool loaf in pan 5 minutes; loosen from sides with knife, then lift up ends of foil and set loaf on a heated serving platter; slide out foil.

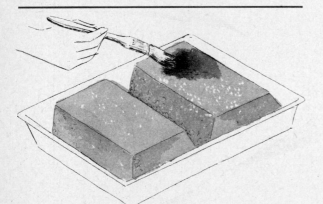

Cooksaver tip:

To have plenty for seconds when serving a crowd, or an on-hand treat to slice cold for sandwiches, mix a double batch of meat loaf and bake as "twins." Saves time and dishwashing — and oven heat too

BEEF-MACARONI LOAF
(Pictured on page 43)

Bake at 350° for 1 hour.
Makes 6 to 8 servings

Macaroni Layers
1 package (8 ounces) elbow macaroni
2 tablespoons butter or margarine
2 tablespoons flour
1 teaspoon salt
¼ teaspoon pepper
1 egg
2 cups milk
½ cup grated Parmesan cheese
Meat Layer
1 small onion, chopped (¼ cup)
1 tablespoon butter or margarine
1½ pounds ground beef
1 egg
1 can condensed tomato soup
1 teaspoon salt
¼ teaspoon pepper
Sauce
1 can (8 ounces) tomato sauce
1 teaspoon sugar
¼ teaspoon basil

1. Grease a loaf pan, 9x5x3; line bottom and ends with a double-thick strip of foil, leaving a 1-inch overhang; grease foil.
2. Make macaroni layers: Cook macaroni, following label directions; drain; return to kettle. Stir in butter or margarine; sprinkle flour, salt, and pepper over; toss to mix well.
3. Beat egg; stir in milk; pour over macaroni mixture. Cook, stirring constantly, over medium heat, until thickened; remove from heat. Stir in Parmesan cheese.
4. Make meat layer: Saute onion in butter or margarine until soft; add ground beef and brown, breaking meat up with a fork as it cooks.
5. Beat egg; stir in ½ can of the tomato soup, salt, and pepper; stir into cooked meat mixture.
6. Spoon half of the macaroni mixture in an even layer in prepared pan; top with all of the meat mixture, then remaining macaroni mixture.
7. Bake in moderate oven (350°) 1 hour, or until firm and brown on top.
8. Make sauce: While loaf bakes, heat tomato sauce with remaining ½ can of tomato soup, sugar, and basil to boiling; simmer 2 to 3 minutes to blend flavors.
9. Cool loaf in pan 10 minutes; loosen from sides with knife, then lift up ends of foil and set loaf on a heated serving platter; slide out foil. Frame platter and top loaf with steamed green and red pepper rings, if you wish. Slice loaf; serve sauce separately to spoon over.

Bound to be a hit with meat-and-potato fans is this hearty, different Mock Pot Roast with Vegetables *(recipe on page 32)*. Zippy-seasoned meat loaf, plus potatoes, onions, carrots, and peas cook together, are ready for the table in just about an hour

49

GIVE MEAT LOAF A NEW LOOK WITH A NEW SHAPE

Your hands and a few everyday kitchen tools are the only helpers you need

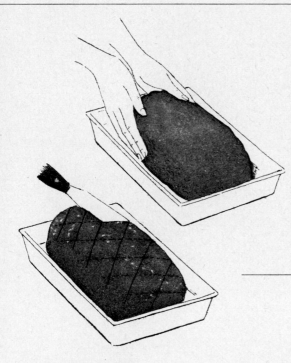

Chunky oblong

Pretty to look at and so easy to do. Just place the meat in a large shallow pan and pat it into a neat thick rounded loaf. Dress top with deep crisscross marks made with a knife or spatula

Jumbo roll

For this trim loaf, use a long baking pan and shape the meat into a big "log." If meat is very lean, top with halved slices of bacon for extra moistness and flavor, then slice between bacon pieces so each serving has a bonus crisp topping

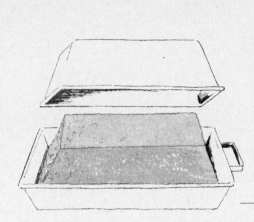

Most-popular loaf

A jiffy — that's all this shaping trick takes.
Press meat into a bread pan, then invert
into a shallow pan for baking. Want to go simpler
still? Bake the loaf right in the pan

Casserole easy

A shallow baking dish — round, square, or oblong —
makes an ideal mold for meat loaf, and most
are attractive enough to carry right to the
table for serving. For a subtle flavor
touch, top loaf with a bay leaf before baking

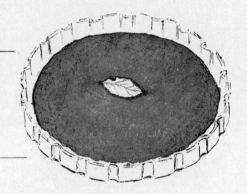

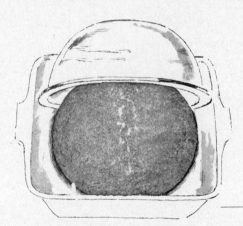

Bowl-'em-over round

Here's another molding trick with a
casserole, or you can use a regular mixing
bowl. Place the meat in the bowl and
turn it upside down into a pan; lift off
bowl. Serving tip: Divide the loaf
into quarters and slice each quarter

Easy-as-pie whirligig

A pie plate is the baker for this inviting
loaf. After pressing meat into the
plate, mark it into wedges and
outline each with a ribbon of catsup.
Cut between marks after baking; lift
out each sauce-topped wedge with a spatula

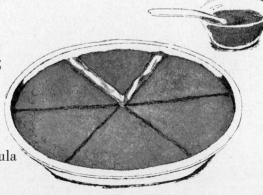

SPANISH MEAT LOAF

Bake at 350° for 1 hour.
Makes 6 servings

1½ pounds ground beef
1 large onion, chopped (1 cup)
1 clove garlic, minced
1 teaspoon chili powder
½ teaspoon salt
¼ teaspoon pepper
2 tablespoons salad oil
¼ cup flour
1 cup water
2 tablespoons lemon juice
   Onion Pastry (recipe follows)
½ cup sliced stuffed green olives
¼ cup seedless raisins
2 tablespoons chili sauce

1. Mix ground beef lightly with onion, garlic, chili powder, salt, and pepper. Shape into a large patty; brown in salad oil in a large frying pan 5 minutes on each side, then break up into chunks.
2. Sprinkle with flour, then stir in with water and lemon juice. Cook, stirring constantly, until mixture thickens and boils 1 minute; remove from heat.
3. Make ONION PASTRY. Roll out to a rectangle, 16x14, on a cooky sheet. (To prevent slipping, set cooky sheet on a damp towel.)
4. Spread half of the meat mixture evenly down middle of pastry, leaving a border of 4 inches on sides and 2 inches at ends. Mix olives, raisins, and chili sauce; spread over meat layer; top with remaining meat mixture. Fold ends of pastry over filling, then fold up sides and overlap to cover filling. Press all edges together to seal; cut several slits in top to let steam escape.
5. Bake in moderate oven (350°) 1 hour, or until pastry is golden-brown and filling bubbles up through slits in pastry.
6. Cut loaf into 2-inch-thick slices. Serve plain or with canned mushroom gravy, if you wish.

ONION PASTRY—Combine 2 cups sifted regular flour, 1 tablespoon instant minced onion, and 1 teaspoon salt in a medium-size bowl; cut in ⅔ cup shortening with a pastry blender until mixture is crumbly. Sprinkle 4 to 5 tablespoons cold water over, 1 tablespoon at a time; mix lightly with a fork until pastry holds together and leaves side of bowl clean.

RICE SCRAMBLE LOAF

Bake at 350° for 50 minutes.
Makes 8 servings

1 large onion, chopped (1 cup)
1 cup chopped celery
3 tablespoons butter or margarine
2 pounds meat-loaf mixture (ground beef, pork, and veal)
2 cups cooked rice
1½ teaspoons salt
1 teaspoon Worcestershire sauce
2 eggs
¼ cup milk
½ cup grated white American cheese
2 tablespoons chopped parsley
2 tablespoons toasted slivered almonds

1. Saute onion and celery in butter or margarine until soft. Combine half with meat-loaf mixture and remaining with cooked rice.
2. Mix meat-loaf–onion mixture lightly with salt, Worcestershire sauce, 1 of the eggs, and milk until well-blended; pat into a square pan, 8x8x2; unmold into a shallow baking pan.
3. Bake in moderate oven (350°) 30 minutes.
4. Mix rice-onion mixture with cheese, parsley, and remaining egg until well-blended; spread over meat loaf; sprinkle with almonds.
5. Bake 20 minutes longer, or until rice is set.

MEAT LOAF ITALIANO

Bake at 350° for 1 hour and 15 minutes.
Makes 8 servings

1½ cups coarse Italian-bread crumbs
1 small can evaporated milk (⅔ cup)
2 pounds ground beef
1 can (8 ounces) spaghetti sauce with mushrooms
1 tablespoon chopped parsley
1½ teaspoons salt
1 teaspoon oregano
3 sweet Italian sausages (about ½ pound)

1. Combine bread crumbs and evaporated milk; let stand about 5 minutes. Mix lightly with ground beef, ½ cup of the spaghetti sauce, parsley, and seasonings until well-blended. Pat half into a loaf pan, 9x5x3.
2. Squeeze sausage meat from casings; pat over meat mixture in pan; top with remaining meat mixture. Unmold into a shallow baking pan; spread with remaining spaghetti sauce.
3. Bake in moderate oven (350°) 1 hour and 15 minutes, or until richly browned.

GLAZED BEEF PATTY

Bake at 350° for 1 hour.
Makes 8 servings

1½ pounds ground beef
½ pound ground pork
2 eggs
2 teaspoons salt
1 teaspoon mixed salad herbs
¼ teaspoon pepper
1 package (8 ounces) mozzarella cheese, sliced
1 red onion, peeled and sliced
   OR: 1 Bermuda onion, peeled and sliced
¼ cup bottled barbecue sauce

1. Mix ground beef and pork lightly with eggs, salt, salad herbs, and pepper until well-blended.
2. Shape half into a 9-inch round in a large shallow baking pan; top with layers of cheese and onion slices, then remaining meat mixture.
3. Bake in moderate oven (350°) 45 minutes; brush with barbecue sauce.
4. Bake 15 minutes longer, or until richly glazed. Cut into wedges.

APPLETIME BEEF SQUARE

Bake at 375° for 1 hour.
Makes 8 servings

2 pounds meat-loaf mixture (ground beef, pork, and veal)
1 cup soft bread crumbs (2 slices)
1 egg
½ cup apple cider
2 teaspoons salt
1 teaspoon fines herbes
¼ teaspoon pepper
1 package (8 ounces) sliced Muenster cheese, cut in strips
2 tablespoons apple jelly

1. Mix meat-loaf mixture, bread crumbs, egg, cider, salt, herbes, and pepper until well-blended.
2. Shape half into a 9-inch square in a shallow baking pan; top with a layer of cheese strips, then remaining meat mixture.
3. Bake in moderate oven (375°) 45 minutes; spread apple jelly over top.
4. Bake 15 minutes longer, or until richly glazed. Cut into squares or oblongs.

LELANI MEAT LOAF

Bake at 375° for 1 hour.
Makes 8 servings

Pineapple Layer
1 medium-size onion, chopped (½ cup)
2 tablespoons salad oil
1 can (about 9 ounces) crushed pineapple
1 tablespoon bottled steak sauce
2 teaspoons soy sauce
½ teaspoon ground ginger
1 clove garlic, peeled
2 teaspoons cornstarch
Meat Layers
2 pounds meat-loaf mixture (ground beef, pork, and veal)
1 egg
½ cup coarse unsalted cracker crumbs
¼ cup catsup
¼ cup water
¼ cup finely chopped parsley
1½ teaspoons salt

1. Make pineapple layer: Saute onion in salad oil until soft in a medium-size frying pan; stir in pineapple and syrup, steak and soy sauces, ginger, and whole clove of garlic.
2. Smooth cornstarch to a paste with a little water; stir into pineapple mixture. Cook, stirring constantly, until sauce thickens and boils 3 minutes; remove garlic.
3. Make meat layers: Mix meat-loaf mixture lightly with remaining ingredients until well-blended.
4. Pat half into a loaf pan, 9x5x3, lined with foil, following directions on page 47; top with all of the pineapple mixture, then remaining meat mixture.
5. Bake in moderate oven (375°) 1 hour, or until brown.
6. Cool loaf in pan 5 minutes; loosen from sides with knife, then lift up ends of foil and set loaf on a heated serving platter; slide out foil.

Variation:
DIXIE MEAT LOAF—Make peach layer: Drain syrup from 1 can (8 ounces) cling peach slices into a small saucepan; chop peach slices coarsely. Stir ½ teaspoon cinnamon, ⅛ teaspoon ground allspice, and 2 tablespoons cider vinegar into syrup; cook until syrup is slightly thickened. Smooth 1 tablespoon cornstarch to a paste with a little water; stir into hot syrup; cook, stirring constantly, until mixture thickens and boils 3 minutes; stir in peaches. Make meat layers, following recipe above; put together with peach filling and bake, following Steps 4 and 5 above.

This hearty Spaghetti Bowl *(recipe on page 56)* with
mildly seasoned meat balls poached in a quick-mix
sauce takes only a half hour from frying pan to table

54

CHAPTER 4

GO PLAIN, GO FANCY WITH
MEAT BALLS

Popular spaghetti with meat balls, dainty Swedish meat balls, hearty soup with meat balls, company-good meat balls—whatever your menu need, you'll find plenty of choices here.

In making meat balls, handle the meat mixture with a light touch and you'll be rewarded with the tenderest, juiciest morsels. Pan-fry, bake, or poach them—they're that adaptable. Serve them with noodles, rice, potatoes, or vegetables—they go with all. Make them into a quick family dish or a guest-night treat—they're perfect any time. And if you're giving a party, there's a whole section on appetizer meat balls in Chapter 7.

Yes, for plain or fancy eating, we vote meat balls tops—and hope you do too.

So-good meat balls for family meals

MACARONI DINNER

Makes 4 servings

    3 slices bacon
    1 pound ground beef
    2 tablespoons minced green pepper
    1 teaspoon salt
    ⅛ teaspoon pepper
    1 medium-size onion, peeled and sliced
    1 can (about 1 pound) red kidney beans
    1 can condensed tomato soup
    1 soup-can water
    ½ cup catsup
    2 teaspoons chili powder
    ¾ cup uncooked elbow macaroni

1. Saute bacon until crisp in a large frying pan; remove and drain on paper toweling, then crumble.
2. Mix ground beef lightly with crumbled bacon, green pepper, salt, and pepper until well-blended; shape into 16 balls.
3. Brown with onion in drippings in same pan. Stir in kidney beans and liquid, soup, water, catsup, chili powder, and macaroni; cover.
4. Simmer, stirring often, 25 minutes, or until macaroni is tender.

GERMAN CASSEROLE

Bake at 350° for 45 minutes.
Makes 4 servings

    2 cups (half an 8-ounce package) noodles
    1 can (about 1 pound) sauerkraut, drained
    1 pound ground beef
    1 egg
    ½ cup soft caraway-rye bread crumbs
    ¼ cup milk
    1 teaspoon salt
    ⅛ teaspoon pepper
    1 tablespoon butter or margarine
    1 can (about 1 pound) stewed tomatoes

1. Cook noodles and drain, following label directions; stir in drained sauerkraut.
2. Mix ground beef lightly with egg, bread crumbs, milk, salt, and pepper until well-blended; shape into 24 balls. Brown in butter or margarine in a large frying pan; stir in tomatoes.
3. Spoon half of the noodle-sauerkraut mixture into an 8-cup baking dish; top with half of the meatball mixture; repeat layers; cover.
4. Bake in moderate oven (350°) 45 minutes, or until bubbly hot in center.

SPAGHETTI BOWL

(Pictured on page 54)

Makes 4 servings

    1 package (1 pound) spaghetti
    2 envelopes spaghetti-sauce mix
    2 cans (8 ounces each) tomato sauce
    3 cups water
    ¼ cup salad oil
    1 pound ground beef
    1 small onion, grated
    ¼ cup chopped parsley
    1 egg
    ½ cup ready-mix bread stuffing
    1 teaspoon salt
    ⅛ teaspoon marjoram
       Grated Parmesan cheese

1. Cook spaghetti, following label directions; drain.
2. Combine spaghetti-sauce mix, tomato sauce, water, and salad oil in a large frying pan; simmer 15 minutes to blend flavors.
3. Mix ground beef lightly with onion, parsley, egg, bread stuffing, salt, and marjoram until well-blended; shape into 24 balls. Place in hot sauce.
4. Simmer 10 minutes, or until cooked through.
5. Layer cooked spaghetti and meat balls and sauce onto a deep serving platter; serve with Parmesan cheese to sprinkle over.

SPRING BEEF RAGOUT

Makes 4 servings

- 1 pound ground beef
- 1 cup soft bread crumbs (2 slices)
- 1 egg
- ¼ cup milk
- 1 teaspoon salt
- 1 tablespoon salad oil
- 1 can (12 ounces) mixed vegetable juices
- ½ teaspoon sugar
- ⅛ teaspoon pepper
- 5 whole allspice
- 1 bay leaf
- 12 small carrots, pared
- 1 package (9 ounces) frozen French-style green beans

1. Mix ground beef lightly with bread crumbs, egg, milk, and ½ teaspoon of the salt until well-blended; shape into 12 balls.
2. Brown in salad oil in a large frying pan; drain off all drippings.
3. Stir in mixed vegetable juices, remaining ½ teaspoon salt, sugar, pepper, allspice, and bay leaf. Push meat balls to one side of pan; place carrots alongside meat; cover. Simmer 30 minutes.
4. Place frozen green beans in a third pile in pan; cook 15 minutes longer, or just until beans are tender. Remove allspice and bay leaf.
5. Serve with hot mashed potatoes, if you wish.

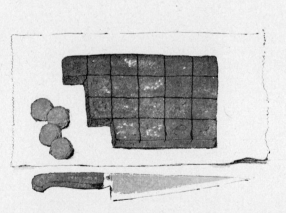

Cooksaver tip:

Meat balls will be even size if you pat meat into a rectangle about an inch thick, then divide it: First in half, then quarters, eighths, and sixteenths, depending on what size ball you want

SUPPER SOUP

Makes 6 servings

- 4 slices bacon
- 1 pound ground beef
- 1 egg
- 2 tablespoons water
- ½ cup soft whole-wheat bread crumbs
- ½ teaspoon salt
- ⅛ teaspoon thyme
- 1 can condensed minestrone soup
- 1 can condensed tomato soup
- 2 soup-cans water

1. Saute bacon until crisp in a large saucepan; remove and drain on paper toweling; crumble and set aside for garnish. Pour off all drippings, then measure 1 tablespoonful and return to pan.
2. Mix ground beef lightly with egg, water, bread crumbs, and seasonings until well-blended; shape into 48 balls.
3. Brown, half at a time, in drippings in pan; pour off any remaining drippings. Return all meat balls to pan; stir in soups and water; cover.
4. Simmer, stirring several times, 20 minutes to blend flavors. Ladle into soup bowls; sprinkle with crumbled bacon.

CHILI RICE MEAT BALLS

Makes 8 servings

- 1 pound ground beef
- 1 pound ground pork
- 1 egg
- ½ cup milk
- ⅔ cup uncooked rice
- 1 small onion, chopped (¼ cup)
- ¼ cup chopped parsley
- 2 teaspoons chili powder
- 2 teaspoons salt
- 2 tablespoons butter or margarine
- 1 can (about 1 pound) tomatoes
- 1 can condensed tomato soup
- 2 soup-cans water

1. Mix ground beef and pork lightly with egg, milk, rice, onion, parsley, 1 teaspoon of the chili powder, and salt; shape into 24 balls.
2. Brown, half at a time, in butter or margarine in a kettle or Dutch oven; remove with a slotted spoon and set aside. Pour off all drippings.
3. Combine tomatoes, soup, water, and remaining 1 teaspoon chili powder in same kettle; heat to boiling. Place meat balls in sauce; cover.
4. Simmer, stirring several times, 1 hour, or until rice is puffed out around meat balls and is tender.

SWEDISH BEEF BALLS

Makes 6 servings

1½ pounds ground beef
2 cups mashed peeled cooked potatoes
1 small onion, grated
¼ cup chopped peeled cooked beets
2 tablespoons chopped dill pickle
2 eggs
½ cup light or table cream
2 teaspoons salt
¼ teaspoon pepper
4 tablespoons (½ stick) butter or margarine
3 tablespoons flour
1½ cups water

1. Mix ground beef lightly with mashed potatoes, onion, beets, dill pickle, eggs, cream, 1 teaspoon of the salt, and pepper until well-blended; shape into 36 balls, then flatten each slightly.
2. Brown, a few at a time, in butter or margarine in a large frying pan, adding butter or margarine as needed. Remove with a slotted spoon and set aside.
3. Blend flour and remaining 1 teaspoon salt into drippings in pan; stir in water. Cook, stirring constantly, until the gravy thickens and boils 1 minute.
4. Place meat balls in gravy; heat just until bubbly.

MEAT-BALL CHOWDER

Makes 6 servings

1 pound ground beef
¼ cup chopped parsley
1 teaspoon salt
6¼ cups water
1 tablespoon bottled steak sauce
2 tablespoons butter or margarine
1 envelope onion-soup mix
1 cup chopped celery
½ cup uncooked rice
1 carrot, pared and grated

1. Mix ground beef lightly with parsley, salt, ¼ cup of the water, and steak sauce; shape into 36 balls.
2. Brown, half at a time, in butter or margarine in a large saucepan; remove with a slotted spoon and set aside. Pour off all drippings.
3. Heat remaining 6 cups water to boiling in same pan; stir in soup mix, celery, and rice; cover.
4. Simmer 15 minutes; stir in carrot and meat balls. Cook 5 minutes longer, or until rice is tender.
5. Ladle into soup bowls; garnish with chopped parsley, if you wish.

PORCUPINES

Makes 6 servings

1 egg
½ cup water
1 envelope onion-soup mix
1½ pounds ground beef
½ cup uncooked rice
1 can (46 ounces) tomato juice
1 teaspoon sugar

1. Beat egg slightly with water and 2 tablespoons of the soup mix. Mix lightly with ground beef and ¼ cup of the rice; shape into 12 balls. Roll in remaining ¼ cup rice, pressing it lightly into meat.
2. Heat tomato juice to boiling; stir in remaining onion-soup mix and sugar. Place meat balls in sauce; cover.
3. Simmer, stirring several times, 50 minutes, or until rice puffs out around meat and is tender.

SCALLOPED MEAT BALLS

Bake at 375° for 30 minutes.
Makes 4 servings

2 cups sliced pared raw potatoes
1 cup sliced pared raw carrots
1 medium-size onion, peeled and sliced
2 teaspoons salt
1 pound ground beef
1 egg
¼ cup fine dry bread crumbs
⅓ cup milk
¼ teaspoon thyme
2 tablespoons butter or margarine
1 can condensed cream of mushroom soup
1 cup (8-ounce carton) dairy sour cream
½ teaspoon paprika

1. Parboil potatoes with carrots, onion, and 1 teaspoon of the salt in a small amount of boiling water 5 minutes; drain.
2. Mix ground beef lightly with egg, bread crumbs, milk, thyme, and remaining 1 teaspoon salt until well-blended; shape into 16 balls.
3. Brown in butter or margarine in a large frying pan; remove with a slotted spoon and set aside. Pour off all drippings.
4. Stir soup, sour cream, and paprika into frying pan; heat, stirring constantly, just until hot.
5. Layer half each of the cooked vegetables, meat balls, and soup mixture into an 8-cup baking dish; repeat layers; cover.
6. Bake in moderate oven (375°) 30 minutes, or until bubbly hot in center.

ITALIAN MEAT-BALL RAGOUT

Makes 4 servings

- 1 pound ground beef
- 1 egg
- ½ cup soft bread crumbs (1 slice)
- 1 tablespoon chopped parsley
- 2 teaspoons salt
- 2 tablespoons salad oil
- 1 large onion, chopped (1 cup)
- 1 clove garlic, minced
- 1 small eggplant, pared and diced (4 cups)
- 1 can (about 1 pound) tomatoes
- 1 teaspoon sugar
- 1 teaspoon cumin seeds

1. Mix ground beef lightly with egg, bread crumbs, parsley, and 1 teaspoon of the salt until well-blended; shape into 24 balls.
2. Brown, half at a time, in salad oil in a large frying pan; remove with a slotted spoon and set aside.
3. Stir onion and garlic into drippings in pan; saute just until soft; add eggplant and meat balls.
4. Mix tomatoes with remaining 1 teaspoon salt, sugar, and cumin seeds; pour over meat balls and eggplant; cover.
5. Simmer, stirring several times, 30 minutes, or until eggplant is tender.

CHINESE MEAT BALLS

Makes 6 servings

- 1½ pounds ground beef
- 2 eggs
- 1½ teaspoons salt
- ¼ teaspoon pepper
- 3 tablespoons salad oil
- 3 medium-size onions, peeled and sliced
- 2 cups thinly sliced celery
- 1 can condensed beef broth
- 1 teaspoon sugar
- 1 can (1 pound) bean sprouts, drained
- 2 tablespoons cornstarch
- 3 tablespoons soy sauce
- 1 tablespoon water
  Hot cooked rice
- 1 can (3 ounces) Chinese fried noodles

1. Mix ground beef lightly with eggs, salt, and pepper until well-blended; shape into 36 balls.
2. Brown, half at a time, in salad oil in a kettle or Dutch oven; remove with a slotted spoon and set aside.
3. Stir onions and celery into drippings in kettle; cook, stirring constantly, just until soft, then stir in beef broth, sugar, bean sprouts, and meat balls; cover.
4. Simmer, stirring several times, 15 minutes to blend flavors.
5. Blend cornstarch with soy sauce and water; stir into meat-ball mixture. Cook, stirring constantly, until mixture thickens and boils 3 minutes.
6. Serve with hot cooked rice, Chinese fried noodles, and more soy sauce, if you wish.

Cooksaver tip:
Rice is simple to cook right

Follow label directions, or steam or bake it these no-watch ways and it will come out plump, tender, and fluffy every time.
The two easy secrets: Accurate measuring and a snug cover for your cooking pot. To make four cups cooked rice, you'll need:

- 2½ cups water
- 1 tablespoon butter or margarine
- 1 teaspoon salt
- 1 cup uncooked long-grain or processed white rice

To steam: Measure the 2½ cups water, butter or margarine, and salt into the top of a double boiler; heat to boiling over direct heat; stir in rice; cover. Place top of double boiler over bottom half filled with boiling water; turn heat to medium. Cook 45 minutes, or until water is absorbed completely and rice is fluffy-dry and tender. Toss lightly with a fork to fluff up, season as you wish, and serve.
To bake: Combine rice, salt, and butter or margarine in a 6-cup baking dish. Heat the 2½ cups water to boiling and pour over; stir well; cover. Bake in moderate oven (350°) 1 hour, or until water is absorbed and rice is tender. Fluff up with a fork, season as you wish, and serve.

Versatile meat balls go really grand as company choices. Left to right: Easy-on-the hostess Scandinavian Ragout *(recipe on page 62)*, little cream-topped Saucy Dill Meat Balls *(recipe on page 66)*, and Oriental-inspired Pacific Potluck *(recipe on page 63)*

Dressed-up meat balls for company nights

MEAT BALLS HAWAIIAN

Makes 4 servings

- 1 pound ground beef
- ½ teaspoon salt
- ¼ teaspoon ground ginger
- 1 egg
- 1 teaspoon water
- ¼ cup flour
- 3 tablespoons salad oil
- 1 can (about 14 ounces) pineapple chunks
- ¼ cup firmly packed brown sugar
- 2 tablespoons cornstarch
- ¼ cup cider vinegar
- 1 tablespoon soy sauce
- 2 green peppers, halved, seeded, and cut in strips
- Hot cooked noodles

1. Mix ground beef lightly with salt and ginger; shape into 16 balls. Beat egg slightly with water; dip balls into egg mixture, then into flour to coat well.
2. Brown in salad oil in a large frying pan; remove with a slotted spoon and set aside.
3. Drain syrup from pineapple into a 1-cup measure; add water to make 1 cup; stir into drippings in pan. Mix brown sugar with cornstarch, vinegar, and soy sauce; stir into pineapple-juice mixture; cook, stirring constantly, until sauce thickens and boils 3 minutes.
4. Arrange meat balls, pineapple chunks, and pepper strips in separate piles in pan; stir each gently to coat with sauce; cover. Simmer 10 minutes, or until meat balls are cooked through.
5. Serve with hot cooked noodles; garnish with chopped macadamia nuts, if you wish.

SCANDINAVIAN RAGOUT
(Pictured on page 60)

Bake at 350° for 30 minutes.
Makes 6 servings

- 1 pound ground beef
- ½ pound ground veal
- 1 cup soft bread crumbs (2 slices)
- 1 egg
- 1 small can evaporated milk (⅔ cup)
- 1 small onion, grated
- 1 teaspoon grated lemon rind
- 1½ teaspoons salt
- ¼ cup salad oil
- 6 medium-size potatoes, pared and cut French-fry style
- 1 medium-size cucumber, halved lengthwise and sliced ¼ inch thick
- 1 can (12 or 16 ounces) whole-kernel corn
- 1 tablespoon flour
- ⅛ teaspoon pepper
- 1 cup (8-ounce carton) dairy sour cream
- 1 tablespoon dill weed

1. Mix ground beef and veal lightly with bread crumbs, egg, evaporated milk, onion, lemon rind, and 1 teaspoon of the salt until well-blended; shape into 36 balls.
2. Brown, half at a time, in salad oil; place in a mound in one third of a greased 12-cup baking dish. (Set frying pan with drippings aside for making gravy.)
3. Parboil potato strips in a small amount of boiling salted water 5 minutes. Remove with a slotted spoon and mound in second third of baking dish; set potato water aside.
4. Parboil cucumber slices in a small amount of boiling water 3 minutes; drain, adding liquid to potato water. Drain corn, adding liquid to potato-cucumber water, if needed, to make 1 cup. Toss corn with cucumber; spoon into remaining space in baking dish.
5. Blend flour, remaining ½ teaspoon salt, and pepper into drippings in frying pan; stir in the 1 cup saved vegetable liquid. Cook, stirring constantly, until gravy thickens and boils 1 minute. Blend a few tablespoonfuls into sour cream, then stir back into remaining in pan; stir in dill weed; heat just to boiling.
6. Pour over meat balls and vegetables; stir lightly with a fork so gravy will flow to bottom; cover.
7. Bake in moderate oven (350°) 30 minutes, or until bubbly hot. To serve as pictured, spoon meat balls and vegetables into mounds on a heated serving platter; garnish with a pickled red pepper.

PACIFIC POTLUCK
(Pictured on page 61)

Bake at 350° for 25 minutes.
Makes 8 servings

- 2 pounds ground beef
- 1 small onion, grated
- 2 eggs
- 2½ teaspoons salt
- ⅛ teaspoon pepper
- 2 tablespoons soy sauce
- 2 tablespoons salad oil
- 1 can (5 ounces) whole blanched almonds (1 cup)
- 1 can (about 14 ounces) pineapple chunks
- 1 can (1 pint, 2 ounces) pineapple juice
- ½ cup sugar
- ¼ cup cornstarch
- ½ cup cider vinegar
- 3 cups frozen peas (from a 1½-pound bag), cooked and drained
- Hot cooked rice

1. Mix ground beef lightly with onion, eggs, 2 teaspoons of the salt, and pepper; shape into 32 balls; dip in soy sauce.
2. Brown, half at a time, in salad oil in a large frying pan; remove with a slotted spoon and place in a 10-cup baking dish. Stir almonds into drippings in pan; heat 1 to 2 minutes; sprinkle over meat balls.
3. Drain syrup from pineapple chunks and combine with pineapple juice. (There should be about 3 cups.) Mix sugar with cornstarch and remaining ½ teaspoon salt; stir in pineapple-juice mixture and vinegar. Cook in same frying pan, stirring constantly, until sauce thickens and boils 3 minutes.
4. Combine pineapple chunks and peas with meat balls and almonds in baking dish; pour sauce over; cover.
5. Bake in moderate oven (350°) 25 minutes to blend flavors.
6. Serve from baking dish with cooked rice, or to serve as pictured, mound meat balls in center of a large shallow dish; spoon cooked rice around edge. Pass little bowls of diced bananas, chopped green onions, and East Indian chutney to spoon on top, if you wish.

CASSEROLE MEAT BALLS

Bake at 450° for 20 minutes,
then at 350° for 15 minutes.
Makes 8 servings

Meat Balls
- 1 pound ground beef
- 1 pound ground veal
- 2 cups soft bread crumbs (4 slices)
- 3 eggs
- 1 large tart apple, pared, quartered, cored, and grated
- 1 small onion, grated
- ¼ cup chopped parsley
- 2 teaspoons seasoned salt
- 1 teaspoon ground ginger

Gravy
- 2½ cups hot water
- 4 tablespoons (½ stick) butter or margarine
- 6 tablespoons flour
- 1 teaspoon salt
- 1 tall can evaporated milk (1⅔ cups)
- ½ teaspoon fines herbes

1. Make meat balls: Mix ground beef and veal lightly with bread crumbs, eggs, apple, onion, parsley, seasoned salt, and ginger until well-blended; shape into 48 balls. Place in a single layer in a greased large shallow baking pan.
2. Bake in very hot oven (450°), turning balls once, 20 minutes, or until lightly browned. Remove with a slotted spoon and mound in the center of a shallow 8-cup baking dish. Lower heat to moderate (350°).
3. Make gravy: Pour hot water into baking pan; stir to mix with drippings and baked-on meat juices; strain into a 4-cup measure. Melt butter or margarine in a saucepan; blend in flour and salt; cook, stirring constantly, just until bubbly. Stir in drippings mixture and evaporated milk; cook, stirring constantly, until gravy thickens and boils 1 minute; stir in herbes. Pour around meat balls; cover.
4. Bake in moderate oven (350°) 15 minutes to blend flavors.

Cooksaver tip:

Try this early-bird fixing trick when you're making lots of meat balls for a party. Season them, shape, and dust lightly with flour to keep them from sticking together (see Cooksaver Tip, page 65), then pile them into a big bowl and chill. Another hint: Use a slotted spoon for turning and lifting them from the pan so all of the fat will drip back

MEAT BALLS VERONIQUE

Bake at 400° for 10 minutes.
Makes 8 servings

Meat Balls
1½   pounds ground beef
 1   large green apple, pared, quartered, and
       cored
 1   large pear, pared, quartered, and cored
 1   small Bermuda onion, peeled and
       quartered
 1   small green pepper, halved and seeded
 2   eggs
 1   cup crushed corn flakes
 1   teaspoon salt
⅛   teaspoon pepper
 1   teaspoon nutmeg
     Dash of ground allspice
Sauce
½   cup toasted slivered almonds (from a
       5-ounce can)
 2   tablespoons butter or margarine
 2   tablespoons cornstarch
 1   tablespoon brown sugar
 2   envelopes instant chicken broth
     OR: 2 chicken bouillon cubes
1½   cups water
 1   jar (about 5 ounces) baby-pack strained
       apricots and apples
 1   cup seeded halved green grapes

1. Make meat balls: Put ground beef, apple, pear, onion, and green pepper through a food chopper, using fine blade; mix lightly with eggs, corn flakes, and seasonings until well-blended. Shape into 48 balls. Place in a single layer in a greased large shallow baking pan.
2. Bake in hot oven (400°) 10 minutes, then broil 1 to 2 minutes to brown tops.
3. Make sauce: Saute almonds, stirring often, in butter or margarine in a large saucepan just until golden; remove from heat.
4. Stir in cornstarch, brown sugar, instant chicken broth or bouillon cubes, and water, crushing cubes, if using, with a spoon. Cook, stirring constantly, until sauce thickens and boils 3 minutes; stir in apricots and apples and grapes.
5. Place meat balls in sauce; simmer, stirring often, 10 minutes to blend flavors.

Cooksaver tip:

Green grapes out of season? Substitute red Tokays or the big purple variety—either tastes equally delicious

BEEF PORKERS

Makes 4 servings

½   pound ground beef
½   pound sausage meat
 1   egg
½   cup soft bread crumbs (1 slice)
¼   cup milk
 1   small onion, minced
 1   teaspoon salt
     Dash of pepper
 3   tablespoons flour
 1   tablespoon salad oil
 2   large onions, peeled, halved, and sliced

1. Mix ground beef and sausage meat lightly with egg, bread crumbs, milk, minced onion, salt, and pepper until well-blended; shape into 16 balls; roll in flour to coat well.
2. Brown in salad oil in a large frying pan; remove with a slotted spoon and set aside.
3. Saute sliced onions in drippings in same pan 10 minutes, or just until soft; return meat balls to pan; cover.
4. Simmer, stirring often, 15 minutes, or until meat balls are cooked through.

DUCHESS MEAT BALLS

Makes 4 servings

 1   pound ground beef
 1   egg
¼   cup milk
½   cup soft bread crumbs (1 slice)
½   cup chopped pecans
 2   tablespoons chopped parsley
½   teaspoon salt
     Dash of pepper
 2   tablespoons butter or margarine
 1   can condensed tomato soup
     Seasoned hot mashed potatoes

1. Mix ground beef lightly with egg, milk, bread crumbs, pecans, parsley, salt, and pepper until well-blended; shape into 24 balls.
2. Brown in butter or margarine in a large frying pan; stir in tomato soup; cover.
3. Simmer, stirring several times, 10 minutes to blend flavors.
4. Spoon seasoned hot mashed potatoes in a ring on a serving plate; spoon meat balls and sauce in center.

MEAT-BALL STEW WITH DUMPLINGS

Makes 6 servings

- 1 pound ground beef
- 1 medium-size onion, chopped (½ cup)
- 6 tablespoons chopped parsley
- 1 egg
- ½ cup soft bread crumbs (1 slice)
- 2 teaspoons salt
- ¼ teaspoon pepper
- 1 teaspoon dry mustard
- 2 tablespoons salad oil
- 1 can (1 pint, 2 ounces) tomato juice
- ½ cup water
- 1 clove garlic, minced
- 1 bay leaf
- 1 teaspoon chili powder
- 12 small white onions, peeled
- 12 small carrots, pared and cut in 2-inch pieces
- 1½ cups biscuit mix
- ½ cup milk
- 1 package (10 ounces) frozen lima beans

1. Mix ground beef lightly with chopped onion, 4 tablespoons of the parsley, egg, bread crumbs, 1 teaspoon of the salt, ⅛ teaspoon of the pepper, and mustard until well-blended; shape into 36 balls.
2. Brown, half at a time, in salad oil in a kettle or Dutch oven; remove with a slotted spoon and set aside. Pour off all drippings.
3. Combine tomato juice, water, garlic, bay leaf, chili powder, and remaining 1 teaspoon salt and ⅛ teaspoon pepper in same kettle; heat to boiling. Add white onions and carrots; cover. Simmer 30 minutes.
4. While vegetables cook, mix biscuit mix with remaining 2 tablespoons parsley; add milk all at once; stir lightly just until flour is moistened.
5. Return meat balls to kettle; add lima beans; heat to boiling. Drop dumpling mixture in 6 mounds on top.
6. Cook, uncovered, 10 minutes; cover; cook 10 minutes longer, or until dumplings are fluffy-light. Remove bay leaf before serving.

Cooksaver tip:

Flouring meat balls? Speed up the job by sprinkling the flour from a shaker, or toss the meat balls, a few at a time, in flour in a paper bag to coat well. Place salt, pepper, spices, or herb seasonings in the bag, too—another timesaver step

CURRIED MEAT BALLS

Makes 6 servings

- 1½ pounds ground beef
- 1 cup soft bread crumbs (2 slices)
- 1 cup tomato juice
- 1½ teaspoons salt
- ⅛ teaspoon pepper
- ¼ cup flour
- 2 tablespoons butter or margarine
- 2 medium-size onions, peeled and sliced
- 1 medium-size apple, pared, quartered, cored, and diced
- 1 teaspoon curry powder
- 2 teaspoons sugar
- 1 envelope instant beef broth
  OR: 1 beef-flavor bouillon cube
- 1 cup hot water
  Hot cooked rice

1. Mix ground beef lightly with bread crumbs, ½ cup of the tomato juice, salt, and pepper; shape into 36 balls; roll in flour to coat well.
2. Brown, half at a time, in butter or margarine in a large frying pan; remove with a slotted spoon and set aside.
3. Stir onions, apple, and curry powder into drippings in pan; saute, stirring often, just until onion is soft.
4. Return meat balls; stir in sugar, instant beef broth or bouillon cube, water, and remaining ½ cup tomato juice, crushing cube, if using, with a spoon; cover. Simmer, stirring often, 20 minutes to blend flavors.
5. Serve over hot cooked rice.

MEAT BALLS IN CREAM

Makes 6 servings

- 1 cup milk
- 2 cups soft caraway-rye bread crumbs (about 3 large slices)
- 1 pound ground beef
- ½ pound ground pork
- 1 small onion, grated
- 1 egg
- 6 tablespoons chopped parsley
- 2 teaspoons salt
- ⅛ teaspoon pepper
- 2 tablespoons salad oil
- 2 tablespoons flour
- 1 can (3 or 4 ounces) sliced mushrooms
- 1 cup cream for whipping

1. Pour milk over bread crumbs; let stand until milk is absorbed, then beat with a fork.
2. Mix lightly with ground beef and pork, onion, egg, 4 tablespoons of the parsley, 1½ teaspoons of the salt, and pepper until well-blended; shape into 36 balls.
3. Brown, a few at a time, in salad oil in a large frying pan; remove with a slotted spoon and set aside.
4. Pour off all drippings from frying pan, then measure 2 tablespoonfuls and return to pan. Stir in flour and remaining ½ teaspoon salt; cook, stirring constantly, just until bubbly. Drain liquid from mushrooms into a 1-cup measure; add water to make 1 cup; stir into flour mixture. Cook, stirring constantly, until gravy thickens and boils 1 minute.
5. Stir in mushrooms, cream, and meat balls; cover. Simmer 15 minutes, or until meat balls are cooked through; stir in remaining 2 tablespoons parsley.
6. Serve with buttered noodles, fluffy rice, or mashed potatoes, if you wish.

SAUCY DILL MEAT BALLS

(Pictured on pages 60-61)

Makes 10 to 12 servings

Meat Balls
- 1½ pounds ground beef
- 1 pound ground veal
- 1 can (4½ ounces) deviled ham
- 1 small can evaporated milk (⅔ cup)
- 2 eggs
- 1 cup soft whole-wheat bread crumbs (2 slices)
- 1 small onion, grated
- ½ teaspoon salt
- ¼ teaspoon ground cloves
- ¼ teaspoon pepper
- ¼ cup shortening
- ¼ cup water

Sauce
- 2 tablespoons butter or margarine
- 2 tablespoons flour
- ½ teaspoon salt
- 1 cup water
- 1 cup (8-ounce carton) dairy sour cream
- 1 tablespoon catsup
- 1 tablespoon dill weed

1. Make meat balls: Mix ground beef and veal and deviled ham lightly with evaporated milk, eggs, bread crumbs, onion, and seasonings until well-blended; shape into 72 balls.
2. Brown, a few at a time, in shortening in a large frying pan; pour off all drippings. Return all meat balls to pan; add water; cover. Simmer 20 minutes, or until cooked through.
3. Make sauce: Melt butter or margarine in a small saucepan; blend in flour and salt; stir in water. Cook, stirring constantly, until sauce thickens and boils 1 minute. Stir a few tablespoonfuls into sour cream, then stir back into remaining in saucepan. Stir in catsup and dill weed; heat just to boiling.
4. Spoon meat balls into a chafing dish or heated serving bowl; pour hot sauce over.

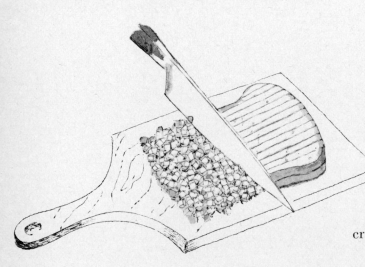

Cooksaver tip:

Lots of recipes call for soft bread crumbs, and here's the easy way to fix them. Lay bread slice on a board, and cut it in matchlike strips lengthwise, then crosswise. One regular slice bread will give ½ cup crumbs. Need more? Stack two or three slices together and cut them at the same time

Saucy-rich meat balls for all occasions

POACHED BURGER BALLS

Makes 8 servings

- 2 pounds meat-loaf mixture (ground beef, pork, and veal)
- 2 eggs
- 1 cup crushed pretzels
- ¼ cup chopped parsley
- 1 tablespoon instant minced onion
- 1 tablespoon lemon juice
- 1 teaspoon paprika
- ½ teaspoon salt
- 1 can (46 ounces) mixed vegetable juices
- 2 envelopes instant beef broth
  OR: 2 beef-flavor bouillon cubes
- 4 tablespoons (½ stick) butter or margarine
- 4 tablespoons flour
- ½ teaspoon prepared mustard

1. Mix meat-loaf mixture lightly with eggs, pretzels, parsley, onion, lemon juice, paprika, and salt until well-blended; shape into 16 balls.
2. Combine mixed vegetable juices and instant beef broth or bouillon cubes in a kettle or Dutch oven; heat, crushing cubes, if using, with a spoon, to boiling; add meat balls.
3. Simmer 25 minutes, or until cooked through. Remove with a slotted spoon and set aside. Pour liquid into a 4-cup measure. (There should be 3 cups.)
4. Melt butter or margarine in same kettle; blend in flour, then stir in the 3 cups liquid and mustard. Cook, stirring constantly, until mixture thickens and boils 1 minute. Return meat balls; heat just until bubbly hot.
5. Serve with hot cooked noodles or mashed potatoes, if you wish.

PENNSYLVANIA DUTCH BEEF BALLS

Makes 4 servings

- 1 pound ground beef
- 1 small onion, chopped (¼ cup)
- 1 teaspoon curry powder
- 1 teaspoon salt
- ½ teaspoon poultry seasoning
- 2 tablespoons salad oil
- 3 envelopes instant beef broth
  OR: 3 beef-flavor bouillon cubes
- 3 cups water
- ¾ cup seedless raisins
  Dash of pepper
- 9 gingersnaps, crumbled (about ½ cup)
- 1½ teaspoons cider vinegar
  Hot cooked noodles

1. Mix ground beef lightly with onion, curry powder, salt, and poultry seasoning; shape into 16 balls.
2. Brown in salad oil in a frying pan; add instant beef broth or bouillon cubes, water, raisins, and pepper, crushing cubes, if using, with a spoon; cover.
3. Simmer, stirring several times, 20 minutes to blend flavors.
4. Stir in crumbled gingersnaps and vinegar, being careful not to break meat balls. Cook, stirring constantly, until gravy is thick and smooth.
5. Serve with hot cooked noodles.

BEEF-HAM PUFFS IN MUSHROOM SAUCE

Makes 4 servings

- 1 pound ground beef
- 1 can (2¼ or 3 ounces) deviled ham
- ½ cup soft bread crumbs (1 slice)
- 2 cups milk
- 1 egg
- 2 tablespoons butter or margarine
- 1 envelope mushroom-soup mix
- 1 cup water

1. Mix ground beef lightly with deviled ham, bread crumbs, ½ cup of the milk, and egg until well-blended; shape into 32 balls.
2. Brown, half at a time, in butter or margarine in a large frying pan; remove with a slotted spoon and set aside.
3. Blend mushroom-soup mix into drippings in pan; slowly stir in water, then remaining 1½ cups milk. Cook, stirring constantly, until sauce thickens and boils 1 minute.
4. Return meat balls; cover. Simmer 15 minutes to blend flavors.

CHILI BURGER BALLS

Makes 8 servings

    2 pounds meat-loaf mixture (ground beef
        and pork)
    1 egg
    ½ cup soft whole-wheat bread crumbs
        (1 slice)
    ¼ cup milk
    2 teaspoons salt
    1 teaspoon paprika
    2 tablespoons salad oil
    1 bottle (12 ounces) chili sauce
    1 cup water
    1 tablespoon brown sugar
    1 teaspoon prepared mustard

1. Mix meat-loaf mixture lightly with egg, bread crumbs, milk, salt, and paprika until well-blended; shape into 16 balls.
2. Brown in salad oil in a kettle or Dutch oven; remove and set aside. Pour off all drippings.
3. Stir chili sauce, water, brown sugar, and mustard into kettle; return meat balls; cover.
4. Simmer, stirring several times, 30 minutes, or until meat balls are cooked through.
5. Serve with mashed potatoes or hot cooked rice or noodles, if you wish.

BAKED SAUCY MEAT BALLS

Bake at 375° for 1 hour.
Makes 8 servings

    1½ pounds ground beef
    ½ pound sausage meat
    1 jar (8 ounces) junior applesauce
    1 cup soft bread crumbs (2 slices)
    8 prunes, pitted and chopped
    1 teaspoon salt
    ¼ teaspoon pepper
    1 can condensed tomato soup
    ¼ cup water

1. Mix ground beef and sausage meat lightly with applesauce, bread crumbs, prunes, salt, and pepper until well-blended; shape into 24 balls. Place in an 8-cup baking dish.
2. Blend tomato soup and water; pour over meat balls; cover.
3. Bake in moderate oven (375°) 1 hour, or until meat balls are cooked through and mixture is bubbly hot.

SKILLET DINNER
(Pictured at right)

Makes 8 servings

    2 pounds meat-loaf mixture (ground beef,
        pork, and veal)
    2 eggs
    1 cup soft bread crumbs (2 slices)
    ¼ cup chopped parsley
    1½ teaspoons salt
    1 large onion, chopped (1 cup)
    1 medium-size head of cabbage (about 2
        pounds)
    1 cup sliced pared carrots
    1 cup mixed vegetable juices
    ½ teaspoon basil
    ¼ teaspoon pepper
    1 package (10 ounces) frozen Fordhook
        lima beans, partly thawed
    1 package (10 ounces) frozen peas, partly
        thawed

1. Mix meat-loaf mixture lightly with eggs, bread crumbs, parsley, and 1 teaspoon of the salt until well-blended; shape into 48 small balls.
2. Brown, half at a time, in a large frying pan; remove and set aside.
3. Pour all drippings from pan, then measure 3 tablespoonfuls and return to pan. Stir in onion and saute just until soft. (This much cooking can be done ahead, if you wish.)
4. Cut cabbage in half; slice one half in 8 wedges, then shred other half finely to make about 6 cups. Stir shredded cabbage into onion in pan; cook 2 minutes, or just until wilted.
5. Stir in carrots, mixed vegetable juices, remaining ½ teaspoon salt, basil, and pepper. Arrange cabbage wedges around edge; cover. Heat to boiling, then simmer 15 minutes.
6. Stir partly thawed limas and peas into vegetables in frying pan; top with meat balls; cover. Cook 15 minutes longer, or until limas are tender and meat balls are heated through.
7. Serve right from the frying pan, or spoon into a heated shallow serving bowl, arranging cabbage wedges around edge.

Mildly seasoned ground beef, pork, and veal, plus four garden-good vegetables, go into this hearty Skillet Dinner *(recipe at left)*. With the meat seasoned, shaped, and browned ahead, the dish takes only about a half hour to finish cooking just before mealtime

MEAT BALLS STROGONOFF

Makes 4 servings

- 1 pound ground beef
- 1 small onion, grated
- 1 teaspoon salt
- ⅛ teaspoon nutmeg
- ⅛ teaspoon ground cloves
   Dash of pepper
- 1 tablespoon salad oil
- 2 tablespoons flour
- 1 teaspoon dry mustard
- 1 envelope instant beef broth
   OR: 1 beef-flavor bouillon cube
- 1 cup water
- 1 cup (8-ounce carton) dairy sour cream
- 2 tablespoons chopped parsley

1. Mix ground beef lightly with onion, salt, nutmeg, cloves, and pepper; shape into 36 balls.
2. Brown, half at a time, in salad oil in a large frying pan; remove and set aside. Pour off drippings, then measure 1 tablespoonful and return to pan.
3. Blend in flour and mustard; stir in instant beef broth or bouillon cube and water, crushing cube, if using, with a spoon. Cook, stirring constantly, until sauce thickens and boils 1 minute.
4. Return meat balls; cover; simmer 5 minutes, or until cooked through.
5. Mix sour cream and parsley; blend in about ½ cup of the hot sauce, then stir back into remaining in pan. Heat slowly just until hot.
6. Serve with hot cooked rice, noodles, or mashed potatoes, if you wish.

CREAMED BEEF-ONION BALLS

Makes 4 servings

- 1 pound ground beef
- 1 egg
- 1 tablespoon chopped parsley
- 1 teaspoon seasoned salt
- 2 tablespoons butter or margarine
- 1½ cups water
- 2 packages (9 ounces each) frozen onions in cream sauce

1. Mix ground beef lightly with egg, parsley, and seasoned salt; shape into 24 balls.
2. Brown in butter or margarine, turning often, in a medium-size frying pan; stir in water; add frozen onions; cover.
3. Heat to boiling, then cook 5 to 8 minutes, or until onions are tender.
4. Spoon over mashed potatoes, buttered toast, or toasted corn-bread squares, if you wish.

CRUNCH-BURGER BALLS

Makes 6 servings

- 1 envelope onion-soup mix
- 1 cup soft bread crumbs (2 slices)
- ½ cup scalded milk
- 1 pound ground beef
- ½ pound ground pork
- 1 egg
- ½ cup chopped parsley
- ½ cup chopped walnuts
- 2 tablespoons salad oil
- 1 tablespoon flour
- 2 cups water
- 2 tablespoons catsup
   Hot cooked rice

1. Mix 1 tablespoon of the onion-soup mix with bread crumbs and milk; let stand 5 minutes. Mix with ground beef and pork, egg, and parsley.
2. Saute walnuts in salad oil until richly browned in a large frying pan; remove with a slotted spoon. Stir into meat mixture; shape into 18 balls.
3. Stir remaining onion-soup mix into drippings in pan; blend in flour, then water and catsup; cook, stirring constantly, until sauce thickens.
4. Place meat balls in sauce. Simmer 20 minutes, or until cooked through.
5. Pile hot cooked rice in the center of a heated dish; spoon meat balls and sauce around edge.

CANADIAN MEAT BALLS IN CREAM GRAVY

Makes 6 servings

- 4 slices Canadian-style bacon, diced
- 1 medium-size onion, chopped (½ cup)
- 1½ pounds ground beef
- 1 egg
- 1 teaspoon salt
- ¼ teaspoon ground allspice
- 2 tablespoons butter or margarine
- 2 tablespoons flour
- 1 can condensed beef broth
- 1 small can evaporated milk (⅔ cup)

1. Saute Canadian bacon lightly in a large frying pan; stir in onion; saute until soft.
2. Mix ground beef lightly with egg, salt, and allspice; stir in bacon-onion mixture; shape into 36 balls. Brown in butter or margarine in same frying pan; push to one side; blend in flour and beef broth.
3. Cook, stirring constantly, until gravy thickens slightly, then simmer 10 minutes. Stir in evaporated milk; heat just to boiling.

MEAT-BALL GOULASH

Makes 6 servings

- 1 pound ground beef
- 1 medium-size onion, chopped (½ cup)
- ½ cup soft bread crumbs (1 slice)
- 1 egg
- 2 teaspoons salt
- ⅛ teaspoon pepper
- ¼ teaspoon thyme
- 2 tablespoons shortening
- 3 cups water
- 1 can condensed cream of mushroom soup
- 1 can (8 ounces) tomato sauce
- 1 bay leaf
- 6 ounces thin spaghetti, broken into 2-inch pieces (about 2 cups)

1. Mix ground beef lightly with half of the chopped onion, bread crumbs, egg, 1 teaspoon of the salt, pepper, and thyme until well-blended; shape into 30 balls.
2. Brown, all at one time, in shortening in a kettle or Dutch oven. Stir in water, soup, tomato sauce, bay leaf, and the remaining chopped onion and 1 teaspoon salt.
3. Heat to boiling; stir in spaghetti; cover. Simmer, stirring often, 20 minutes, or until spaghetti is tender. Remove bay leaf before serving.

BUFFET MEAT BALLS

Makes 8 servings

- 1½ pounds ground beef
- 1 can (12 ounces) pork luncheon meat
- 1 cup light or table cream
- 2 eggs
- 1 medium-size onion, grated
- 1 cup soft bread crumbs (2 slices)
- ½ teaspoon ground allspice
- ¼ teaspoon pepper
- 2 tablespoons butter or margarine
- 2 tablespoons flour
- 1½ cups milk

1. Put ground beef and pork luncheon meat through a food chopper, using fine blade; mix lightly with ½ cup of the cream, eggs, onion, bread crumbs, allspice, and pepper until well-blended; shape into 48 balls.
2. Brown, a few at a time, in butter or margarine in a large frying pan; remove with a slotted spoon and set aside.
3. Blend flour into drippings in pan; stir in milk and remaining ½ cup cream; cook, stirring constantly, until gravy thickens and boils 1 minute.
4. Return meat balls to pan; heat just to boiling.

MOSCOWS

Makes 4 servings

- 1 pound ground beef
- 1 egg
- ½ cup soft rye-bread crumbs (1 slice)
- 1 tablespoon prepared beet-horseradish
- ½ teaspoon salt
- 1 tablespoon butter or margarine
- 1 tablespoon flour
- 1 envelope instant beef broth
- ¾ cup water
- ½ cup dairy sour cream
- 2 tablespoons grated Cheddar cheese

1. Mix ground beef lightly with egg, bread crumbs, beet-horseradish, and salt until well-blended; shape into 24 balls.
2. Brown in butter or margarine in a large frying pan; sprinkle with flour and instant beef broth; stir in water. Cook, stirring constantly, until mixture thickens and boils 1 minute, then simmer 5 minutes; remove from heat.
3. Stir about ½ cup of the hot sauce from meat mixture into sour cream, then stir back into remaining mixture in pan. Heat over *very low* heat just until hot. (Do not let it boil, for sour cream may curdle.)
4. Just before serving, sprinkle with cheese. Spoon over buttered toast or noodles, if you wish.

BAVARIAN DINNER

Makes 8 servings

- 1½ pounds ground beef
- ½ pound ground pork
- 1 teaspoon salt
- ½ cup soft bread crumbs (1 slice)
- 2 tablespoons chili sauce
- 2 tablespoons salad oil
- 1 medium-size onion, chopped (½ cup)
- 1 large apple, pared, cored, and chopped
- 2 cans (about 1 pound each) sauerkraut, drained
- 1 can (about 6 ounces) apple juice
- 1 tablespoon brown sugar
- ½ teaspoon caraway seeds

1. Mix ground beef and pork lightly with salt, bread crumbs, and chili sauce until well-blended; shape into 24 balls. Brown in salad oil in a large frying pan; remove with a slotted spoon.
2. Saute onion and apple until soft in drippings in pan; stir in sauerkraut. Place meat balls on top; pour apple juice over; sprinkle with brown sugar and caraway seeds.
3. Simmer 40 minutes to blend flavors.

Specially tempting on a brisk day is this savory
Continental Meat-ball Pie *(recipe on page 74)*.
Tiny beef balls and peppery sausages simmer first
in a tomato-rich sauce, then bake with carrots,
zucchini, and onions under a cap of golden pastry

CHAPTER 5

MAKE BUSY DAYS EASY DAYS WITH

ONE-DISH MEALS

Planning dinner around one hearty dish is a happy answer when you're looking for something new, something different, something special, or something fast. And here's a whole chapter packed with almost five dozen choices.

Some are casseroles that can be put together ahead and baked later; others are meat-rich pies and stews, garden-fresh vegetables stuffed with savory fillings, or skillet speedies that cook on top of the range with little or no watching. And with everything—meat, potato, and vegetable—in one dish, serving and cleanup are a snap.

Busy days or easy days, they're all ideas you'll be glad to have in your file to use the year round.

For an old-time treat, bake a hearty meat pie

CHEESEBURGER PIE

Bake at 400° for 40 minutes.
Makes 6 servings

- 1½ pounds ground beef
- 1 egg
- ¼ cup dairy sour cream
- ⅓ cup quick-cooking rolled oats
- ½ teaspoon seasoned salt
- 2 tablespoons bottled Russian salad dressing
- 1 package piecrust mix
- ½ cup process cheese spread (from an 8-ounce jar)

1. Mix ground beef lightly with egg, sour cream, rolled oats, seasoned salt, and Russian dressing until well-blended.
2. Prepare piecrust mix, following label directions. Roll out half to a 12-inch round; fit into a 9-inch pie plate; trim overhang to ½ inch. Pack meat filling lightly into shell; spoon cheese spread over top.
3. Roll out remaining pastry to an 11-inch round; cut several slits near center to let steam escape; cover pie. Trim overhang to ½ inch; turn under, flush with rim; flute.
4. Bake in hot oven (400°) 40 minutes, or until crust is golden-brown. Cut into wedges.

CONTINENTAL MEAT-BALL PIE
(Pictured on page 72)

Bake at 425° for 30 minutes.
Makes 6 to 8 servings

- 1½ pounds meat-loaf mixture (ground beef, pork, and veal)
- 3 tablespoons flour
- 3 tablespoons salad oil
- 2 Italian hot sausages, sliced ½ inch thick
- 3 cups water
- 1 envelope spaghetti-sauce mix
- 1 can (6 ounces) tomato paste
- 12 small carrots, pared and cut in 1-inch-long pieces
- 6 small zucchini, washed and sliced 1 inch thick
- 1 can (1 pound) whole white onions, drained
- 1 package piecrust mix
- 1 egg, slightly beaten

1. Shape meat-loaf mixture into about 18 balls; roll in flour to coat evenly. Brown in salad oil in a large frying pan; push to one side; add sausages and brown lightly.
2. Stir water, spaghetti-sauce mix, and tomato paste into frying pan; cover. Simmer 15 minutes.
3. Cook carrots and zucchini together in boiling salted water 15 minutes, or just until tender; drain well.
4. Spoon meat-ball mixture, carrots and zucchini, and drained onions into a shallow 12-cup baking dish.
5. Prepare piecrust mix, following label directions, or make pastry from your own favorite two-crust recipe. Roll out to a rectangle, 15x12; cut out 9 about-1-inch-wide strips.
6. Save 3 strips for rim of pie, then weave remaining over pie to make a crisscross top; trim ends. Cover rim with saved strips, pressing down lightly all around. Cut out tiny fancy shapes from remaining pastry with a truffle or small cooky cutter. (Bake any leftover pastry for nibbles.)
7. Brush pastry strips with beaten egg; place cut-outs around rim; brush again.
8. Bake in hot oven (425°) 30 minutes, or until pastry is golden and filling bubbles up.

FRIJOLE PIE

Bake at 400° for 30 minutes.
Makes 6 servings

- 1 medium-size onion, chopped (½ cup)
- 1 clove garlic, minced
- 2 tablespoons salad oil
- 1 pound ground beef
- 1 can (about 1 pound) red kidney beans, drained
- 1 can (8 ounces) tomato sauce
- ½ medium-size green pepper, seeded and chopped
- 1 teaspoon salt
- ½ teaspoon sugar
- ½ teaspoon prepared mustard
- ½ teaspoon chili powder
- ½ teaspoon oregano
- ⅛ teaspoon celery salt
- 1 tablespoon cornstarch
- 2 tablespoons water
- 1 package piecrust mix

1. Saute onion and garlic lightly in salad oil; push to one side of pan. Shape ground beef into a large patty in same pan; brown 5 minutes on each side, then break up into chunks.
2. Stir in beans, tomato sauce, green pepper, and seasonings; cover. Simmer, stirring often, 20 minutes.
3. Mix cornstarch with water until smooth; stir into bean mixture; cook, stirring constantly, until thickened.
4. While filling cooks, prepare piecrust mix, following label directions. Roll out half to a 12-inch round on a lightly floured pastry cloth or board; fit into a 9-inch pie plate; trim overhang to ½ inch. Spoon hot meat mixture into shell.
5. Roll out remaining pastry to an 11-inch round; cut several slits near center to let steam escape; cover pie. Trim overhang to ½ inch; turn under, flush with rim; flute.
6. Bake in hot oven (400°) 30 minutes, or until golden-brown. Cut into wedges.

Cooksaver tip:

Have trouble transferring rolled-out pastry from board to pie plate without tearing it? Just roll pastry around the rolling pin, lift over plate, and unroll carefully, keeping overhang even all the way around

HERB-STUFFED MEAT PIE

Bake at 350° for 40 minutes.
Makes 6 servings

- 1 egg
- ¼ cup milk
- 2½ cups herb-seasoned stuffing croutons (from a 7-ounce package)
- 1½ pounds ground beef
- 1 teaspoon salt
- 1 small onion, peeled and sliced
- 1 medium-size apple, pared, quartered, cored, and chopped
- ¼ cup chopped celery
- 1 medium-size carrot, pared and grated
- 3 tablespoons butter or margarine
- ½ cup hot water

1. Beat egg with milk; stir in ½ cup of the croutons; let stand 5 minutes. Mix in ground beef and salt lightly until well-blended. Press into a 9-inch pie plate, making a ½-inch-high edge.
2. Saute onion, apple, celery, and carrot in butter or margarine just until onion is soft; stir in water and remaining croutons. Spoon into meat shell.
3. Bake in moderate oven (350°) 40 minutes, or until top is golden-brown.
4. Pour off any drippings; cut pie into wedges.

BEEF AND SPINACH COBBLER PIE

Bake at 375° for 30 minutes.
Makes 6 servings

- 2 packages refrigerated plain or buttermilk biscuits
- ½ cup chopped celery
- 1 small onion, chopped (¼ cup)
- 3 tablespoons butter or margarine
- 1 package (10 ounces) frozen chopped spinach
- 1 pound ground beef
- 2 eggs, beaten
- 1½ teaspoons salt

1. Flatten biscuits to ¼-inch thickness; stand 11 around side of a greased 10-inch pie plate; place remaining, overlapping, in bottom.
2. Saute celery with onion in 2 tablespoons of the butter or margarine just until soft. Add spinach; cover. Heat just until spinach thaws.
3. Stir in ground beef, eggs, and salt; spoon into biscuit-lined pie plate.
4. Bake in moderate oven (375°) 30 minutes, or until biscuits are crusty-brown.
5. Melt remaining 1 tablespoon butter or margarine; brush over biscuit edge. Cut pie into wedges.

COBBLE BEEF PIE

Bake at 425° for 25 minutes.
Makes 4 servings

- 1   pound ground beef
- 1   egg
- ½   cup soft bread crumbs (1 slice)
- 1   teaspoon Worcestershire sauce
- ½   teaspoon salt
- ⅛   teaspoon pepper
- 2   tablespoons butter or margarine
- 1   can (1 pound) beans and franks in tomato sauce
- 1   can (8 ounces) tomato sauce
- 1   tablespoon brown sugar
- 2   teaspoons prepared mustard
- 1   cup biscuit mix
- 1   small onion, grated
- ½   cup finely diced process American cheese
- ⅓   cup milk

1. Mix ground beef lightly with egg, bread crumbs, Worcestershire sauce, salt, and pepper until well-blended; shape into 16 balls.
2. Brown in butter or margarine in a large frying pan. Stir in beans, tomato sauce, brown sugar, and mustard; heat to boiling, then spoon into an 8-cup baking dish.
3. Mix biscuit mix with onion, cheese, and milk to make a soft dough; drop by teaspoonfuls in mounds on top of hot meat-ball mixture.
4. Bake in hot oven (425°) 25 minutes, or until top is golden-brown.

CREOLE EGGBURGER PIE

Bake at 350° for 35 minutes.
Makes 4 servings

- 1   can condensed tomato soup
- 2   tablespoons pickle relish
- 1   small onion, minced
- 2   tablespoons minced celery
- 2   tablespoons minced green pepper
- 1   teaspoon salt
- 1   teaspoon Worcestershire sauce
- 1½   pounds ground beef
- 4   eggs
     Dash of pepper
- 2   tablespoons grated Parmesan cheese

1. Mix tomato soup, pickle relish, onion, celery, green pepper, salt, and Worcestershire sauce in a small saucepan. Measure out ⅓ cup, then simmer remaining 5 minutes.
2. Mix ground beef lightly with the ⅓ cup sauce mixture; press into a 9-inch pie plate. Mark lightly into quarters, then make a deep hollow in each with a tablespoon.
3. Bake in moderate oven (350°) 15 minutes; pour off all drippings.
4. Spoon 1 teaspoonful of the hot sauce into each hollow in meat; break an egg into each; sprinkle with pepper. Spoon remaining sauce around eggs; sprinkle cheese over all.
5. Bake 20 minutes longer, or until eggs are cooked as you like them.
6. Cut into quarters with an egg for each serving.

Cooksaver tip:

These picture-directions show at a glance how easy it is to make Creole Eggburger Pie. Another time, after baking for 25 minutes and pouring off the drippings, following Step 3 at right, above, stack slices of hard-cooked egg in each hollow, top each with sauce and several strips of process American cheese. Slide back into the oven for 10 minutes, or until cheese melts. A wide spatula is a good serving tool

DOUBLE-CORN PIE

Bake at 375° for 30 minutes.
Makes 6 to 8 servings

Filling
1½ pounds ground beef
  2 packages (10 ounces each) frozen
      succotash, cooked and drained
  1 cup chopped celery
  1 large onion, chopped (1 cup)
  3 tablespoons flour
  1 teaspoon salt
  1 teaspoon basil
  1 teaspoon Worcestershire sauce
  1 can (about 1 pound) tomatoes
Topping
  1 cup yellow or white corn meal
  4 tablespoons flour
  1 tablespoon sugar
  2 teaspoons baking powder
 ½ teaspoon salt
  1 egg
 ½ cup milk
  4 tablespoons (½ stick) butter or
      margarine, melted

1. Make filling: Shape ground beef into a large
patty in a large frying pan; brown 5 minutes on
each side, then break up into chunks. Spoon into
a 10-cup baking dish; stir in succotash and celery.
2. Saute onion until soft in drippings in pan; stir in
flour, salt, basil, Worcestershire sauce, and tomatoes. Cook, stirring constantly, until mixture
thickens and boils 1 minute. Pour over meat and
vegetables; stir lightly to mix.
3. Make topping: Combine corn meal, flour, sugar,
baking powder, and salt.
4. Beat egg with milk; stir into flour mixture just
until blended; stir in melted butter or margarine.
Pour over hot mixture in baking dish.
5. Bake in moderate oven (375°) 30 minutes, or
until top is golden-brown.

DEEP-DISH BEEF PIE

Bake at 375° for 40 minutes.
Makes 6 to 8 servings

  2 pounds meat-loaf mixture (ground beef,
      pork, and veal)
  1 medium-size onion, chopped (½ cup)
 ½ cup chopped celery
  1 can condensed cream of mushroom soup
 ¼ cup light or table cream
  1 tablespoon dried parsley flakes
  1 bay leaf
  1 tablespoon soy sauce
 ½ package piecrust mix
 ½ cup grated process American cheese

1. Mix meat-loaf mixture lightly with onion and
celery; shape into a large patty; brown 5 minutes
on each side, then break up into chunks.
2. Stir in mushroom soup, cream, parsley flakes, bay
leaf, and soy sauce; cover. Simmer, stirring several times, 15 minutes; remove bay leaf. Spoon
meat mixture into a baking pan, 9x9x2.
3. While meat cooks, combine piecrust mix and
grated cheese; prepare pastry, following label
directions. Roll out to a square, 10x10; trim edges
even; place over hot meat filling, pressing against
edges of pan to seal; cut several slits in top to let
steam escape.
4. Bake in moderate oven (375°) 40 minutes, or
until crust is golden and filling bubbles up.

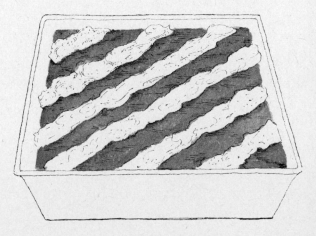

HARVEST PIE

Bake at 375° for 20 minutes.
Makes 6 servings

1½ pounds ground beef
 1 egg
 ¼ cup catsup
 1 tablespoon prepared horseradish-
      mustard
 1 cup soft bread crumbs (2 slices)
 ½ cup milk
1½ teaspoons salt
 ¼ cup flour
 4 tablespoons (½ stick) butter or
      margarine
 1 can (about 1 pound) tomatoes
 ¼ cup water
 1 tablespoon soy sauce
 4 medium-size carrots, pared and sliced
 1 cup sliced celery
 1 large onion, peeled and sliced
 ½ pound green beans, diced
 1 package refrigerated crescent rolls

1. Mix ground beef lightly with egg, catsup, horse-radish-mustard, bread crumbs, milk, and salt until well-blended; shape into 24 balls; roll in flour to coat well.
2. Brown, half at a time, in 3 tablespoons of the butter or margarine in a kettle or Dutch oven; remove with a slotted spoon and set aside.
3. Stir tomatoes, water, soy sauce, carrots, celery, and onion into kettle; cover. Simmer 20 minutes; return meat balls and add green beans; cook 10 minutes longer, or just until vegetables are tender. Spoon into a greased 12-cup round baking dish.
4. Separate crescent rolls into triangles, following label directions; place each flat, spoke fashion, on top of meat mixture so points meet in center.
5. Bake in moderate oven (375°) 20 minutes, or until topping is golden-brown. Melt remaining 1 tablespoon butter or margarine; brush over top.

Cooksaver tip:

See how a twist of the wrist turns triangles of dough from refrigerated crescent rolls into this whirligig topper for the Harvest Pie above?

SOUTH-OF-THE-BORDER PIE

Bake at 375° for 35 minutes.
Makes 6 servings

 2 slices bacon
 1 pound ground beef
 1 medium-size onion, chopped (½ cup)
 1 can (about 1 pound) tomatoes
 1 can (8 ounces) tomato sauce
 1 tablespoon chili powder
 1 teaspoon salt
 1 package corn-muffin mix

1. Saute bacon until crisp; drain on paper toweling, then crumble. Pour off all drippings; measure 2 tablespoonfuls and return to pan.
2. Mix ground beef lightly with onion. Shape into a large patty in same pan; brown 5 minutes on each side, then break up into chunks. Stir in crumbled bacon, tomatoes, tomato sauce, and seasonings; heat to boiling.
3. Prepare corn-muffin mix, following label directions for muffins.
4. Spread half of batter evenly over bottom of a greased shallow 6-cup baking dish; spoon hot meat mixture over; drop remaining batter by tablespoonfuls on top.
5. Bake in moderate oven (375°) 35 minutes, or until top is puffed and golden-brown.

QUICK SUPPER PIE

Bake at 400° for 10 minutes.
Makes 4 to 6 servings

 1 pound ground beef
 1 large onion, chopped (1 cup)
 2 tablespoons butter or margarine
 ⅓ cup flour
 1 teaspoon salt
 2 cups milk
 1 small can evaporated milk (⅔ cup)
 1 can (8 ounces) peas
 2 pimientos, diced
 4 slices buttered bread, halved diagonally

1. Shape ground beef into a large patty in a frying pan; brown 5 minutes on each side, then break up into chunks.
2. Stir in onion and butter or margarine; continue cooking lightly just until onion is soft. Blend in flour, salt, milk, and evaporated milk.
3. Cook, stirring constantly, until mixture thickens and boils 1 minute. Stir in peas and liquid and pimientos. Pour into a greased shallow 8-cup baking dish; top with overlapping bread slices.
4. Bake in hot oven (400°) 10 minutes, or until bread is toasty-golden.

Cooksaver tip:

Turnover Pasties are fun to eat and fun to shape. After folding biscuit-dough squares over meat filling, use a fork to press the edges together to seal. Cut a few slits in the top to let the steam escape, or go fancy and make a tiny cutout with a truffle cutter

TURNOVER PASTIES

Bake at 400° for 15 minutes.
Makes 8 pasties

    1 medium-size onion, chopped (½ cup)
    1 tablespoon salad oil
    ¾ pound ground beef
    ¼ cup chili sauce
    1 tablespoon soy sauce
    ½ teaspoon salt
  2¼ cups biscuit mix
    1 package (3 ounces) pimiento cream
         cheese
    ½ cup milk

1. Saute onion lightly in salad oil; push to one side of pan. Shape ground beef into a large patty in same pan; brown 5 minutes on each side, then break up into chunks; pour off all drippings.
2. Stir in chili sauce, soy sauce, salt, and ¼ cup of the biscuit mix. Remove from heat.
3. Cut pimiento cream cheese into remaining 2 cups biscuit mix until crumbly; stir in milk to make a soft dough. Turn out on a floured board and knead a few times. Divide dough in half; roll out each to a 10-inch square; trim edges even, then cut each in quarters.
4. Place about ⅓ cup of the meat filling on each square; fold into a triangle and press edges to seal; cut several slits in top to let steam escape. Place pasties on a greased cooky sheet.
5. Bake in hot oven (400°) 15 minutes, or until golden-brown.
6. Serve hot, plain or with hot canned beef gravy, if you wish, or cold as a picnic or lunch-box meat.

JIFFY BEEF DUMPLINGS

Bake at 375° for 20 minutes.
Makes 8 dumplings

    1 pound ground beef
    ½ cup catsup
    2 tablespoons pickle relish
    1 teaspoon dry mustard
    1 teaspoon salt
    ⅛ teaspoon pepper
    1 tablespoon salad oil
    ½ package piecrust mix
    1 can (about 11 ounces) meatless
         spaghetti sauce

1. Mix ground beef lightly with catsup, pickle relish, mustard, salt, and pepper until well-blended; shape into 8 balls. Brown in salad oil.
2. Prepare piecrust mix, following label directions. Roll out to a rectangle, 20x10; trim edges even, then cut into 8 squares.
3. Place a browned meat ball on each square; fold pastry up and around meat balls; moisten edges, then pinch to seal. Place dumplings, without touching, in a shallow baking pan.
4. Bake in moderate oven (375°) 20 minutes, or until golden-brown.
5. Heat spaghetti sauce to boiling; spoon over hot dumplings.

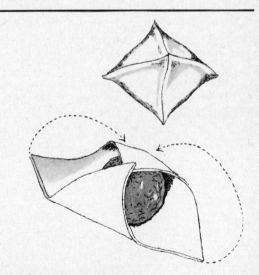

Cooksaver tip:

Jiffy Beef Dumplings are another fun twist on a meat pie. To make even-shape dumplings, place the meat ball right in the center of pastry square; fold opposite sides of dough up over the meat to cover completely, then pinch the edges lightly with your fingers to crimp and seal

BEEF-CROWNED ONION PIE

Bake at 400° for 45 minutes.
Makes 6 servings

Onion Pie
1 package piecrust mix
3 large onions, peeled and sliced thin
4 tablespoons (½ stick) butter or
    margarine
2 large potatoes, pared and sliced thin
2 teaspoons salt
½ teaspoon pepper

Beef Crown
1½ pounds ground beef
½ cup chili sauce
¼ cup milk
1¼ teaspoons salt
⅛ teaspoon pepper

1. Make onion pie: Prepare piecrust mix, following label directions. Roll out to a rectangle, 18x13; fit into a jelly-roll pan, 15x10x1. Trim overhang to ½ inch; turn under, flush with rim; flute.
2. Saute onions in butter or margarine 10 minutes, or just until barely soft; stir in potatoes; sprinkle with salt and pepper, tossing lightly to mix. Spread in an even layer in pastry shell.
3. Bake in hot oven (400°) 45 minutes, or until potatoes are tender and pastry is golden.
4. Make beef crown: Mix ground beef lightly with chili sauce, milk, salt, and pepper; shape into 12 patties about ½ inch thick. Place in a shallow baking pan.
5. Bake in oven with onion pie 15 minutes, or until meat is done as you like it.
6. Cut pie into 12 pieces; top each with a meat patty.

Cooksaver tip:

A pastry brush is a good investment to short-cut many kitchen jobs. Use it to spread a buttery topper or beaten egg over a pastry crust, or to brush a glaze on meat loaf. It's handy, too, for barbecue cooking

Time aflying?
Cook dinner
in a skillet

CHOW MEIN BOWL

Makes 6 servings

1 medium-size onion, chopped (½ cup)
2 tablespoons salad oil
1 pound ground beef
1 can (about 1 pound) Chinese vegetables
1 can (about 1 pound) bean sprouts
1 envelope instant beef broth
    OR: 1 beef-flavor bouillon cube
2 tablespoons cornstarch
1 tablespoon sugar
2 tablespoons soy sauce
2 cups thinly sliced broccoli flowerets
½ teaspoon salt
1 can (3 ounces) Chinese fried noodles

1. Saute onion in salad oil just until soft in a large frying pan; push to one side.
2. Shape ground beef into a large patty in same pan; brown 5 minutes on each side, then break up into chunks.
3. Drain liquids from Chinese vegetables and bean sprouts into a 2-cup measure; add 1¼ cups to meat mixture with instant beef broth or bouillon cube. Heat, stirring constantly and crushing bouillon cube, if using, with a spoon, to boiling.
4. Blend cornstarch with sugar and soy sauce; stir into meat mixture. Cook, stirring constantly, until mixture thickens and boils 3 minutes.
5. Lay broccoli on top of meat mixture; cover. Cook over low heat, stirring often, 10 minutes, or just until broccoli is tender.
6. Stir in drained vegetables, bean sprouts, and salt; cover. Cook 5 minutes longer, or until bubbly hot. Serve with Chinese fried noodles.

KIMA

Makes 4 servings

- 1 large onion, chopped (1 cup)
- 1 tablespoon curry powder
- 3 tablespoons butter or margarine
- 1 pound ground beef
- 2 tomatoes, peeled and diced
- 1 can (about 9 ounces) peas
- 1 teaspoon salt
- 1 teaspoon paprika
- ½ teaspoon chili powder
- ½ teaspoon garlic salt
  Brown-butter Rice (*recipe follows*)

1. Saute onion with curry powder lightly in butter or margarine in a large frying pan; push to one side.
2. Shape ground beef into a large patty in same pan; brown 5 minutes on each side, then break up into chunks.
3. Stir in tomatoes, peas and liquid, and seasonings; cover. Simmer 30 minutes to blend flavors.
4. Serve with BROWN-BUTTER RICE.

BROWN-BUTTER RICE — Prepare 1 package (7 ounces) precooked rice, following label directions. Heat 4 tablespoons (½ stick) butter or margarine slowly in a small frying pan, shaking pan often as butter bubbles up and turns a rich brown. (Watch that it does not burn.) Stir into hot rice; toss lightly with a fork to mix; sprinkle with pepper.

HAMBURGER HOT POT

Makes 6 servings

- 4 medium-size potatoes, pared and sliced thin
- 1½ pounds ground beef
- 3 medium-size onions, peeled and sliced thin
- 1 teaspoon salt
- ¼ teaspoon pepper
- 2 tablespoons butter or margarine
- 2 tablespoons chopped parsley
- ½ cup canned condensed beef broth

1. Place one third of the potato slices in the bottom of a buttered electric skillet; top with even layers of half of the ground beef and half of the onion slices. Repeat layers, ending with potato slices arranged in an attractive pattern on top.
2. Sprinkle with salt and pepper; dot with butter or margarine; sprinkle with parsley. Pour beef broth over; cover. Set heat control at 225°, following manufacturer's directions.
3. Simmer 1 hour, or until potatoes are tender.

SPAGHETTI RAGOUT

Makes 6 servings

- 4 slices bacon, diced
- 1 pound ground beef
- 1 medium-size onion, peeled and sliced
- ½ cup sliced celery
- 1 medium-size carrot, pared and sliced
- ¼ pound chicken livers, coarsely chopped
- ¼ cup catsup
- 2 envelopes instant beef broth
  OR: 2 beef-flavor bouillon cubes
- 1½ cups water
- ½ teaspoon salt
- ⅛ teaspoon nutmeg
- ½ cup cream for whipping
- 1 package (8 ounces) spaghetti
  Grated Parmesan cheese

1. Saute bacon until crisp in a large frying pan; add ground beef, onion, celery, and carrot. Brown meat, breaking it up as it cooks.
2. Stir in chicken livers, catsup, instant beef broth or bouillon cubes, water, salt, and nutmeg, crushing cubes, if using, with a spoon; cover.
3. Simmer, stirring several times, 30 minutes. Blend in cream slowly; heat just until bubbly.
4. While sauce simmers, cook spaghetti, following label directions; drain. Pour sauce over; toss lightly to mix. Serve with Parmesan cheese to sprinkle over.

BURGER BURGOO

Makes 6 servings

- 2 pounds ground beef
- 1 large onion, chopped (1 cup)
- 1 cup diced celery
- 1 clove garlic, minced
- 1 tablespoon sugar
- 1 tablespoon basil
- 2 teaspoons salt
- ⅛ teaspoon pepper
- 1 bay leaf
- 1 can (46 ounces) mixed vegetable juices
- 1 cup uncooked rice

1. Shape ground beef into a large patty in a large frying pan; brown 5 minutes on each side, then break up into chunks. Push to one side.
2. Stir in onion, celery, and garlic; saute lightly.
3. Stir in seasonings, mixed vegetable juices, and rice; heat to boiling; cover.
4. Simmer 45 minutes, or until rice is tender and liquid is almost absorbed. Remove bay leaf before serving.

HOPPING JOHN

Makes 8 servings

2 slices bacon, cut in 1-inch pieces
1 pound meat-loaf mixture (ground beef, pork, and veal)
1 medium-size onion, chopped (½ cup)
1 cup chopped celery
2 packages (10 ounces each) frozen blackeye peas, partly thawed
1 teaspoon salt
1 teaspoon basil
½ teaspoon thyme
1 bay leaf
Few drops red-pepper seasoning
1 envelope instant beef broth
½ cup water
½ cup precooked rice
1 cup tomato juice

1. Saute bacon until crisp in a large frying pan; remove with a slotted spoon and drain on paper toweling; set aside.
2. Shape meat-loaf mixture into a patty in same pan; brown 5 minutes on each side, then break up into chunks; push to one side. Add onion to pan and saute just until soft. Stir in cooked bacon, celery, blackeye peas, seasonings, beef broth, and water. Heat to boiling; cover.
3. Simmer 30 minutes, or until blackeye peas are tender.
4. Stir in rice and tomato juice; cover again. Simmer 10 minutes longer, or until rice is tender. Remove bay leaf before serving.

SKILLET BEEF AND BEANS

Makes 4 servings

1 pound ground beef
1 teaspoon salt
½ teaspoon thyme
⅛ teaspoon pepper
2 cans (1 pound each) white kidney beans, drained
1 can (1 pound) small whole onions, drained
1 cup apple cider
½ cup chopped parsley

1. Shape ground beef into a large patty in a large frying pan. Brown 5 minutes on each side, then break up into chunks.
2. Stir in remaining ingredients, except parsley; cover.
3. Simmer, stirring several times, 30 minutes. Sprinkle with chopped parsley.

FRYING-PAN MOUSSAKA

Makes 6 servings

1½ pounds ground beef
1 large onion, chopped (1 cup)
1 clove garlic, minced
1 large eggplant, pared and cubed
4 cans (8 ounces each) tomato sauce
2 teaspoons salt
1 teaspoon oregano
1 teaspoon basil
1 teaspoon sugar
¼ cup chopped parsley

1. Shape ground beef into a large patty in a large frying pan. Brown 5 minutes on each side, then break up into chunks; push to one side.
2. Stir onion and garlic into pan; saute just until onion is soft. Stir in eggplant, tomato sauce, and seasonings; cover.
3. Simmer, stirring several times, 25 minutes, or just until eggplant is tender. Sprinkle with chopped parsley.

SPANISH RICE AND MEAT BALLS

Makes 4 servings

4 slices bacon
1 pound ground beef
1 egg
½ cup soft bread crumbs (1 slice)
2 teaspoons salt
1 large onion, chopped (1 cup)
½ cup chopped celery
½ cup chopped green pepper
1 teaspoon chili powder
1 cup uncooked rice
1 can (about 1 pound) tomatoes
1 cup water

1. Saute bacon until crisp in a large frying pan; remove and drain on paper toweling.
2. Mix ground beef lightly with egg, bread crumbs, and 1 teaspoon of the salt until well-blended; shape into 16 small balls.
3. Brown in bacon drippings in same pan; push to one side.
4. Stir onion, celery, green pepper, and chili powder into pan; saute just until vegetables are soft.
5. Stir in rice, tomatoes, water, and remaining salt; heat to boiling, stirring lightly to mix; cover.
6. Simmer, adding more water if mixture seems dry, 45 minutes, or until rice is tender and liquid is absorbed. Garnish with saved bacon.

HAMBURGER CHOP-CHOP

Makes 8 servings

  1 pound ground beef
  ½ pound ground pork
  1 tablespoon peanut oil
  1 large onion, peeled and sliced
  1 cup thinly sliced celery
  6 small carrots, pared and sliced
         ½ inch thick
  1 envelope instant beef broth
  ½ cup water
  4 cups shredded Chinese cabbage
  1 tablespoon cornstarch
  1 tablespoon brown sugar
  2 tablespoons soy sauce

1. Mix ground beef and pork and shape into a large patty in a large frying pan; brown in peanut oil 5 minutes on each side, then break up into small chunks. Push to one side.
2. Stir onion and celery into pan; saute just until onion is soft. Stir in carrots, instant beef broth, and water; heat to boiling; cover.
3. Simmer 20 minutes, or until carrots are crisply tender. Spread cabbage over meat-vegetable mixture; cover again. Cook 7 to 10 minutes, or until cabbage is tender.
4. Mix cornstarch and brown sugar with soy sauce; stir into meat-vegetable mixture. Cook, stirring constantly, until mixture thickens and boils 3 minutes.
5. Serve with Chinese fried noodles and more soy sauce, if you wish.

MACARONI-AND-BEEF CANCAN

Makes 6 servings

  1½ pounds ground beef
  1 large onion, chopped (1 cup)
  1 can (15 ounces) macaroni in
        cheese sauce
  1 can (about 1 pound) tomatoes
  1 can (7 ounces) whole-kernel corn,
        drained
  1 can (6 ounces) sliced mushrooms
  1 teaspoon salt
  ½ teaspoon sugar

1. Shape ground beef into a large patty in a large frying pan; brown 5 minutes on each side, then break up into small chunks; push to one side.
2. Stir onion into pan and saute just until soft; stir in remaining ingredients.
3. Heat to boiling; simmer 15 minutes, or until heated through.

PLATTER DINNER

Makes 4 servings

  1 pound ground beef
  1 can condensed beef broth
  ¼ cup fine dry bread crumbs
  1 small onion, grated
  1 teaspoon salt
  ⅛ teaspoon pepper
  2 tablespoons butter or margarine
  3 medium-size yellow squashes, trimmed
        and sliced 1 inch thick
  8 small carrots, pared
  ½ cup evaporated milk
  1 tablespoon instant-type flour

1. Mix ground beef lightly with ¼ cup of the beef broth, bread crumbs, onion, salt, and pepper; shape into 20 small balls.
2. Brown in butter or margarine; pour remaining broth over. Place squashes and carrots around meat balls; cover.
3. Simmer 25 minutes, or until vegetables are tender.
4. Remove meat balls with a slotted spoon and place in center of a deep serving platter; place vegetables around edge.
5. Blend evaporated milk and flour in a cup; stir into hot liquid in pan. Cook, stirring constantly, until gravy thickens and boils 1 minute. Spoon over meat and vegetables.

CALICO BEEF STEW

Makes 6 servings

  1 pound ground beef
  1 large onion, chopped (1 cup)
  1 cup diced celery
  1 clove garlic, minced
  1 package (12 ounces) smoked sausage
        links, sliced thin
  1 can (about 1 pound) tomatoes
  1 can (about 1 pound) chick peas
  1 can (about 1 pound) sliced carrots
  2 cups shredded cabbage
  1 teaspoon sugar
  1 teaspoon seasoned salt
  1 teaspoon thyme

1. Shape ground beef into a large patty in a frying pan; brown 5 minutes on each side, then break up into chunks; push to one side.
2. Stir onion, celery, and garlic into frying pan; saute just until onion is soft. Stir in remaining ingredients; heat to boiling.
3. Simmer 20 minutes, or until cabbage is tender.

SKILLET GOULASH

Makes 4 servings

1¼ pounds ground beef
2 teaspoons salt
1 can (1 pint, 2 ounces) tomato juice
2 tablespoons corn syrup
½ teaspoon paprika
4 medium-size carrots, pared and quartered
½ medium-size head cabbage, cut in 4 wedges
1 can (1 pound) whole potatoes, drained
1 teaspoon caraway seeds

1. Mix ground beef lightly with 1 teaspoon of the salt; shape into 12 balls; flatten each slightly.
2. Brown meat patties in a large frying pan; remove with a slotted spoon and set aside.
3. Stir tomato juice, remaining 1 teaspoon salt, corn syrup, and paprika into pan; add carrots; cover.
4. Simmer 10 minutes; add cabbage wedges, potatoes, and meat patties; sprinkle with caraway seeds. Simmer 20 minutes longer, or until cabbage and carrots are tender.

NOODLES NAPOLI

Makes 6 servings

1 pound ground beef
½ pound sausage meat
1 medium-size onion, chopped (½ cup)
½ clove garlic, minced
1 package (8 ounces) fine noodles
2 cans (about 1 pound each) tomatoes
½ cup water
1 pimiento, chopped
1½ teaspoons salt
1 cup grated Cheddar cheese (4 ounces)

1. Mix ground beef and sausage meat; shape into a large patty in a large frying pan; brown 5 minutes on each side, then break up into chunks. Remove and set aside.
2. Pour off all drippings, then measure 3 tablespoonfuls and return to pan; stir in onion and garlic and saute just until soft. Add uncooked noodles; continue cooking, stirring often, until noodles are toasty-golden.
3. Stir in tomatoes, water, pimiento, salt, and browned meat; cover.
4. Simmer, stirring often, 10 minutes; stir in cheese; cover again. Cook 10 minutes longer, or until noodles are tender and cheese is melted.

HOT-HOT CHILI CON CARNE

Makes 8 servings

8 medium-size onions, chopped (4 cups)
2 cloves garlic, minced
6 teaspoons chili powder
2 tablespoons bacon drippings
2 pounds ground beef
2 teaspoons salt
3 cups water
3 cans (about 1 pound each) red kidney beans
2 teaspoons ground cumin

1. Saute onions and garlic with chili powder in bacon drippings just until onions are soft in a large heavy frying pan; remove with a slotted spoon and set aside.
2. Shape ground beef into a large patty in same pan; brown 5 minutes on each side, then break up into chunks. Stir in sauteed onion mixture, salt, and water; simmer 45 minutes.
3. Stir in kidney beans and liquid and cumin; simmer 1 hour.
4. Spoon into soup bowls; serve with buttered hard rolls or corn bread.

JIFFY DINNER STEW
(Pictured at right)

Makes 6 servings

½ pound sweet Italian sausages, sliced
1 pound ground beef
2 teaspoons bottled steak sauce
2 cans (about 1 pound each) stewed tomatoes
1 package (9 ounces) frozen Italian green beans, partly thawed
2 cans (1 pound each) whole potatoes, drained
1 teaspoon salt
2 tablespoons flour
2 tablespoons cold water

1. Brown sausages in a large frying pan; push to one side.
2. While sausages brown, shape ground beef lightly into 12 balls; flatten each slightly. Brown on one side in same pan; turn; pour off all drippings.
3. Brush meat patties with steak sauce; pour tomatoes over; add green beans and potatoes. Sprinkle with salt; cover.
4. Cook 20 minutes, or until beans are tender.
5. Smooth flour and cold water to a paste; stir into meat mixture. Cook, stirring constantly, until gravy thickens and boils 1 minute.

Jiffy Dinner Stew (*recipe at left*) owes its different flavor to Italian sausages and its speed to quick-cooking ground beef, frozen green beans, ready-seasoned tomatoes, and canned potatoes. Romaine salad and fruit compote round out the meal

Bake these quick hot breads to dress up a plain meal

Olive-cheese rounds

Roll refrigerated biscuits to 3-inch rounds; drizzle with melted butter or margarine, then top with thinly sliced Cheddar cheese and ripe olives. Place on a greased cooky sheet. Bake in hot oven (400°) 10 minutes, or until cheese melts and bubbles up

Fan-tan loaves

Separate 1 package refrigerated butterflake or gem-flake rolls into 12 pieces; stand 4 each in ungreased toy loaf pans. Brush with melted butter or margarine; sprinkle generously with sesame or celery seeds. Bake in moderate oven (375°) 25 minutes, or until golden. Serve hot

Garlic-bread chunks

Halve a loaf of French bread lengthwise, then quarter crosswise. Make 3 cuts in each piece almost to bottom crust; spread with butter or margarine seasoned with minced garlic or garlic powder. Place on a cooky sheet. Bake in hot oven (425°) 5 minutes, or until crispy-hot

Club toasties

Make 4 or 5 deep cuts diagonally in brown 'n' serve club rolls; spread cuts with butter or margarine seasoned with chopped parsley. Bake, following label directions

Italian herb sticks

Halve Italian bread lengthwise and crosswise; split each quarter. Brush cut sides with melted butter or margarine mixed with oregano or basil. Place on a cooky sheet. Bake in hot oven (425°) 5 minutes, or until toasty-crisp

Cracker crunchies

Split milk crackers with a small sharp-tip knife; brush with melted butter or margarine; sprinkle with seasoned salt. Place on a cooky sheet. Bake in hot oven (400°) 10 minutes, or until toasty. Other seasoners: Caraway seeds, paprika, dill weed

Herb ring-a-round

Separate 2 packages refrigerated butterflake or gem-flake rolls into 12 pieces each. Dip into ¼ cup melted butter or margarine combined with 2 teaspoons mixed salad herbs and a dash of nutmeg. Stand on edge, working from outside to center, in a 9-inch pie plate. Bake in moderate oven (375°) 20 minutes, or until golden. Serve hot

Make stuffed vegetables your main dish

BEEF AND POTATO BOATS

Bake at 400° for 1 hour and 20 minutes
Makes 4 servings

    4 large baking potatoes
    4 slices bacon
    ¾ pound ground beef
    3 green onions, trimmed and sliced
 1½ teaspoons salt
    ½ cup dairy sour cream
    2 tablespoons butter or margarine
        Milk
    ¼ cup grated process American cheese

1. Bake potatoes in hot oven (400°) 1 hour, or until tender.
2. Saute bacon until crisp; drain on paper toweling, then crumble. Pour off all drippings from pan.
3. Mix ground beef lightly with green onions; shape into a large patty in same pan; brown 5 minutes on each side, then break up into small chunks. Stir in ½ teaspoon of the salt, sour cream, and crumbled bacon; remove from heat.
4. Split baked potatoes in half; scoop out centers, being careful not to break shells. Place shells in a shallow baking pan. Mash potatoes; beat in remaining 1 teaspoon salt, butter or margarine, and just enough milk to make them creamy-stiff.
5. Spoon beef mixture into shells, dividing evenly; top with mashed potatoes; sprinkle with cheese.
6. Bake in hot oven (400°) 20 minutes, or until cheese is bubbly hot.

Cooksaver tip:

Best baking potatoes are the big chubby round ones, or thin-skin long or boat-shape varieties. Scrub them, then dry well before baking

PEPPER-BEAN CUPS

Bake at 350° for 30 minutes.
Makes 4 servings

    4 large green peppers
    1 pound ground beef
    1 can (1 pound) pork and beans in tomato sauce
    1 can (about 4 ounces) French fried onion rings
    ½ cup catsup
    1 teaspoon prepared mustard

1. Cut a thin slice from top of each pepper; scoop out seeds and membrane. Parboil peppers in a small amount of boiling salted water 10 minutes; drain well. Stand in a greased shallow baking pan.
2. Shape ground beef into a large patty in a frying pan; brown 5 minutes on each side, then break up into small chunks.
3. Stir in pork and beans, half of the onion rings, catsup, and mustard. Spoon into pepper cups, dividing evenly.
4. Bake in moderate oven (350°) 20 minutes; top with remaining onion rings. Bake 10 minutes longer, or until onions are hot and crisp.

Cooksaver tip:

Give ground beef that is to be mixed with other ingredients a deep rich color and flavor this way: Pat meat lightly into a big patty in a frying pan; saute slowly until crusty on bottom. Cut patty in half for easy turning and brown other side the same way, then break it up into chunks

Cooksaver tip:

Follow these how-to's for making cabbage rolls: First trim off coarse rib of leaf for easier rolling, then place meat in center of leaf; fold leaf over to cover and roll up, jelly-roll fashion

ITALIAN MEAT LOAVES IN SQUASH BOWLS

Bake at 375° for 1 hour and 45 minutes.
Makes 6 servings

    3 medium-size acorn squashes
    2 tablespoons melted butter or margarine
       Salt and pepper (for squashes)
 1½ pounds ground beef
 1½ cups soft bread crumbs (3 slices)
    1 egg
  ⅓ cup catsup
    1 teaspoon salt (for filling)
    1 teaspoon oregano
    2 tablespoons grated Parmesan cheese

1. Halve squashes; scoop out seeds and membrane, but do not pare. Brush hollows with melted butter or margarine; sprinkle lightly with salt and pepper. Place in shallow baking pan.
2. Combine ground beef lightly with bread crumbs, egg, catsup, the 1 teaspoon salt, and oregano until well-blended. Heap into squash halves, dividing evenly. (Mixture will mound well.) Sprinkle with Parmesan cheese.
3. Bake, uncovered, in moderate oven (375°) 45 minutes; cover with foil. Bake 1 hour longer, or until squashes are tender.

CABBAGE ROLLUPS
(Pictured on page 90)

Bake at 375° for 45 minutes.
Makes 4 servings

    8 large cabbage leaves (from a medium-size head)
    1 pound ground beef
  ¼ cup quick-cooking rolled oats
    1 small onion, chopped (¼ cup)
    1 tablespoon chopped parsley
    1 egg
    1 can condensed beef broth
    1 teaspoon salt
  ⅛ teaspoon pepper
    1 tablespoon butter or margarine

1. Trim base of cabbage and carefully break off 8 whole leaves. (Save remaining cabbage to cook for a vegetable or make into salad for another meal.)
2. Place leaves in a large saucepan; pour in water to a depth of 1 inch; cover. Heat to boiling; remove from heat. Let stand 5 minutes, or until leaves wilt; drain well.
3. Mix ground beef lightly with rolled oats, onion, parsley, egg, ⅔ cup of the beef broth, salt, and pepper until well-blended.
4. Lay cabbage leaves flat on counter top; spoon meat mixture onto middle of each, dividing evenly. Fold edges of each leaf over filling and roll up; fasten with wooden picks. Arrange rolls in a single layer in a greased shallow 6-cup baking dish.
5. Pour remaining broth over cabbage rolls; dot with butter or margarine; cover.
6. Bake in moderate oven (375°) 45 minutes, or until cabbage is tender. Lift onto a heated serving platter with a slotted spoon; remove picks. Serve sauce separately to spoon over rolls, if you wish. To serve as pictured, arrange cabbage rolls on top of a platter of hot cooked noodles; spoon sauce over. Garnish with a kebab of pitted ripe olives and a sweet yellow wax pepper.

Cooksaver tip:

Here's another hint for peeling leaves from cabbage without tearing them: Trim base of head and cut out core; place cabbage, cored end up, in a kettle and add boiling water to cover; let stand a few minutes. Holding head with a fork, remove leaves as they wilt. Rest of head can be drained, ready to cook later

This budget-best trio—plump Cabbage Rollups *(recipe on page 89)*, peppery-hot Rancho Beef Dinner *(recipe on page 101)*, and Speedy Party Lasagna *(recipe on page 100)*—looks fancy, yet each stretches a little meat a long way

ZUCCHINI IN A SHELL

Bake at 350° for 30 minutes.
Makes 6 servings

- 6 small zucchini (about 2 pounds)
- 1 pound ground beef
- 1 small onion, chopped (¼ cup)
- 1 tablespoon salad oil
- 1 tablespoon chopped pimiento
- 1 egg, slightly beaten
- 1½ teaspoons salt
- ⅛ teaspoon pepper
- 1 cup soft bread crumbs (2 slices)
- ⅓ cup grated Parmesan cheese

1. Trim ends from zucchini; parboil zucchini whole in boiling salted water 10 minutes; drain. Cut in half lengthwise; scoop out centers, being careful not to break shells. Place in a shallow baking pan. Chop scooped-out centers; drain well. Set aside for Step 3.
2. Shape ground beef into a large patty in a frying pan; brown with onion in salad oil 5 minutes on each side, then break up into small chunks. Remove from heat.
3. Stir in chopped zucchini, pimiento, egg, salt, pepper, and bread crumbs. Spoon into zucchini shells, dividing evenly; sprinkle with cheese.
4. Bake in moderate oven (350°) 30 minutes, or until tops are golden-brown.

STUFFED TOMATO CROWNS

Bake at 350° for 20 minutes.
Makes 6 servings

- 6 medium-size tomatoes
- 1 pound ground beef
- 1 small onion, minced (¼ cup)
- 1 tablespoon butter or margarine
- 3 tablespoons flour
- 1 teaspoon salt
- ⅛ teaspoon pepper
- 1 teaspoon curry powder
- 1 cup milk
- ½ cup buttered bread crumbs

1. Cut a thin slice from tops of tomatoes; scoop out centers carefully and save to use in soup or salad. Turn tomato cups upside down to drain.
2. Mix ground beef lightly with onion; shape into a large patty in a frying pan; brown in butter or margarine 5 minutes on each side, then break up into small chunks.
3. Stir in flour, salt, pepper, curry powder, and milk. Cook, stirring constantly, until mixture thickens and boils 1 minute.
4. Spoon into tomato cups; place in a greased shallow baking pan; sprinkle tops with buttered bread crumbs.
5. Bake in moderate oven (350°) 20 minutes, or until crumbs are golden-brown.

Cooksaver tip:

Easy-does-it when you're fixing zucchini for stuffing. Parboil squash first, then halve lengthwise and carefully scoop out centers. (A measuring spoon does a fast neat job because it has a sharp edge.) Same tool works equally well when you're hollowing out tomatoes or eggplant

SUPPER STUFFED PEPPERS

Bake at 350° for 10 minutes.
Makes 4 servings

    1 cup (half an 8-ounce package) elbow
        macaroni
    4 medium-size green peppers
    ½ pound ground beef
    1 small can evaporated milk (⅔ cup)
    ⅓ cup water
    1 envelope chicken-noodle
        soup mix
    ¼ cup grated process American cheese

1. Cook macaroni in *unsalted* boiling water, following label directions; drain, then return to kettle.
2. Cut a slice from top of each pepper; scoop out seeds and membrane. Chop slices and set aside for filling. Parboil peppers in a small amount of boiling water 10 minutes; drain well. Stand in a greased shallow baking pan.
3. Shape ground beef into a large patty in a frying pan; brown with chopped green pepper 5 minutes on each side, then break up into small chunks. Stir in evaporated milk, water, soup mix, and 2 tablespoons of the cheese.
4. Stir into cooked macaroni; spoon into pepper cups. Sprinkle with remaining cheese.
5. Bake in moderate oven (350°) 10 minutes, or until bubbly hot.

EGGPLANT SUPREME

Bake at 350° for 25 minutes.
Makes 4 servings

    2 medium-size eggplants (about 2 pounds)
    1 pound ground beef
    2 tablespoons salad oil
    1 can (about 1 pound) stewed tomatoes
    1 can (8 ounces) tomato sauce
    1 teaspoon salt
    ¼ teaspoon oregano
    ¼ teaspoon garlic salt
    ½ cup grated Parmesan cheese

1. Trim ends from eggplants; cut a thin slice lengthwise from each; scoop out centers, being careful not to break shells. Place shells in a shallow baking pan. Chop scooped-out centers.
2. Shape ground beef into a large patty in a frying pan; brown in salad oil with chopped eggplant 5 minutes on each side, then break up into chunks. Stir in tomatoes, tomato sauce, and seasonings.
3. Simmer, stirring several times, 25 minutes; stir in cheese. Spoon into eggplant shells.
4. Bake in moderate oven (350°) 25 minutes, or until shells are tender. To serve, cut each in half.

Casseroles... the more, the merrier

MACARONI PAPRIKASH

Bake at 350° for 30 minutes.
Makes 6 servings

    1 package (8 ounces) small twist or elbow
        macaroni
    1 small onion, peeled and sliced
    1 tablespoon butter or margarine
    1 pound ground beef
    2 tablespoons flour
    3 teaspoons paprika
    ½ teaspoon salt
    1 envelope instant beef broth
        OR: 1 beef-flavor bouillon cube
    1 cup milk
    1 can (3 or 4 ounces) chopped mushrooms
    ½ cup water
    1 cup (8-ounce carton) dairy sour cream
    ¼ cup chopped parsley
    1 cup buttered bread crumbs

1. Cook macaroni, following label directions; drain, then return to kettle.
2. Saute onion lightly in butter or margarine in a large frying pan; push to one side. Shape ground beef into a large patty in same pan; brown 5 minutes on each side, then break up into chunks.
3. Blend in flour, 2½ teaspoons of the paprika, and salt; add instant beef broth or bouillon cube, milk, mushrooms and liquid, and water. Cook, stirring constantly, and crushing bouillon cube, if using, with a spoon, until mixture thickens and boils 1 minute.
4. Blend about ½ cup of the hot mixture into sour cream, then stir back into remaining in pan. Stir into cooked macaroni with parsley.
5. Spoon into a greased 8-cup baking dish; sprinkle with buttered bread crumbs and remaining ½ teaspoon paprika.
6. Bake in moderate oven (350°) 30 minutes, or until bubbly hot and crumbs are golden.

MACARONI-AND-CHEESE SURPRISE

Bake at 325° for 30 to 45 minutes.
Makes 6 servings

- 1 package (8 ounces) elbow macaroni
- 1 pound ground beef
- 1 egg
- 2 tablespoons chopped parsley
- 1½ teaspoons salt
- ⅛ teaspoon pepper
- 3 tablespoons butter or margarine
- 2 tablespoons flour
- 1 teaspoon dry mustard
- 1 teaspoon Worcestershire sauce
- 2½ cups milk
- 2 cups grated Cheddar cheese (8 ounces)
- 3 small tomatoes
- 1 cup buttered bread crumbs

1. Cook macaroni, following label directions; drain, then return to kettle.
2. Mix ground beef lightly with egg, parsley, 1 teaspoon of the salt, and pepper; shape into 18 balls.
3. Brown in 1 tablespoon of the butter or margarine in a large frying pan; place 3 in each of 6 greased individual baking dishes, or all in an 8-cup baking dish.
4. Pour off all drippings. Melt remaining 2 tablespoons butter or margarine; blend in flour, remaining ½ teaspoon salt, and mustard; stir in Worcestershire sauce and milk. Cook, stirring constantly, until the sauce thickens and boils 1 minute.
5. Stir in 1 cup of the cheese until melted, then stir into cooked macaroni. Spoon over meat balls; sprinkle with remaining 1 cup cheese.
6. Cut stem ends from tomatoes; halve tomatoes crosswise and sprinkle lightly with sugar, salt, and pepper, if you wish. Place on top of macaroni mixture; sprinkle buttered crumbs around edges.
7. Bake in slow oven (325°) 30 minutes for individual baking dishes, or 45 minutes for large baking dish, or until bubbly hot.

Cooksaver tip:

When you have time to fuss, fancy up tomato halves by giving each a fluted edge this way: Mark a guideline around middle of tomato with a wooden pick, then make even saw-tooth cuts, cutting through to center, above and below marks all around. Pull halves apart gently

DEVILED NOODLES AND BEEF

Bake at 350° for 35 minutes.
Makes 6 servings

- 1 medium-size onion, peeled and sliced
- 1 package noodles with sour-cream—cheese-sauce mix
- 1 pound ground beef
- 1 can condensed cream of mushroom soup
- 1 can (4½ ounces) deviled ham
- ½ cup milk
- ⅛ teaspoon pepper
- ½ cup crushed cheese crackers
- 1 tablespoon melted butter or margarine

1. Stir onion into noodles, then prepare with sauce mix from package, following label directions.
2. Shape ground beef into a large patty in a frying pan; brown 5 minutes on each side, then break up into chunks. Stir in mushroom soup, deviled ham, milk, and pepper; pour over noodle mixture; toss lightly to mix.
3. Spoon into a greased shallow 6-cup baking dish; sprinkle with crushed crackers, then drizzle with butter or margarine.
4. Bake in moderate oven (350°) 35 minutes, or until bubbly in center and top is golden-brown.

POTLUCK BURGER BAKE

Bake at 375° for 45 minutes.
Makes 4 servings

- 1 pound ground beef
- 1 medium-size onion, peeled and sliced
- 1½ teaspoons salt
- ⅛ teaspoon pepper
- 1 teaspoon Worcestershire sauce
- 2 cups (about half an 8-ounce package) fine noodles
- 1 can condensed cream of celery soup
- 1 soup can of water
- 1 can (1 pound) cream-style corn
  Chopped parsley

1. Shape ground beef into a large patty in a frying pan; brown 5 minutes on each side, then break up into chunks. Stir in onion, salt, pepper, and Worcestershire sauce; cook, stirring constantly, 2 to 3 minutes. Spoon into a greased 8-cup baking dish; top with uncooked noodles.
2. Heat soup, water, and corn, stirring constantly, to boiling in same pan. Pour over noodles; stir lightly so sauce will flow to bottom; cover.
3. Bake in moderate oven (375°) 45 minutes, or until noodles are tender. Sprinkle with chopped parsley.

BEEF AND POTATO SCALLOP

Bake at 375° for 55 minutes.
Makes 4 servings

1 pound ground beef
1 teaspoon salt
½ teaspoon paprika
⅛ teaspoon pepper
⅛ teaspoon poultry seasoning
1 envelope onion-sauce mix
1 cup water
1 package (10 ounces) frozen mixed
    vegetables, partly thawed
2 cups thinly sliced pared potatoes
1 cup buttered bread crumbs

1. Mix ground beef lightly with salt, paprika, pepper, and poultry seasoning. Shape into a large
   patty in a frying pan; brown 5 minutes on each
   side, then break up into chunks.
2. Sprinkle onion-sauce mix over; stir in water.
   Heat, stirring constantly, just to boiling; stir in
   mixed vegetables.
3. Spoon one third into a greased 8-cup baking
   dish; top with half of the potatoes. Repeat layers,
   then spoon remaining meat mixture on top;
   cover.
4. Bake in moderate oven (375°) 45 minutes; uncover; sprinkle with buttered bread crumbs.
   Bake 10 minutes longer, or until crumbs are
   golden-brown.

LAREDO BEEF

Bake at 350° for 1 hour.
Makes 6 servings

1 pound ground beef
1 teaspoon chili powder
2 tablespoons salad oil
1 envelope beef-vegetable soup mix
1 can (about 1 pound) stewed tomatoes
1 package (10 ounces) frozen baby lima
    beans, partly thawed
½ cup crushed corn chips (from a 4-ounce
    package)

1. Mix ground beef lightly with chili powder. Shape
   into a large patty in a frying pan; brown in salad
   oil 5 minutes on each side, then break up into
   chunks.
2. Stir in soup mix, stewed tomatoes, and beans;
   heat, stirring several times, to boiling.
3. Spoon into a greased 6-cup baking dish; sprinkle
   corn chips in a ring on top.
4. Bake in moderate oven (350°) 1 hour, or until
   bubbly hot in center.

MERRY MIX-UP

Bake at 350° for 2 hours.
Makes 8 servings

1 package (10 ounces) frozen lima beans,
    partly thawed
1 pound ground beef
1 can (about 1 pound) tomatoes
1 can (12 or 16 ounces) whole-kernel corn
2 cups thinly sliced pared potatoes
1 large onion, chopped (1 cup)
1 large green pepper, halved, seeded, and
    chopped
4 tablespoons flour
1 teaspoon salt
1 teaspoon curry powder
1 cup buttered bread crumbs

1. Combine beans with ground beef, tomatoes, corn,
   potatoes, onion, and green pepper in a greased
   12-cup baking dish.
2. Mix flour with salt and curry powder; sprinkle
   over meat mixture, then stir in; cover.
3. Bake in moderate oven (350°) 1 hour; uncover;
   sprinkle with buttered bread crumbs. Bake, uncovered, 1 hour longer, or until potatoes are
   tender and top is golden-brown.

FIESTA CASSEROLE

Bake at 400° for 30 minutes.
Makes 6 servings

1 large onion, chopped (1 cup)
1 clove garlic, minced
2 tablespoons salad oil
1 pound ground beef
1 can (about 1 pound) tomatoes
1 can (about 1 pound) red kidney beans
1 can (15 ounces) chili con carne without
    beans
1½ teaspoons salt
1 can (11 ounces) tortillas
1 cup grated Cheddar cheese (4 ounces)

1. Saute onion and garlic lightly in salad oil in a
   large frying pan; push to one side.
2. Shape ground beef into a large patty in same
   pan; brown 5 minutes on each side, then break
   up into chunks. Stir in tomatoes, beans and
   liquid, chili con carne, and salt; heat to boiling.
3. Place 3 of the tortillas, overlapping if necessary,
   in a greased 12-cup baking dish; top with about
   1 cup of the sauce. Repeat to make 5 more layers of each. Sprinkle with cheese.
4. Bake in hot oven (400°) 30 minutes, or until
   bubbly hot.

EYE-CATCHING WAYS TO TOP A CASSEROLE

Try these twists with pastry

For an extra-dressy look, twist strips of pastry into ropes, and place diagonally over a meat pie. Or weave plain strips, over and under, to make a crisscross top

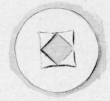

Star-bright—that's this simple design that looks so pretty. Cut a 3-inch cross in pastry round and turn points back so the filling peeks through

No tricks needed for this three-ring design. Just make cutouts in a pastry round with a fluted truffle cutter; lift them out and place in an even pattern on top of pastry

Go gay with cheese

So many casseroles call for cheese toppings and here it's the arrangement that counts. To make the chevron design, cut cheese slices into about-inch-wide strips and arrange as pictured

For this whirling star, start with four square slices of cheese. Cut three in half diagonally to form triangles, then place, points out, around whole slice in center

You couldn't ask for an easier trim than this, but it goes a long way in dressing up a casserole. Cut cheese slices in strips, and place, crisscross fashion, to make a lattice top

Make these fancies with bread

Ring-a-round-a-rosy go thin slices of crusty French bread. Place them on the casserole about 15 minutes before it comes from the oven, so they'll stay crisp, bake just long enough to turn toasty-golden

Here's still another variation of a star. To make it, cut bread slices in quarters diagonally, and place, points in, around the edge of a chicken or beef pie or stew

Inch-size cubes of bread, placed checkerboard style, form an inviting see-through "crust." White bread is always pleasing, but for flavor variety, try sesame-seed, whole-wheat, or pumpernickel

Even party rye gets into the act, and here it's cut in quarters and lined up around the edge of a casserole. Looks special, tastes special, too

Cut a pretty figure with biscuits

Zip open a package of refrigerated biscuits and you're off to all kinds of designs. Separate biscuits, cut rounds from centers with the inside of a doughnut or small biscuit cutter. Lift out rounds; use them for one design, rings, for another. Two other ideas: Cut biscuits in half moons or ovals with a round cutter, or make four cuts in each biscuit, separate slightly to form "petals"

BEEF AND RICE AMANDINE

Bake at 350° for 45 minutes.
Makes 6 servings

- 1 pound ground beef
- 1 can condensed cream of chicken soup
- 1 envelope instant beef broth
  OR: 1 beef-flavor bouillon cube
- 1 cup water
- 1 cup sliced celery
- 1 small onion, peeled and sliced
- ½ cup uncooked rice
- 1 teaspoon soy sauce
- ⅛ teaspoon oregano
- ½ cup toasted slivered almonds

1. Shape ground beef into a large patty in a large frying pan; brown 5 minutes on each side, then break up into chunks.
2. Stir in chicken soup, instant beef broth or bouillon cube, water, celery, onion, rice, soy sauce, and oregano. Heat to boiling, crushing bouillon cube, if using, with a spoon; pour into a greased 8-cup baking dish; cover.
3. Bake in moderate oven (350°) 30 minutes; uncover; sprinkle almonds on top. Bake 15 minutes longer, or until golden-brown.

BEEF AND BEANS AU GRATIN

Bake at 325° for 1 hour.
Makes 6 servings

- 1 clove garlic, minced
- 1 tablespoon salad oil
- 1 pound ground beef
- ½ teaspoon chili powder
- 1 teaspoon Worcestershire sauce
- 1 teaspoon prepared mustard
- ¼ cup chili sauce
- 1 can (about 1 pound) beans in tomato sauce
- 1 can (about 1 pound) red kidney beans, drained
- ½ cup grated Cheddar cheese
- ¼ cup dry bread crumbs

1. Saute garlic lightly in salad oil in a large frying pan; push to one side.
2. Shape ground beef into a large patty in same pan; brown 5 minutes on each side, then break up into chunks. Stir in chili powder, Worcestershire sauce, mustard, chili sauce, and beans. Spoon into a greased 8-cup baking dish.
3. Mix cheese and bread crumbs; sprinkle over top.
4. Bake in slow oven (325°) 1 hour, or until top is crusty-brown.

JIFFY CASSOULET
(Pictured at right)

Bake at 350° for 1 hour.
Makes 8 servings

- 6 slices bacon
- 2 pounds meat-loaf mixture (ground beef and pork)
- 1 can (about 1 pound) red kidney beans, drained
- 1 can (about 1 pound) white kidney beans, drained
- 1 can (about 1 pound) sliced carrots, drained
- 1 can (about 1 pound) stewed tomatoes
- 1 tablespoon dried parsley flakes
- 2 teaspoons salt
- 1 teaspoon thyme
- ¼ teaspoon pepper

1. Saute bacon just until fat starts to cook out in a large frying pan; remove and drain on paper toweling; set aside.
2. Shape meat-loaf mixture into a large patty in same pan; brown 5 minutes on each side. Pour off all drippings, then break meat up into chunks.
3. Stir in drained beans and carrots, tomatoes, and seasonings; heat to boiling. Spoon into a greased 10-cup baking dish; place bacon on top.
4. Bake in moderate oven (350°) 1 hour, or until bubbly hot and bacon is crisp.

LITTLE LASAGNA

Bake at 375° for 45 minutes.
Makes 4 servings

- 2 cups (about half an 8-ounce package) regular noodles
- 1 cup cream-style cottage cheese
- ½ pound ground beef
- 4 slices Muenster cheese (from an 8-ounce package), cut in strips
- 1 can (about 11 ounces) spaghetti sauce with mushrooms
- ¼ cup grated Parmesan cheese

1. Cook noodles, following label directions; drain, then spoon into a greased shallow 6-cup baking dish.
2. Spread cottage cheese over noodles; break up ground beef and sprinkle on top. Place half each of the cheese strips and spaghetti sauce on top; repeat with remaining cheese strips and sauce. Sprinkle with Parmesan cheese.
3. Bake in moderate oven (375°) 45 minutes, or until bubbly in center and top is golden-brown.

Ready-mixed meat-loaf meat and four speedy canned vegetables go into Jiffy Cassoulet *(recipe at left)*, a modern-day version of an old-fashioned French favorite. Serve with zippy corn relish and crusty little rolls or corn-bread squares

MEXICAN JACK CASSEROLE

Bake at 350° for 30 minutes.
Makes 8 servings

  1 medium-size onion, chopped (½ cup)
  ½ cup chopped celery
1½ teaspoons chili powder
  2 tablespoons salad oil
1½ pounds meat-loaf mixture (ground beef, pork, and veal)
  ¼ teaspoon oregano
  1 can (8 ounces) tomato sauce
  2 cans (about 1 pound each) baked beans
  1 cup grated Cheddar cheese (4 ounces)

1. Saute onion and celery with chili powder lightly in salad oil in a frying pan; push to one side.
2. Shape meat-loaf mixture into a large patty in same pan; brown 5 minutes on each side, then break up into chunks. Stir in oregano and tomato sauce; heat to boiling. Place beans, cheese, and meat mixture in a greased 8-cup baking dish.
3. Bake in moderate oven (350°) 30 minutes.

SPEEDY PARTY LASAGNA
(Pictured on page 91)

Bake at 425° for 25 minutes.
Makes 12 servings

  2 packages (1 pound, 8 ounces each) lasagna dinner
  2 packages (10 ounces each) frozen chopped spinach
  1 pound ground beef
  2 cups (1-pound carton) cream-style cottage cheese
  1 egg
  2 teaspoons Italian seasoning
  ½ teaspoon salt

1. Cook noodles from packages of lasagna dinner, following label directions; drain.
2. Cook spinach, following label directions; drain.
3. Shape ground beef into a patty in a frying pan; brown 5 minutes on each side, then break up into chunks. Stir in sauce from lasagna dinner.
4. Mix cottage cheese with egg, Italian seasoning, and salt; stir in spinach.
5. Set aside 6 noodles. Layer half of remaining noodles, cheese mixture, meat sauce, and grated cheese (from packages) into a greased baking dish, 13x9x2. Repeat layers.
6. Roll up saved noodles, jelly-roll fashion; slice in half and press, cut sides down, into sauce.
7. Bake in hot oven (425°) 25 minutes, or until bubbly hot.

MACARONI-BEEF ROYALE

Bake at 350° for 45 minutes.
Makes 6 servings

  1 package (8 ounces) small macaroni shells
  1 package (6 ounces) cream cheese with chives
  1 pound ground beef
  2 cans (8 ounces each) tomato sauce
  1 teaspoon sugar
1½ teaspoons salt
  2 medium-size onions, peeled and sliced
  2 tablespoons butter or margarine
  1 egg
  1 cup (8-ounce carton) dairy sour cream

1. Cook macaroni, following label directions; drain, then return to kettle.
2. Slice cream cheese with chives into macaroni; toss to coat well. Spoon into a greased shallow 8-cup baking dish.
3. Shape ground beef into a large patty in a frying pan; brown 5 minutes on each side, then break up into chunks. Stir in tomato sauce, sugar, and 1 teaspoon of the salt; spoon over macaroni mixture in baking dish.
4. Saute onions in butter or margarine just until soft in same pan; arrange over meat mixture in baking dish.
5. Beat egg slightly; blend in sour cream and remaining ½ teaspoon salt; spoon over onions.
6. Bake in moderate oven (350°) 45 minutes, or until bubbly in center and top is set.

Cooksaver tip:

If you find you're out of the variety of macaroni your recipe calls for, take heart. Other kinds taste just as good, and it's fun to experiment with spaghetti, butterflies, spirals—or mix them, if you like. When making substitutions, choose shapes of about the same size so they'll cook evenly

CABBAGE-BURGER BAKE

Bake at 400° for 1 hour.
Makes 6 servings

 1 small head cabbage (about 2 pounds)
 6 slices bacon
 1 medium-size onion, chopped (½ cup)
 1 cup uncooked rice
 1½ pounds meat-loaf mixture (ground beef and pork)
 1 teaspoon salt
 ⅛ teaspoon pepper
 1 can (about 15 ounces) spaghetti sauce with mushrooms
 3 cups water

1. Shred cabbage. (There should be about 8 cups.) Spread half in a greased shallow baking dish, 13x9x2.
2. Saute bacon just until fat starts to cook out; remove and drain on paper toweling; set aside.
3. Stir onion and rice into drippings in pan; cook, stirring constantly, until onion is soft and rice is lightly browned. Spoon over cabbage in baking dish.
4. Shape meat-loaf mixture into large patty in same pan. Brown 5 minutes on each side, then break up into chunks. Spoon over rice mixture in baking dish; sprinkle with salt and pepper; top with remaining cabbage.
5. Heat spaghetti sauce with water to boiling in same pan. Pour over cabbage, stirring lightly with a fork so sauce will flow to bottom. Top with bacon slices; cover.
6. Bake in hot oven (400°) 50 minutes, or until rice and cabbage are tender; uncover. Bake 10 minutes longer to crisp bacon.

RANCHO BEEF DINNER
(Pictured on pages 90-91)

Bake at 350° for 1 hour.
Makes 6 servings

 1 cup yellow corn meal
 6 slices bacon
 1 pound ground beef
 1½ teaspoons salt
 ⅛ teaspoon pepper
 ¼ cup chopped parsley
 1 large onion, chopped (1 cup)
 ½ cup chopped celery
 ½ clove garlic, crushed
 1 can (about 1 pound) tomatoes
 1 package (6 ounces) cubed Cheddar cheese

1. Stir corn meal slowly into 4 cups boiling water; cook until thick, about 30 minutes. Pour into a greased baking dish, 13x9x2; chill.
2. Saute bacon until crisp in a medium-size frying pan; drain on paper toweling; crumble and set aside. Pour off drippings, then measure 2 tablespoonfuls and return to pan.
3. Mix ground beef lightly with 1 teaspoon of the salt, pepper, and parsley; shape into 24 small balls. Brown in drippings in pan; push to one side.
4. Stir onion, celery, and garlic into pan; saute just until onion is soft. Stir in tomatoes, cheese, and remaining ½ teaspoon salt. Remove from heat.
5. Remove chilled corn-meal mush from dish by turning upside down on a cutting board; cut into about-1-inch blocks.
6. Set aside about 10 for top, then place half of the remaining in the bottom of a greased 8-cup baking dish. Top with half each of the meat balls and sauce and crumbled bacon. Repeat to make another layer of each, mounding meat balls in center; arrange saved corn-meal blocks around edge; cover.
7. Bake in moderate oven (350°) 20 minutes; uncover. Bake 40 minutes longer, or until bubbly hot.

Layers of peppery meat sauce, noodles, and cheese stack up to
Our Favorite Lasagna *(recipe on page 104)*. Recipe fills a
big dish, so if you're planning a party, it's a good easy-
serve choice. Some left? It reheats perfectly in its baker

CHAPTER 6

EVERYBODY HAS FUN AT

COOKOUTS, COOK-INS

Puffs of smoke are curling up from back-yard grills where sizzling-good burgers are regular fare. Kitchens make happy settings, too, when lively teen-agers get together for fill-'em-up food that's fast and easy.

Here you'll find lots of ways to shape, season, grill, and serve hamburgers outdoors and in . . . barbecue sauces to brush on burgers as they cook and toppers to crown your grilled-to-perfection prizes . . . spoonables to dip from a bottomless kettle . . . cook-in and carry-out casseroles, pizza, spaghetti, and chili mixes for a small family gathering as well as a crowd. And yes, even tips for the chef on building the fire.

Whether you cook out or cook in, serve hamburger plain or fancy—you can depend on this favorite to make a hit.

Picnic specials to cook in, carry out

SPAGHETTI FOR A CROWD

Makes 12 servings

- 1 large onion, chopped (1 cup)
- 2 cloves garlic, minced
- ¼ cup olive oil or salad oil
- 2 pounds ground beef
- 2 cans (about 2 pounds each) Italian tomatoes
- 2 cans (6 ounces each) tomato paste
- 1 cup water
- ½ cup chopped celery
- ¼ cup chopped parsley
- 2 bay leaves
- 1 teaspoon basil
- 4 teaspoons salt
- 2 teaspoons sugar
- ¼ teaspoon pepper
- 2 packages (1 pound each) spaghetti
  Grated Parmesan cheese

1. Saute onion and garlic in olive oil or salad oil just until onion is soft in a kettle or Dutch oven; push to one side.
2. Shape ground beef into a large patty in same kettle; brown 5 minutes on each side, then break up into chunks. Stir in remaining ingredients, except spaghetti and cheese.
3. Simmer, stirring several times, 2 hours, or until sauce is thick. Let stand 5 to 10 minutes until fat rises to top, then skim off; remove bay leaves.
4. Cook spaghetti in two kettles, following label directions; drain.
5. Spoon cooked spaghetti and meat sauce into separate large bowls for everyone to dish up his own; serve with grated Parmesan cheese to sprinkle on top.

OUR FAVORITE LASAGNA
(Pictured on page 102)

Bake at 350° for 30 minutes.
Makes 8 servings

- ½ pound sweet Italian sausages
- ½ pound ground beef
- 1 medium-size onion, chopped (½ cup)
- 1 clove garlic, minced
- 1 can (about 2 pounds) Italian tomatoes
- 1 envelope spaghetti-sauce mix
- 1 pound lasagna noodles
- 1 tablespoon salad oil
- 2 eggs
- 2 cups (1 pound) cream-style cottage cheese
- 2 packages (8 ounces each) sliced mozzarella or pizza cheese
- ½ cup grated Parmesan cheese

1. Squeeze sausages from casings; mix meat lightly with ground beef. Shape into a large patty in a frying pan; brown 5 minutes on each side, then break up into chunks; push to one side.
2. Stir in onion and garlic; saute just until soft. Stir in tomatoes and spaghetti-sauce mix; simmer, stirring several times, 30 minutes, or until slightly thickened.
3. While sauce cooks, slide lasagna noodles, one at a time so as not to break, into a kettle of boiling salted water. Add salad oil; cook, following label directions. (Oil keeps noodles from sticking.) Cook, stirring often, 15 minutes, or just until tender. Drain; cover with cold water.
4. Beat eggs slightly; blend in cottage cheese.
5. Line bottom of a lightly oiled baking dish, 13x9x2, with a single layer of drained noodles. (Lift each strip separately from water and hold over kettle to drain.) Cover with a third each of cottage-cheese mixture, meat sauce, and mozzarella or pizza and Parmesan cheeses. Repeat to make two more layers of each. (Our picture shows the top layer of mozzarella cheese arranged in crisscross and triangle designs.)
6. Bake in moderate oven (350°) 30 minutes, or until bubbly hot. Garnish with a ripe-olive "flower" and parsley, if you wish. (To make olive "flower," cut a pitted ripe olive lengthwise into sixths; arrange, petal fashion, around a whole ripe olive.)

Cooksaver tip:

For a change from mild Parmesan cheese, try grated zesty Romano or herb-seasoned Sap Sago cheese

PANAMA JOHNNY

Makes 6 servings

1 pound ground beef
1 large onion, chopped (1 cup)
1 medium-size green pepper, halved,
    seeded, and chopped
1 cup chopped celery
1 clove garlic, minced
½ cup sliced stuffed green olives
1 can (3 or 4 ounces) chopped mushrooms
1 envelope spaghetti-sauce mix
1 can (6 ounces) tomato paste
1 can condensed beef broth
1 soup can of water
¼ pound spaghetti, broken in 2-inch pieces

1. Shape ground beef into a large patty in a kettle or Dutch oven; brown 5 minutes on each side, then break up into chunks.
2. Stir in onion, green pepper, celery, garlic, olives, mushrooms and liquid, spaghetti-sauce mix, tomato paste, beef broth, and water.
3. Cook, stirring often, 1 hour, or until thick.
4. Cook spaghetti, following label directions; drain. Stir into meat mixture; heat just to boiling.

BARBECUED BEEF BAKE

Bake at 350° for 1 hour.
Makes 6 servings

1 small Bermuda onion, peeled and sliced
1 medium-size green pepper, halved,
    seeded, and sliced
2 tablespoons butter or margarine
1½ pounds ground beef
1 cup bottled barbecue sauce
2 cups water
1 can (8 ounces) tomato sauce
1 tablespoon brown sugar
½ teaspoon salt
¾ cup uncooked rice

1. Saute onion and green pepper in butter or margarine just until soft in a large frying pan; remove and set aside.
2. Shape ground beef into a large patty in same pan; brown 5 minutes on each side, then break up into chunks.
3. Stir in remaining ingredients. Heat, stirring several times, just to boiling.
4. Spoon half of the onion–green-pepper mixture into an ungreased 12-cup baking dish; top with all of the meat mixture, then remaining onion–green-pepper mixture; cover.
5. Bake in moderate oven (350°) 1 hour, or until rice is tender.

SKILLET ENCHILADAS
(Pictured on page 109)

Makes 8 servings

Sauce
3 medium-size onions, chopped
    (1½ cups)
1 tablespoon chili powder
2 tablespoons olive oil or salad oil
2 cans (about 1 pound each) tomatoes
2 cans (8 ounces each) tomato sauce
2 teaspoons sugar
1 teaspoon oregano
¼ teaspoon bottled red-pepper seasoning
1 clove garlic

Tortillas and Filling
1 pound ground beef
1 teaspoon chili powder
1 clove garlic, minced
1 can (about 4 ounces) chopped ripe
    olives, drained
1 cup chopped green onions
¼ cup salad oil
8 tortillas (from an 11-ounce can)
1½ cups grated Cheddar cheese (6 ounces)

Topping
Sliced stuffed green olives
Sweet-onion rings

1. Make sauce: Saute onions and chili powder in olive oil or salad oil until onions are soft in a large frying pan; stir in remaining sauce ingredients, sticking garlic onto a wooden pick so it will be easy to remove.
2. Simmer, adding a little water from time to time if mixture seems dry, 45 minutes to blend flavors; remove garlic.
3. Prepare tortillas: Mix ground beef lightly with chili powder and garlic; shape into a large patty in a medium-size frying pan. Brown 5 minutes on each side, then break up into chunks; remove from heat. Stir in ripe olives and green onions.
4. Heat salad oil in a small frying pan; dip each tortilla into the hot oil just until softened. Remove and drain on paper toweling.
5. Spread each with a scant ⅓ cup meat mixture, then sprinkle with 1 tablespoon of the grated cheese. Roll up; place, spoke fashion and seam side down, in sauce in pan.
6. Spoon some of the sauce over rolls; sprinkle with remaining cheese.
7. Arrange topping: Place sliced green olives and onion rings on top of enchiladas; heat slowly just until enchiladas are hot and cheese melts slightly.

DIXIE CASSEROLE

Bake at 350° for 30 minutes.
Makes 4 servings

- 1 medium-size onion, chopped (½ cup)
- 2 tablespoons butter or margarine
- 1 pound ground beef
- 2 tablespoons flour
- 1 teaspoon salt
- ½ teaspoon paprika
- 1 small can evaporated milk (⅔ cup)
- ⅔ cup water
- ½ cup catsup
- 1 cup grated Cheddar cheese (4 ounces)
- 1 can (about 1 pound) hominy, drained
- ¼ cup fine dry bread crumbs
- ¼ cup sliced stuffed green olives

1. Saute onion lightly in butter or margarine in a large frying pan; push to one side.
2. Shape ground beef into a large patty in same pan; brown 5 minutes on each side, then break up into chunks. Stir in flour, salt, and paprika, then evaporated milk, water, and catsup.
3. Cook, stirring constantly, until mixture thickens and boils 1 minute. Stir in ⅓ cup of the cheese and drained hominy.
4. Spoon into a greased 6-cup baking dish; sprinkle with bread crumbs and remaining cheese.
5. Bake in moderate oven (350°) 30 minutes, or until bubbly hot and top is golden-brown. Garnish with a ring of sliced olives.

BEEF AND LENTILS GENOESE

Makes 8 to 10 servings

- 1½ pounds ground beef
- 1 large onion, chopped (1 cup)
- ¼ pound salami, diced
- 1 package (1 pound) dried lentils
- 1 teaspoon Italian seasoning
- ½ teaspoon pumpkin-pie spice
- 1 envelope instant beef broth
    OR: 1 beef-flavor bouillon cube
- 1 teaspoon salt
- 6 cups water

1. Shape ground beef into a large patty in a kettle or Dutch oven; brown 5 minutes on each side, then break up into chunks; push to one side.
2. Stir onion into drippings in kettle; saute just until soft; stir in remaining ingredients. Heat to boiling, crushing bouillon cube, if using, with a spoon; cover.
3. Simmer 1 hour, or until lentils are soft. Ladle into soup plates or small bowls.

RIO CHILI BEANS

Bake at 325° for 1 hour.
Makes 8 servings

- 4 slices bacon, diced
- 1½ pounds ground beef
- 1 medium-size onion, chopped (½ cup)
- ½ cup chopped celery
- 1 clove garlic, minced
- 2 cans (about 1 pound each) red kidney beans
- 1 can (about 1 pound) tomatoes
- 1 can (6 ounces) tomato paste
- 1 tablespoon chili powder
- 1 teaspoon salt
- 1 teaspoon sugar
- ½ teaspoon oregano
- ¼ teaspoon pepper

1. Saute bacon until crisp in a kettle or Dutch oven; remove and set aside. Pour off drippings, then measure 2 tablespoonfuls and return to kettle.
2. Shape ground beef into a large patty in same kettle; brown 5 minutes on each side, then break up into chunks.
3. Stir in onion, celery, and garlic; saute lightly, then stir in kidney beans and liquid and remaining ingredients; heat just to boiling.
4. Spoon into an ungreased 12-cup baking dish; sprinkle bacon on top; cover.
5. Bake in slow oven (325°) 1 hour, or until bubbly.
6. Spoon over your choice of corn chips, toasted corn-bread squares, or toasted English muffins, if you wish.

BARLEY-BEEF STEW

Makes 6 servings

- 1 pound ground beef
- 1 large onion, diced (1 cup)
- 1 cup diced celery
- 1 cup diced pared raw carrots
- 1 cup diced pared white turnip
- ½ cup barley
- 1 envelope instant beef broth
- 2 teaspoons salt
- 4 cups water

1. Shape ground beef into a large patty in a kettle or Dutch oven; brown 5 minutes on each side, then break up into chunks; push to one side.
2. Stir onion and celery into kettle; saute just until soft. Stir in remaining ingredients; heat to boiling; cover.
3. Simmer 1 hour, or until barley is tender. Ladle into soup plates or small bowls.

PICNIC PIES

Bake at 400° for 20 minutes.
Makes 8 pies

    1 pound ground beef
    1 small onion, grated
    1 egg
    ½ cup soft bread crumbs (1 slice)
    1 tablespoon catsup
    ½ teaspoon Worcestershire sauce
    1 teaspoon salt
    ⅛ teaspoon pepper
    1 package piecrust mix

1. Mix ground beef lightly with onion; shape into a large patty in a frying pan; brown 5 minutes on each side, then break up into small chunks.
2. Beat egg slightly; stir in bread crumbs, catsup, Worcestershire sauce, salt, and pepper; drizzle over meat. Cook, stirring constantly, about 1 minute; cool while making pastry.
3. Prepare piecrust mix, following label directions. Roll out half to a 12-inch square; cut into 4 six-inch squares.
4. Spoon about ¼ cup meat mixture onto center of each; fold over to make a triangle. Press edges firmly with a fork to seal, then trim even, if needed. Place pies on an ungreased cooky sheet. Repeat with remaining pastry and meat mixture.
5. Bake in hot oven (400°) 20 minutes, or until pastry is golden. Serve warm.

DANISH BEEF PATTIES

Makes 6 servings

    1½ pounds ground beef
    1   medium-size potato, cooked, peeled, and
        chopped fine
    1   medium-size onion, grated
    3   tablespoons chopped pickled beets
    1   egg
    1   tablespoon chopped parsley
    1   teaspoon salt
    2   tablespoons salad oil
    1   envelope brown-gravy mix
    ½   teaspoon prepared horseradish
    1   cup water

1. Mix ground beef lightly with potato, onion, beets, egg, parsley, and salt until well-blended; shape into 6 patties about 1 inch thick.
2. Pan-fry over medium heat in salad oil 8 minutes on each side, or until meat is done as you like it.
3. Blend gravy mix, horseradish, and water; pour over patties. Heat, stirring constantly, to boiling; cover. Simmer 1 minute to blend flavors.

Cooksaver tip:

If you make the Picnic Pies ahead and want to tote them farther away than your back yard, reheat them, then keep under wraps this way: Bundle each pie in foil and reheat in moderate oven (350°) 10 minutes. Pack all — still in their foil jackets — in a box.
They'll stay warm for about an hour

CONFETTI SCALLOP

Bake at 350° for 1 hour and 10 minutes.
Makes 8 servings

    1   cup (about half an 8-ounce package)
        macaroni twists
    1   pound ground beef
    1   teaspoon salt
    1   teaspoon curry powder
    ¼   teaspoon marjoram
    1   large onion, chopped (1 cup)
    4   cups chopped raw cabbage (about
        1 pound)
    1   can (about 1 pound) tomatoes
    1   can (8 ounces) tomato sauce
    1   can (3 or 4 ounces) chopped mushrooms
    1   cup grated sharp Cheddar cheese
        (4 ounces)
    ¼   cup seedless raisins
    4   slices mozzarella or pizza cheese (from an
        8-ounce package), cut in triangles

1. Cook macaroni, following label directions; drain, then return to kettle.
2. Mix ground beef lightly with salt, curry powder, marjoram, and onion; shape into a large patty in a frying pan; brown 5 minutes on each side, then break up into chunks.
3. Stir into cooked macaroni with cabbage, tomatoes, tomato sauce, mushrooms and liquid, Cheddar cheese, and raisins. Spoon into a greased 12-cup baking dish; cover.
4. Bake in moderate oven (350°) 1 hour; arrange mozzarella or pizza cheese on top. Bake 10 minutes longer, or until cheese melts slightly.

Help yourself, everybody, to sizzling Burgers Kun Koki *(recipe on page 117)* to pop into a big roll. Slumgullion-on-a-bun *(recipe on page 113)* and Skillet Enchiladas *(recipe on page 105)* are choices to cook indoors, then whisk off to your outdoor eating spot

TEXAS TACOS
(Pictured on page 132)

Bake at 325° for 30 minutes.
Makes 6 servings

Filling
   2 pounds ground beef
   1 envelope onion-soup mix
   1 can (1 pint, 2 ounces) tomato juice
   1 cup catsup
  ¼ cup firmly packed brown sugar
   2 tablespoons cider vinegar
   2 tablespoons Worcestershire sauce
   2 teaspoons salt

Pancakes
   3 eggs
 1½ cups milk
   1 cup sifted regular flour
   1 teaspoon salt
  ½ cup white or yellow corn meal
   2 tablespoons melted butter or margarine

Topping
   2 cups (16-ounce carton) dairy sour cream
   1 package (4 ounces) shredded sharp
       Cheddar cheese
   1 medium-size green pepper, seeded and
       cut in thin rings
       Cherry tomatoes

1. Make filling: Shape ground beef into a large patty in a large frying pan; brown 5 minutes on each side, then break up into small chunks. Stir in remaining filling ingredients; cover.
2. Simmer, stirring often, 1 hour, or until thick.
3. Make pancakes: Beat eggs with milk; sift in flour and salt, then stir in corn meal and melted butter or margarine; beat just until smooth.
4. Heat a 7-inch heavy frying pan over low heat; lightly grease with butter or margarine. Pour in batter, a scant ¼ cup at a time, tipping pan to cover bottom completely. Bake until pancake top appears dry and underside is golden; turn; brown other side. Repeat, lightly buttering pan before each baking, to make 12 pancakes.
5. Spoon about ¼ cup of the filling onto each pancake as it is baked; roll up and place, seam side down, in a double row in a buttered shallow baking dish, 13x9x2.
6. Keep pancake rolls warm in very slow oven (250°) until all are filled. (Pancakes may be filled ahead, then chilled until ready to bake.)
7. Make topping: Spoon sour cream in a ribbon between pancake rows; sprinkle with cheese; spoon any remaining filling beside sour cream.
8. Bake in slow oven (325°) 30 minutes, or until top is bubbly and pancakes are heated through. (If filled pancakes have been chilled, increase baking time to 45 minutes.) Garnish with green-pepper rings and cherry tomatoes.

WESTERN CASSEROLE

Bake at 350° for 1¼ hours.
Makes 4 servings
   1 pound ground beef
  ½ cup grated process American cheese
 1½ teaspoons salt
   1 tablespoon salad oil
  ¾ cup uncooked rice
   1 medium-size onion, chopped (½ cup)
   1 can condensed tomato soup
   1 soup can of water
  ½ teaspoon oregano
  ¼ teaspoon dry mustard
   1 can (about 1 pound) cut green beans,
       drained
   1 can (12 or 16 ounces) whole-kernel
       corn, drained

1. Mix ground beef lightly with cheese and 1 teaspoon of the salt until well-blended; shape into 12 balls.
2. Brown in salad oil in a large frying pan; remove with a slotted spoon and place in an ungreased 8-cup baking dish; sprinkle with uncooked rice and onion.
3. Stir soup, water, oregano, mustard, and remaining ½ teaspoon salt into drippings in pan; heat slowly, stirring several times, to boiling. Pour over meat mixture; cover.
4. Bake in moderate oven (350°) 45 minutes; stir with a fork to mix well. Spoon drained green beans and corn in a double ring on top, then cover again.
5. Bake 30 minutes longer, or until rice is tender and vegetables are heated through.

Cooksaver tip:

When baking pancakes, make sure your frying pan is heated to the proper temperature before pouring in batter. Here's how to test: Sprinkle a few drops of water into the pan; when they bounce about, temperature is right. Using a griddle? Test it the same way

Cooksaver tip:

No canned sweet potatoes or yams on hand for French Beef Bake? Just substitute either fresh variety this way: Pare the potatoes and slice ¼ inch thick, then parboil in boiling, slightly salted water about 10 minutes. Drain well; layer into baking dish, as below. You'll need about a pound, the same as the canned ones

FRENCH BEEF BAKE

Bake at 350° for 1½ hours.
Makes 8 servings

- 2 pounds ground beef
- ¼ cup flour
- 2 teaspoons salt
- 1 teaspoon curry powder
- ¼ teaspoon pepper
- 1 can (about 1 pound) whole sweet potatoes or yams, drained and cut into ¼-inch-thick slices
- 4 leeks, trimmed and sliced
- 1 package (10 ounces) frozen peas, partly thawed
- ¼ cup sliced stuffed green olives
- 1¼ cups boiling water
- 1 tablespoon butter or margarine

1. Shape ground beef into a large patty in a large frying pan; brown 5 minutes on each side, then break up into chunks; stir in flour.
2. Mix salt, curry powder, and pepper.
3. Layer vegetables and ground-beef mixture into a 12-cup baking dish this way: Half each of the sliced sweet potatoes, leeks, ground-beef mixture, peas, and olive slices; sprinkle with half of the seasoning mixture. Repeat with remaining vegetables, meat, and seasoning mixture.
4. Pour in boiling water slowly; dot with butter or margarine; cover.
5. Bake in moderate oven (350°) 1½ hours, or until vegetables are tender.

CAMPER'S STEW

Makes 6 servings

- 2 pounds ground beef
- 2 teaspoons salt
- 2 cans (about 11 ounces each) beef gravy
- 1 can (8 ounces) spaghetti sauce with mushrooms
- 1 can (1 pound) mixed vegetables
- 1 can (1 pound) small white potatoes, drained
- 1 can (1 pound) small whole onions, drained

1. Mix ground beef lightly with salt; shape into 6 patties about 1 inch thick.
2. Pan-fry in a large heavy frying pan 8 minutes on each side for medium, or until meat is done as you like it. Pour off all drippings.
3. Stir in beef gravy, spaghetti sauce, mixed vegetables and liquid, and drained potatoes and onions. Heat just until bubbly hot.
4. Spoon a meat patty into each of six soup bowls; spoon vegetables and gravy over.

BRUNSWICK BEEF

Makes 12 servings

- 4 pounds ground beef
- 2 cans (about 1 pound each) tomatoes
- 2 cans (1 pound each) cream-style corn
- 2 cans (1 pound each) peas
- 1 can (about 14 ounces) chicken broth
- 1 envelope French salad-dressing mix
- ¼ cup instant minced onion
- 1 tablespoon sugar
- ¼ teaspoon pepper
- 1 package (8 ounces) fine noodles
  OR: 1 package (8 ounces) regular noodles
- ½ cup chopped parsley

1. Shape ground beef into 4 large patties; brown, one at a time, 5 minutes on each side in a kettle or Dutch oven. Pour off all drippings. Return all meat to kettle; break up into small chunks.
2. Stir in tomatoes, corn, peas and liquid, chicken broth, salad-dressing mix, onion, sugar, and pepper; heat to boiling. Simmer, stirring several times, 5 minutes.
3. Stir in noodles; cook 10 to 15 minutes longer, or just until noodles are tender; stir in parsley.
4. Serve with big squares of hot corn bread, if you wish.

Spoonburgers to please every taste

CHUCK-WAGON CHILI BUNS

Makes 12 to 16 servings

- 3 pounds ground beef
- 1 pound sausage meat
- 2 large onions, chopped (2 cups)
- 1 clove garlic, minced
- 2 cups chopped celery
- 1 small green pepper, halved, seeded, and chopped
- 2 teaspoons chili powder
- 2 cans (about 1 pound each) red kidney beans
- 1 bottle (14 ounces) catsup
- 2 tablespoons brown sugar
- 1 tablespoon dry mustard
- 3 teaspoons salt
- 2 teaspoons paprika
- ½ teaspoon pepper
- 3½ cups water
- ¼ cup cider vinegar
- 2 tablespoons Worcestershire sauce
- 12 split hamburger buns, toasted and buttered
  Grated Cheddar cheese
  Sweet onion rings

1. Mix ground beef lightly with sausage meat; shape into two large patties. Brown, one at a time, in a kettle or Dutch oven 5 minutes on each side; remove and set aside.
2. Pour off all drippings, then measure 2 tablespoonfuls and return to kettle. Add onions and garlic; saute just until soft. Stir in celery, green pepper, and chili powder; cook just until celery is soft.
3. Return browned meat to kettle and break up into chunks. Stir in kidney beans and liquid, catsup, brown sugar, mustard, salt, paprika, pepper, water, vinegar, and Worcestershire sauce.
4. Simmer, stirring often, 1 hour, or until thick.
5. Spoon onto hamburger buns; top with grated cheese and onion rings.

PENNSYLVANIA BARBECUE

Makes 6 servings

- ½ pound sausage meat
- 1½ pounds ground beef
- 1 large onion, chopped (1 cup)
- 1 cup diced celery
- 1 bottle (12 ounces) chili sauce
- 1 can (8 ounces) tomato sauce
- 1½ cups water
- 2 tablespoons prepared mustard
- 1 teaspoon celery salt
- 1 teaspoon salt
- ¼ teaspoon pepper
- 6 split hamburger buns, toasted and buttered

1. Saute sausage meat 3 to 5 minutes in a kettle or Dutch oven; remove and set aside. Pour off all drippings; return 1 tablespoonful to kettle.
2. Shape ground beef into a large patty in same kettle; brown 5 minutes on each side, then break up into chunks; remove with a slotted spoon and add to sausage meat.
3. Stir onion and celery into drippings in pan; saute just until onion is soft.
4. Return browned meats to kettle; stir in chili sauce, tomato sauce, water, mustard, and seasonings. Simmer, stirring often, 45 minutes, or until thick.
5. Spoon onto hamburger buns.

TAMALE HOT POT

Makes 6 servings

- 1 large onion, chopped (1 cup)
- 2 tablespoons bacon drippings
- 1 pound ground beef
- 1 to 2 teaspoons chili powder
- 1 teaspoon salt
- 2 cans (about 1 pound each) red kidney beans
- 1 can condensed tomato soup
- 2 cans (about 1 pound each) tamales

1. Saute onion in bacon drippings just until soft in a kettle or Dutch oven; push to one side.
2. Shape ground beef into a large patty in same pan; brown 5 minutes on each side, then break up into chunks. Stir in chili powder, salt, kidney beans and liquid, tomato soup, and sauce from tamales; heat to boiling.
3. Remove wrappers from tamales; cut tamales into 1-inch pieces; stir into meat mixture. Heat slowly just until tamales are hot.
4. Spoon over hot corn bread, if you wish.

BARBECUE BEANIES

Makes 8 servings

 4 slices bacon, diced
 1 large onion, peeled and sliced
 1 clove garlic, minced
 1 teaspoon chili powder
1½ pounds ground beef
 2 cans (about 1 pound each) baked beans
 1 can condensed tomato soup
 1 teaspoon salt
 ¼ teaspoon pepper
 1 can (about 7 ounces) pitted ripe olives, drained and sliced
 8 hard rolls, split

1. Saute bacon just until crisp in a kettle; remove and drain on paper toweling.
2. Stir onion, garlic, and chili powder into drippings in kettle; saute just until onion is soft; push to one side.
3. Shape ground beef into a large patty in kettle; brown 5 minutes on each side, then break up into chunks.
4. Stir in baked beans and sauce, tomato soup, salt, and pepper. Cook, stirring often, 15 minutes. Stir in olives.
5. Toast rolls and butter, if you wish. Top with hot hamburger mixture; sprinkle with bacon.

SLUMGULLION-ON-A-BUN
(Pictured on pages 108-109)

Makes 8 servings

 2 pounds ground beef
 1 large onion, chopped (1 cup)
 1 clove garlic, minced
 1 envelope spaghetti-sauce mix
 1 can (1 pint, 2 ounces) tomato juice
 1 cup chopped celery
 1 can (12 or 16 ounces) whole-kernel corn
 ½ cup chopped dill pickle
 8 split hamburger buns

1. Shape ground beef into a large patty in a kettle or Dutch oven. Brown 5 minutes on each side, then break up into chunks; push to one side.
2. Add onion and garlic; saute just until soft. Stir in spaghetti-sauce mix, tomato juice, celery, and corn and liquid; cover.
3. Simmer 30 minutes, or until thick; stir in chopped pickle.
4. Spoon over hamburger buns. Top with chopped sweet onions or grated cheese, if you wish.

TEEN PARTY SUBS

Makes 6 servings

 ½ pound sweet Italian sausages
 1 clove garlic, minced
 1 small onion, peeled and sliced
 ½ medium-size green pepper, seeded and cut in strips
 2 tablespoons salad oil
 1 can (1 pint, 2 ounces) tomato juice
 1 can (about 1 pound) tomatoes
 1 teaspoon sugar
 ½ teaspoon salt
 ¼ teaspoon pepper
 ½ teaspoon oregano
 1 pound ground beef
 1 egg
 2 tablespoons water
 ¼ cup fine dry bread crumbs
 ¼ cup grated Parmesan cheese
 6 hero rolls, split, toasted, and buttered

1. Cut sausages in 1-inch pieces. Saute with garlic, onion, and green pepper in salad oil in a kettle or Dutch oven 5 minutes. Stir in tomato juice, tomatoes, sugar, salt, pepper, and oregano until well-blended.
2. Simmer, uncovered, stirring several times, 30 minutes to blend flavors.
3. Mix ground beef lightly with egg, water, bread crumbs, and cheese until well-blended; shape into 36 balls.
4. Place in hot sauce; simmer, stirring several times, 25 minutes, or until meat balls are cooked through and sauce is thick.
5. Spoon 6 meat balls and some of the sauce, sandwich style, into each buttered roll.

Cooksaver tip:

Teen-agers love to eat spoonburgers out of hand, so wrap them, picnic style, in big paper napkins. For the grownups who prefer plates, make outdoor eating carefree with the paper variety. With so many colorful patterns available today, you can go plain or fancy to suit your mood

CHILI-CHEESE TOAST

Makes 6 servings

- 1 pound ground beef
- 1 medium-size onion, chopped (½ cup)
- ⅛ teaspoon garlic salt
- 1 tablespoon flour
- 1½ teaspoons chili powder
- ½ teaspoon salt
- 1 can (about 1 pound) tomatoes
- 1 can (12 or 16 ounces) whole-kernel corn
- 1 can (about 2 ounces) chopped ripe olives, drained
- 1 package (4 ounces) shredded Cheddar cheese
- 6 slices white bread, toasted and buttered

1. Mix ground beef lightly with onion and garlic salt. Shape into a large patty in a kettle or Dutch oven; brown 5 minutes on each side, then break up into chunks.
2. Stir in flour, chili powder, and salt, then tomatoes, corn and liquid, and olives; cover. Simmer, stirring several times, 15 minutes. Stir in cheese just until melted.
3. Spoon over toast; top with chopped bread-and-butter pickles, if you wish.

ONION-GRAVY BURGERS

Makes 4 servings

- 1 pound ground beef
- ½ cup corn-flake crumbs (from an about 10-ounce package)
- 1 envelope onion-soup mix
- ¼ cup milk
- 1 egg
- 1 can (3 or 4 ounces) sliced mushrooms
- 1½ cups water
- 2 tablespoons flour
- ½ teaspoon Italian seasoning
- 4 split hamburger buns, toasted

1. Mix ground beef lightly with corn-flake crumbs, half of the soup mix, milk, and egg until well-blended; shape into 8 patties about ½ inch thick.
2. Pan-fry just until brown on both sides.
3. Mix remaining soup mix, mushrooms and liquid, water, flour, and Italian seasoning; pour over patties. Heat, stirring constantly, to boiling; cover. Simmer, stirring once or twice, 20 minutes to blend flavors.
4. Spoon a meat patty and some of the sauce over each bun half.

HUMPTY-DUMPTIES

Makes 12 servings

- 2 tablespoons salad oil
- 1 clove garlic, minced
- 2 envelopes spaghetti-sauce mix
- 1 can (about 1 pound) tomatoes
- 1 can (12 ounces) mixed vegetable juices
- 1½ cups water
- 2 teaspoons sugar
- ¼ cup chopped parsley
- 2 pounds ground beef
- 1 medium-size onion, grated
- 2 eggs
- 1 cup soft bread crumbs (2 slices)
- 2 teaspoons salt
- 1 teaspoon dry mustard
- ½ cup milk
- 12 onion rolls or English muffins, split and toasted
  Grated Parmesan cheese
  OR: Grated Romano cheese

1. Heat salad oil and garlic in a saucepan; stir in spaghetti-sauce mix, tomatoes, mixed vegetable juices, water, sugar, and parsley. Simmer 20 minutes to blend flavors.
2. Mix ground beef lightly with onion, eggs, bread crumbs, salt, and mustard until well-blended; shape into 36 balls. Place in hot sauce; simmer 15 minutes, or until meat balls are cooked through. Remove from heat. Slowly stir in milk until well-blended.
3. Spoon 3 meat balls and some of the sauce into each roll or muffin, sandwich style; sprinkle with Parmesan cheese or Romano cheese. Serve with potato chips, if you wish.

Cooksaver tip:

If you like the flavor of garlic but prefer not to eat it, try this easy trick: String the peeled whole clove on a wooden pick and drop it into your cooking pot, then scoop it out before serving. Or substitute a dash of garlic salt or powder; both come in handy shaker-top or easy-measure jars

If you're serving Burger Shortcakes for a big crowd, save yourself time by making the mashed potatoes with your favorite instant packaged variety— either plain or seasoned. Label tells you clearly what quantity you will need

BURGER SHORTCAKES

Makes 4 servings

1½ pounds ground beef
1 small onion, grated
1 teaspoon salt
⅛ teaspoon pepper
2 tablespoons flour
¼ teaspoon paprika
1 can (3 or 4 ounces) sliced mushrooms
½ cup water
1 envelope instant chicken broth
   OR: 1 chicken-bouillon cube
½ cup dairy sour cream
2 tablespoons chili sauce
   Hot mashed potatoes

1. Mix ground beef lightly with onion, salt, and pepper until well-blended; shape into 8 patties about ½ inch thick.
2. Brown on both sides in a large frying pan; remove with a slotted spoon and set aside while making sauce.
3. Blend flour and paprika into drippings in pan; cook, stirring constantly, just until bubbly. Stir in mushrooms and liquid, water, and instant chicken broth or bouillon cube. Continue cooking and stirring, crushing bouillon cube, if using, with a spoon, until sauce thickens and boils 1 minute.
4. Return meat patties to pan; cover. Simmer 15 minutes.
5. Mix sour cream and chili sauce; stir in about ¼ cup of the hot sauce, then stir back into remaining sauce in pan. Heat slowly just until hot.
6. Put each two patties together, sandwich style, with mashed potatoes; spoon sauce over top.

TORPEDOES

Makes 8 servings

1½ pounds ground beef
½ pound ground veal
½ cup quick-cooking rolled oats
2 eggs
1 tablespoon instant minced onion
2 teaspoons seasoned salt
½ teaspoon dry mustard
¼ teaspoon nutmeg
¼ teaspoon pepper
½ cup milk
2 tablespoons shortening
2 tablespoons flour
1 envelope instant beef broth
   OR: 1 beef-flavor bouillon cube
1½ cups water
1 cup (8-ounce carton) dairy sour cream
8 hero rolls, split and toasted

1. Mix ground beef and veal lightly with rolled oats, eggs, instant minced onion, seasoned salt, mustard, nutmeg, pepper, and milk until well-blended. Shape into 64 balls.
2. Brown, part at a time, in shortening in a large frying pan; remove with a slotted spoon and set aside.
3. Stir flour into drippings; cook, stirring constantly, just until bubbly. Stir in instant beef broth or bouillon cube, and water; continue cooking and stirring, crushing cube, if using, with a spoon, until sauce thickens and boils 1 minute.
4. Place meat balls in sauce; cover. Simmer 10 minutes.
5. Stir a generous ½ cup of the sauce into sour cream; stir back into remaining mixture in pan. Heat slowly, just until hot.
6. Spoon, sandwich style, into hero rolls.

Cooksaver tip:

When serving a big crowd, you can fix Torpedoes ahead through simmering meat balls in sauce, then chill. Just before party eating time, reheat to boiling; finish making sauce, following Step 5. Special for new cooks: Stirring part of the hot sauce into the cold sour cream first, then into cooking pan, and heating very slowly just until hot, prevents curdling

Sandwich bests to grill to your order

BEEFBURGER ROLLUP

Makes 6 servings

- 1½ pounds ground beef
- 2 cups soft bread crumbs (4 slices)
- ½ cup evaporated milk
- 1 medium-size onion, chopped (½ cup)
- ½ cup chopped stuffed green olives
- 1 clove garlic, minced
- 2 eggs
- 1 teaspoon salt
- ½ teaspoon paprika
- ¼ teaspoon pepper
- ½ cup bottled barbecue sauce
- 6 split hamburger buns, toasted

1. Mix ground beef lightly with bread crumbs, evaporated milk, onion, chopped olives, garlic, eggs, salt, paprika, and pepper until well-blended.
2. Shape meat into a 12-inch-long roll on a sheet of heavy foil; wrap tightly and seal lengthwise with a drugstore fold. Fold one end over and over to seal; stand roll on end; tap gently to settle meat; seal other end. (This much can be done early in the day and roll chilled until cooking time.)
3. Take roll from refrigerator when you start the grill fire. When coals are white-hot, place roll in its foil cover on grill. Grill, turning roll a quarter turn every 10 minutes, 40 minutes.
4. Slide roll far enough from heat to unwrap; open foil and crush it around roll to form a cooking pan. Brush roll generously all over with barbecue sauce. Continue grilling, turning and brushing often with sauce, until meat is richly browned and done as you like it.
5. Cut into thick slices; make into jumbo sandwiches with toasted hamburger buns.

HAMBURGER FOLDOVERS

Makes 8 servings

- 2 pounds ground beef
- 1½ teaspoons salt
- ¼ teaspoon pepper
- 1 package (4 ounces) shredded Cheddar cheese
- ¼ cup bottled steak sauce
- 8 split hamburger buns
- 2 medium-size tomatoes, sliced
- 1 large onion, peeled, sliced, and separated in rings

1. Mix ground beef lightly with salt and pepper; divide into 8 portions.
2. Pat each into a 6-inch round on a piece of waxed paper or foil; spoon about 2 tablespoons cheese in center. Fold round in half, using paper or foil to lift meat; press edges together to seal. Brush patties with steak sauce.
3. Grill over hot coals, turning and brushing with more steak sauce, until meat is done as you like it.
4. Toast buns on grill, then butter, if you wish. Put together, sandwich style, with meat patties, tomato slices, and onion rings.

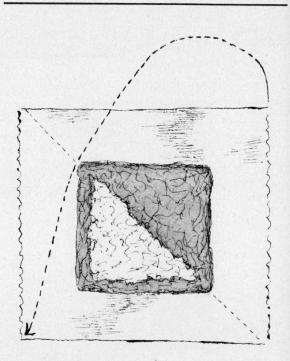

Cooksaver tip:

Big thin hamburger patties or squares are easy to fold in half moons or triangles if patted out first on foil or waxed paper to use as a "lifter"

BURGERS KUN KOKI

(Pictured on page 108)

Makes 8 servings

¼ cup salad oil
¼ cup soy sauce
2 tablespoons corn syrup
1 tablespoon lemon juice
½ teaspoon ground ginger
¼ teaspoon garlic powder
2 green onions, sliced thin
2 pounds ground beef
8 split hamburger buns, buttered

1. Mix salad oil, soy sauce, corn syrup, lemon juice, ginger, garlic powder, and green onions in a large shallow pan.
2. Shape ground beef into 8 patties about ¾ inch thick. Dip in sauce mixture to coat both sides, then place in a single layer in same pan. Chill 3 to 4 hours to season.
3. When ready to cook, remove patties from sauce and grill over hot coals, brushing several times with the remaining sauce, until meat is done as you like it.
4. Toast buns on grill, if you wish; put together, sandwich style, with meat patties.

BURGERS MILANESE

Makes 8 servings

2 pounds ground beef
½ cup bottled Italian salad dressing
1 package (8 ounces) sliced mozzarella or pizza cheese, cut in triangles
16 slices Italian bread, toasted

1. Shape ground beef into 8 patties about ¾ inch thick; place in a shallow dish. Pour salad dressing over; turn patties to coat well with dressing; chill, turning several times, about 15 minutes to season.
2. When ready to cook, remove patties from dressing. Grill over hot coals, brushing several times with remaining dressing in dish, until meat is almost as done as you like it.
3. Top each patty with 2 or 3 cheese triangles; continue grilling 1 to 2 minutes longer, or just until cheese melts slightly.
4. Put each patty together, sandwich style, with toasted bread slices.

SMOKY BEEF BURGERS

Makes 8 servings

2 pounds ground beef
1 medium-size onion, grated
2 teaspoons salt
½ teaspoon oregano
¼ teaspoon pepper
½ cup bottled smoke-flavor barbecue sauce
3 tablespoons water
8 English muffins, split and toasted

1. Mix ground beef lightly with onion, salt, oregano, pepper, and 2 tablespoons of the barbecue sauce; shape into 8 patties about ¾ inch thick. Mix remaining barbecue sauce and water.
2. Grill patties over hot coals, brushing several times with barbecue-sauce mixture, until meat is done as you like it.
3. Put together, sandwich style, with toasted muffins.

YORKVILLE SPECIAL

Makes 6 servings

2 pounds ground beef
2 teaspoons salt
½ teaspoon caraway seeds
2 cups coleslaw (from a 1-pound container)
6 slices rye bread, buttered
Paprika

1. Mix ground beef lightly with salt and caraway seeds; shape into 6 patties about 1 inch thick.
2. Grill patties over hot coals until meat is done as you like it.
3. Drain coleslaw well; spoon onto each slice of bread to form a nest; top with a meat patty; sprinkle with paprika.

Cooksaver tip:

Prefer to fix your own coleslaw? Here's how for 4 cups: Finely shred enough cabbage to measure 4 cups; toss with 1 tablespoon sugar, then chill. When ready to serve, toss again with a mixture of 1 tablespoon each mayonnaise or salad dressing, lemon juice, and cream; season with salt and pepper

This tiered Pacifica Patio Burger *(recipe at right)* with crisp potato chips and relishes makes a satisfying main course. The soup—a blend of buttermilk and mixed vegetable juices served frosty cold—can double as the appetizer and beverage

BURGER-BACON GRILL

Makes 6 servings

- 1 can (8 ounces) tomato sauce
- 1 envelope garlic salad-dressing mix
- 1½ pounds ground beef
- 1 egg
- 12 slices bacon
- 6 split hamburger buns, buttered

1. Mix tomato sauce and salad dressing mix.
2. Mix ground beef lightly with egg and ½ cup of the tomato-sauce mixture; shape into 6 patties about 1 inch thick.
3. Grill over hot coals, brushing often with remaining sauce, until meat is done as you like it.
4. While patties cook, thread bacon, accordion style, onto long skewers; grill until crisp.
5. Put patties together, sandwich style, with buttered buns; top each with 2 slices bacon.

PATIO CHEESEBURGERS

Makes 12 servings

- 2 pounds ground beef
- 2 cups grated process American cheese (8 ounces)
- 1 medium-size onion, chopped (½ cup)
- 1 teaspoon salt
- ⅛ teaspoon pepper
- 12 split hamburger buns, buttered

1. Mix ground beef lightly with cheese, onion, salt, and pepper until well-blended; shape into 12 patties about ½ inch thick.
2. Stack with waxed paper or foil between; cover lightly and chill until ready to cook.
3. Grill over hot coals until meat is done as you like it.
4. Put together, sandwich style, with buttered buns.

Cooksaver tip:

Lots of foods take to kebab-cooking, and it's fun to grill a few to serve with your burgers. Try: Mushroom caps, cherry tomatoes, canned small onions, or chunks of green pepper threaded onto a long skewer, brushed with melted butter or margarine, and grilled just until hot

TERIYAKI STICKS

Makes 8 servings

- 2 pounds ground beef
- 1 small onion, grated
- ½ cup soy sauce
- ½ cup chili sauce
- 1 tablespoon molasses
  Few drops red-pepper seasoning
- 8 split frankfurter rolls, toasted

1. Mix ground beef lightly with onion; shape into 16 sticks about 1 inch thick. Place in a shallow baking dish, 10x6x2.
2. Combine remaining seasonings; pour over meat; turn to coat well. Chill about 30 minutes.
3. Grill over hot coals, brushing with remaining sauce in dish, until meat is done as you like it.
4. Put each two together, sandwich style, with toasted rolls.

PACIFICA PATIO BURGERS
(Pictured at left)

Makes 4 servings

- 1½ pounds ground beef
- 1 small onion, grated
- 2 teaspoons Worcestershire sauce
- 1 teaspoon salt
- ¼ teaspoon pepper
- 3 slices process Swiss cheese, cut into thin strips
- 4 split hamburger buns, toasted and buttered
  Lettuce
- 4 thick slices tomato
  Mayonnaise or salad dressing
  Onion rings
  Red-pepper relish

1. Mix ground beef lightly with onion, Worcestershire sauce, salt, and pepper; shape into 4 patties about 1 inch thick.
2. Grill over hot coals until meat is almost as done as you like it. Crisscross cheese strips on top, dividing evenly; grill 1 minute longer, or until cheese melts.
3. Cover bottom halves of buns with lettuce. Spread tomato slices with mayonnaise or salad dressing; place on top of lettuce, then top with a broiled meat patty. Garnish with a few onion rings and a generous spoonful of red-pepper relish. Serve with remaining bun halves. Our pictured plate shows a serving of potato chips, dill pickles, and olives and a refreshing cooler of equal parts chilled mixed vegetable juices and buttermilk.

OUTDOOR CHEFS: THESE BARBECUE TIPS ARE FOR YOU

Starting point: The fire

Getting the fire going is the same, whether your grill is a fancy store-bought model or a simple rack propped up on two stones. Unless you live where slow-burning wood is abundant, it's best to buy charcoal briquettes, sold by the bag in varying weights in most supermarkets. They start fast, burn slowly without spitting out sparks, and give an intense heat. Knowing how much charcoal to use is also important, and while you'll learn through practice, here's a good guide: Hamburgers cook quickly, so a single layer of briquettes usually will be enough.

Lighting the fire

For easy starting, buy one of the many packaged starter fuels on the market. Choices are many—liquid, jelly, a combination box of charcoal and lighter, even an electric lighter to plug into an outdoor outlet. Be sure to read label directions, and for complete safety follow them to the letter. Other tips: Keep youngsters away from the grill while you're starting the fire and cooking, and before starting any fire, know how to put it out—fast! Sand is your best helper, so it's smart to keep a small pailful handy.

Be patient

A single layer of briquettes will take a minimum of 30 minutes to heat through. Briquettes are ready when they turn ashgray. At night, you can also detect a red glow, but the ash-gray look is your best

guide. They hold their heat for a long time, so you needn't be in a rush to start cooking. Budget note: If your fire bed is still active when you finish cooking, pick out the briquettes with tongs, dunk them in water, and dry, ready to use another time.

"First aid" for regulating fire

If your food choices seem to be cooking too slowly, it may be that you need a bigger fire bed, or should simply wait awhile before loading the grill. Another possibility is to tap the ash off the briquettes, for it's an insulator. For a fire that appears to be too hot, know-how is simple, too. Lower the firebox or raise the grill, if they're adjustable. Or move the food to the edge of the grill, away from intense heat.

What about tools?

You can do nicely with a few carefully chosen ones or go all out—even to a chef's hat. Whatever your choice, do buy good-quality utensils, for they will reward you in long service. A few musts for the new chef:

A long-handle pancake turner for flipping hamburgers, plus a matching spoon for stirring spoonables.

A dipper to use for serving.

A wire broiler basket such as the one shown at right for grilling and turning several hamburgers at a time.

A two-inch quality paintbrush and heavy saucepan with a flat bottom and heatproof handle for sauce spreader and container.

Sharp knives and a cutting board.

Large easy-grasp salt and pepper shakers.

Asbestos pot holders or mitts.

Roll of heavy foil for all kinds of jobs, from lining the firebox (foil reflects heat faster) to making disposable pans for cooking little burgers if the wire mesh on your grill is wide.

Serving tips for the chef's helper

Keep a supply of paper plates, cups, bowls, platters, and napkins on hand, for they make eating out fun and cleanup easy.

Save up a few empty 46-ounce cans (the kind fruit and vegetable juices come in) and small ones, too, for they make perfect containers for heating barbecue sauces and buttery spreads. They cost nothing and, what's best, are disposable.

Use washcloths for napkins when you entertain, for they stay put in a breeze, wash easily with no ironing, and, if dampened, are ideal for finger-style eating. And your guests will appreciate your thoughtfulness.

Turn oven racks into trays if you need extra-large ones. They're perfect for toting all the paraphernalia that's needed for outdoor cooking.

A few simple tricks with burgers

Grill burgers good and brown before turning. And, as when cooking indoors, flip only once.

Prevent sticking by brushing grill or patties with a little salad oil; or for meat, use salad oil mixed with a seasoner of your choice.

Shape hamburger patties around a small piece of cracked ice. As the meat grills, the ice will melt and give the burger a special juiciness. Or moisten both sides of the patty with a few drops of cold water.

Make one giant 1-inch-thick patty instead of several individual burgers and, as it grills, brush with barbecue or Worcestershire sauce for a deep rich color. Simply cut into wedges for serving.

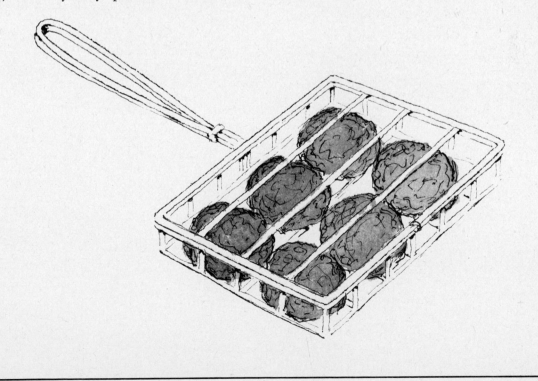

GOLDEN GATE SAUCY BURGERS
(Pictured on pages 126-127)

Makes 12 servings

- 3 pounds ground beef
- 1 large onion, grated
- 1 egg
- 1 cup canned applesauce
- 2 teaspoons salt
- ¼ teaspoon pepper
- 12 split hamburger buns, toasted and buttered
  Chili Topping *(recipe follows)*
  Salty-nut Topping *(recipe follows)*
  Rarebit Topping *(recipe follows)*
  Spaghetti Topping *(recipe follows)*

1. Mix ground beef lightly with onion, egg, applesauce, and seasonings until well-blended; shape into 12 patties about 1 inch thick.
2. Grill 8 minutes on each side for medium, or over hot coals, or until meat is done as you like it.
3. Place each patty on half a roll; spoon a topping of your choice over; put together with remaining halves of rolls.

Chili Topping

Makes about 4 cups

- 1 medium-size onion, chopped (½ cup)
- 2 teaspoons chili powder
- 2 tablespoons olive oil or salad oil
- 1 can (1 pound) red kidney beans
- 1 can (about 1 pound) stewed tomatoes
- ½ teaspoon salt
- ¼ teaspoon pepper
- 1 cup sliced pitted ripe olives

1. Saute onion with chili powder in olive oil or salad oil just until onion is soft in a large frying pan; stir in remaining ingredients except olives; cover.
2. Simmer, stirring several times, 30 minutes to blend flavors; stir in olives.

Salty-nut Topping

Makes about 1½ cups

- ¼ pound (1 stick) butter or margarine
- 1 can (8 ounces) walnuts, chopped
- 1 teaspoon seasoned salt

1. Melt butter or margarine in a small saucepan; stir in walnuts and seasoned salt.
2. Saute, stirring often, 5 minutes, or until walnuts are buttery-hot.

Rarebit Topping

Makes about 3 cups

- 2 tablespoons butter or margarine
- 2 tablespoons flour
- 1 teaspoon salt
- ¼ teaspoon dry mustard
- 1 tablespoon Worcestershire sauce
- 2 cups milk
- 1 pound process American cheese, cut into pieces

1. Melt butter or margarine in a saucepan; blend in flour, salt, mustard, and Worcestershire sauce; cook just until bubbly. Stir in milk; continue cooking, stirring constantly, until sauce thickens and boils 1 minute.
2. Stir in cheese; cook, stirring constantly, just until cheese melts.

Spaghetti Topping

Makes about 7 cups

- 2 envelopes spaghetti-sauce mix
- 1 can (6 ounces) tomato paste
- 1 can (8 ounces) tomato sauce
- 4 tablespoons salad oil
- 3 cups water
- 1 package (8 ounces) thin spaghetti
- ½ cup grated Parmesan cheese

1. Blend spaghetti-sauce mix with tomato paste and tomato sauce in a large saucepan; stir in salad oil and water.
2. Heat to boiling; simmer, stirring once or twice, 25 to 30 minutes to blend flavors.
3. While sauce simmers, cook spaghetti, following label directions; drain. Spoon sauce over; sprinkle with cheese. Toss to mix well.

KONA COAST GRILL

Makes 6 servings

- 1½ pounds ground beef
- 1 teaspoon instant coffee
- 1 teaspoon salt
- 2 tablespoons cream
- 12 slices cracked-wheat bread, toasted and buttered

1. Mix ground beef lightly with coffee, salt, and cream until well-blended; shape into 6 patties about ¾ inch thick.
2. Grill patties over hot coals until meat is done as you like it.
3. Put together, sandwich style, with toasted bread slices. Serve with sweet-pickle relish and potato salad, if you wish.

Cooksaver tip:

Hamburgers take to so many stylings, and it's fun to make rounds, squares, logs, rectangles, or triangles to fit different shapes of bread, buns, and rolls. "Doughnut" patty even has a custom-made center to hold catsup or mustard. Tiny balls molded around an olive and strung on a skewer are best skillet-grilled, for meat is soft

GRILLED FOUR-SQUARES

Makes 8 servings

- 2 pounds ground beef
- 2 eggs
- 1 medium-size onion, chopped (½ cup)
- 1 cup finely chopped raw spinach
- 1 cup grated Cheddar cheese (4 ounces)
- 2 teaspoons salt
- ½ teaspoon celery salt
- ¼ teaspoon pepper
- 16 slices bread

1. Mix ground beef lightly with eggs, onion, spinach, cheese, and seasonings until well-blended; divide into 8 portions.
2. Press each into a square the same size as bread slice on a square of waxed paper or foil.
3. Grill squares over hot coals until meat is done as you like it.
4. Toast bread on grill, then butter, if you wish. Put together, sandwich style, with meat squares. Serve plain or with catsup, prepared horseradish-mustard, or canned French fried onion rings.

MULHOLLAND BURGERS

Makes 8 servings

- 2 pounds ground beef
- 1 envelope instant meat marinade
- ⅔ cup water
- 8 large poppy-seed rolls, split and toasted

1. Shape ground beef into 8 patties about ¾ inch thick; place in a shallow dish; chill.
2. Just before cooking, mix meat marinade and water, following label directions; pour over patties; turn to coat all over.
3. Grill over hot coals, brushing several times with remaining marinade in dish, until meat is done as you like it.
4. Put together, sandwich style, with toasted rolls. Serve with sweet pickles and potato or corn chips, if you wish.

Quick and easy tricks to vary hamburgers

"GUESS WHAT" GRILLED BURGERS

Makes 8 servings

2 **pounds ground beef**
2 **teaspoons salt**
¼ **teaspoon freshly ground pepper**

Mix ground beef lightly with salt and pepper. Stir in 1 medium-size onion, grated, if you wish. Shape any of these ways, stacking each two patties with waxed paper or foil between:

Sixteen thin rounds to fit hamburger buns, round bread slices, or large baking powder biscuits.

Sixteen rectangles to fit frankfurter rolls, club rolls, or 3-inch pieces of French bread.

Sixteen squares to fit sliced sandwich bread.

Put each two patties together with any of these fillings:

Thinly sliced tomatoes sprinkled lightly with seasoned salt and grated Parmesan cheese.

Canned baked beans seasoned with crumbled crisp bacon and a dash of catsup.

Chili con carne spooned right from the can.

Canned French fried onions, coarsely crushed.

Drained canned chopped or sliced mushrooms.

Dill, sweet, or crisp cucumber pickle slices.

Assorted sliced cheeses: American, Swiss, pimiento, sharp Cheddar.

Crumbled or mashed blue cheese mixed with an equal amount of cream cheese.

Grated Parmesan cheese or sharp cheese spread plain or mixed with a little chili sauce.

Thinly sliced frankfurters topped with mustard.

Pickle relish blended with chopped celery, grated carrot, and a little mayonnaise or salad dressing.

Grill this way: Press edges of filled patties together to seal. Grill over hot coals until meat is done as you like it. Put together, sandwich style, with your choice of buns or bread.

MORE-AND-MORE BURGERS

Makes 4 servings

1 **pound ground beef**
1 **teaspoon salt**
⅛ **teaspoon pepper**

Mix ground beef lightly with salt and pepper, then mix in one of these special seasoners before shaping patties:

¼ cup bottled barbecue sauce.

1 or 2 green onions, sliced thin.

1 can (2¼ or 3 ounces) deviled ham, 1 teaspoon prepared mustard, and 1 tablespoon pickle relish.

½ cup grated Cheddar cheese and ¼ cup catsup.

⅓ cup chopped walnuts, peanuts, or toasted almonds.

¼ cup dairy sour cream, 1 tablespoon chopped parsley, and a generous dash of thyme and oregano.

½ cup chopped fresh mushrooms or drained canned ones.

¼ cup chopped stuffed green olives or 2 tablespoons each chopped pimiento and ripe olives.

½ cup grated pared carrot, 2 tablespoons grated radishes, and 1 teaspoon grated onion.

¼ cup grated Parmesan cheese, ¼ cup canned tomato sauce, and ¼ teaspoon oregano.

½ cup cooked rice, 2 teaspoons soy sauce, and 1 sliced green onion.

3 slices crumbled crisp bacon and ½ cup canned applesauce.

½ cup crushed cheese crackers or other flavored crackers, or plain or seasoned potato chips or corn chips.

Shape into patties. Grill over hot coals until meat is done as you like it. Put together, sandwich style, with your choice of buns or bread.

TOPPERS FOR PLAIN BURGERS

Makes enough for 4 to 6 sandwiches

Make plain burgers and grill over hot coals until meat is done as you like it, then top with any of these seasoning extras:

1 tablespoon butter or margarine heated with ¼ cup chili sauce and ¼ teaspoon chili powder just until bubbly.

½ package (3 or 4 ounces) pimiento, relish, or chives cream cheese blended with ¼ cup dairy sour cream.

1 tablespoon each melted butter or margarine and bottled garlic-flavor French dressing mixed with 1 teaspoon chopped parsley and ½ teaspoon cut chives.

1 tablespoon flour blended with 1 tablespoon butter or margarine, ¼ teaspoon curry powder, ¼ teaspoon salt, and 1 can (3 or 4 ounces) chopped mushrooms and liquid, and cooked until sauce thickens and boils 1 minute.

½ can French fried onions heated with ¼ cup catsup just until bubbly.

2 tablespoons butter or margarine heated with ¼ cup catsup and 1 tablespoon bottled steak sauce.

2 cups shredded cabbage seasoned with bottled coleslaw dressing and a few sliced stuffed green olives and bits of crisp bacon.

½ can (1 pound) barbecue beans or baked beans heated with ½ cup grated Cheddar cheese.

Instant mashed potatoes blended with 1 or 2 sliced green onions.

Cooksaver tip:

Hot cooked burgers taste twice as good topped with frosty butter drops to melt in 'way down deep. To fix them, choose any of the buttery spreads listed at right. Drop, a teaspoonful at a time, into a tiny mound in a foil- or waxed-paper—lined ice-cube tray; chill until firm. At cookout time, pile them into a bowl half-filled with ice, ready to put on burgers

BUTTERY SPREADS FOR BUNS AND BREADS

Makes enough for 4 to 6 sandwiches

Start with 4 tablespoons (½ stick) softened butter or margarine and blend in any of these seasoners, then spread on buns, rolls, or bread:

1 tablespoon chopped parsley and 1 teaspoon finely cut chives.

1 can (2¼ ounces) deviled ham and ½ teaspoon prepared horseradish-mustard.

1 tablespoon hamburger or hot-dog relish.

1 teaspoon bottled steak sauce and ½ teaspoon chili powder.

1 tablespoon chopped stuffed green olives or chopped ripe olives.

2 tablespoons crumbled blue cheese and ½ teaspoon Worcestershire sauce.

¼ cup mashed peeled avocado, 1 tablespoon chili sauce, and ¼ teaspoon onion salt.

¼ teaspoon curry powder and 2 tablespoons catsup or chili sauce.

1 small onion, minced, and ¼ cup chili sauce.

1 tablespoon mayonnaise or salad dressing, 1 tablespoon chopped dill pickle, and ¼ teaspoon garlic salt.

¼ cup grated Cheddar cheese and 2 tablespoons pickle relish.

2 tablespoons grated Parmesan cheese and a dash of oregano.

¼ cup smoky-cheese spread (from a 5-ounce jar) and ½ teaspoon prepared mustard.

1 tablespoon catsup, 1 teaspoon lemon juice, ½ teaspoon prepared mustard, and ¼ teaspoon chili powder.

1 tablespoon finely chopped walnuts, peanuts, or almonds and ½ teaspoon seasoned salt.

Teen-agers find so many excuses for a party, and here's fare to please all:
Golden Gate Saucy Burgers with Spaghetti and Rarebit Toppings *(recipes on
page 122)*, assorted relishes, and a big tubful of icy bottled beverages

Zippy sauces to brush on burgers as they grill

ALL-PURPOSE BARBECUE SAUCE

Makes 3 cups

1 cup light molasses
1 cup prepared mustard
1 cup cider vinegar

Combine all ingredients in a 4-cup jar with tight-fitting lid; shake well to mix. Store in refrigerator.

Variations:
GINGER-RICH SAUCE—Mix 1 cup ALL-PURPOSE BARBECUE SAUCE with ½ cup ginger marmalade and 1 teaspoon ground ginger. Makes 1½ cups.
ZING SAUCE — Mix 1 cup ALL-PURPOSE BARBECUE SAUCE with ¼ cup catsup, ¼ cup salad oil, and 2 tablespoons Worcestershire sauce. Makes 1½ cups.
ITALIAN HERB SAUCE—Mix 1 cup ALL-PURPOSE BARBECUE SAUCE with ½ cup chili sauce and ½ teaspoon oregano. Makes 1½ cups.
PEPPY TOMATO SAUCE — Mix 1 cup ALL-PURPOSE BARBECUE SAUCE with ½ cup tomato juice and ½ teaspoon cracked or freshly ground pepper. Makes 1½ cups.

DIABLE SAUCE

Makes about 2 cups

¾ cup prepared mustard
½ cup molasses
½ cup cider vinegar
1 tablespoon Worcestershire sauce
¼ teaspoon bottled red-pepper seasoning

1. Combine all ingredients in a small bowl; beat until well-blended.
2. Spread sparingly on hamburgers, for this sauce is **hot.**
3. Store any left over in a tightly covered jar in the refrigerator.

RED SOY SAUCE

Makes 2½ cups

2 cans (8 ounces each) tomato sauce
1 medium-size onion, chopped (½ cup)
1 clove garlic, minced
¼ cup soy sauce
2 tablespoons sugar
1 teaspoon dry mustard
⅛ teaspoon cayenne

1. Combine all ingredients in a medium-size bowl; stir until well-blended.
2. Store any left over in a tightly covered jar in the refrigerator.

Gourmet sauces to top your cooked burgers

JAVANESE PEANUT SAUCE

Makes 1¼ cups

1 small onion, finely chopped (¼ cup)
2 tablespoons peanut oil or salad oil
¼ teaspoon ground cardamom
½ cup cream-style peanut butter
¼ cup firmly packed brown sugar
¼ cup soy sauce
¼ cup lemon juice
¼ teaspoon bottled red-pepper seasoning

1. Saute onion in peanut oil or salad oil just until soft in a small frying pan; stir in cardamom. Let stand to cool slightly.
2. Blend peanut butter with brown sugar in a small bowl; stir in remaining ingredients, then cooled onion mixture.
3. Let stand at room temperature until serving time.

HORSERADISH-ALMOND SAUCE

Makes about 1¼ cups

¼ cup toasted slivered almonds (from a
    5-ounce can)
2 teaspoons butter or margarine
2 teaspoons flour
1 teaspoon sugar
¼ teaspoon salt
1 small can evaporated milk (⅔ cup)
⅓ cup milk
2 tablespoons prepared horseradish

1. Saute almonds in butter or margarine until golden-brown in a small saucepan; remove from heat.
2. Stir in flour, sugar, and salt; cook, stirring constantly, just until bubbly. Stir in evaporated milk and milk; continue cooking and stirring until sauce thickens and boils 1 minute.
3. Stir in horseradish; serve warm.

MOCK BEARNAISE SAUCE

Makes about 1 cup

½ cup apple juice
1 tablespoon tarragon vinegar
1 tablespoon finely chopped onion
    or shallots
⅛ teaspoon freshly ground pepper
1 sprig parsley
½ teaspoon dried tarragon leaves
2 egg yolks
½ cup (1 stick) butter or margarine, melted
    Dash of cayenne
1 teaspoon chopped parsley

1. Combine apple juice, vinegar, onion or shallots, pepper, parsley sprig, and tarragon in a small saucepan. Heat to boiling, then simmer, uncovered, 8 to 10 minutes, or until liquid measures about ⅓ cup; strain into a cup.
2. Beat egg yolks slightly in the top of a double boiler; stir in about ⅓ of the melted butter or margarine. Place top over simmering, *not boiling*, water.
3. Beat in strained liquid, alternately with remaining melted butter or margarine; continue beating, keeping top over simmering water, until mixture is fluffy-thick. Remove from heat at once.
4. Stir in cayenne and chopped parsley. Serve warm.

Fancy relishes to serve with plain burgers

RIPE-OLIVE CHOP-CHOP

Makes about 5 cups

3 cans (2¼ ounces each) chopped
    ripe olives
1½ cups finely chopped celery
1 cup finely chopped dill pickle
    (about 4 medium-size)
½ cup finely chopped onion
1 clove garlic, minced
1 can (2 ounces) anchovy fillets
½ cup salad oil
¼ cup wine vinegar or cider vinegar
¼ teaspoon pepper

1. Combine olives, celery, dill pickle, onion, and garlic; toss lightly to mix.
2. Drain oil from anchovies into olive mixture; cut anchovies into tiny pieces and stir in with salad oil, vinegar, and pepper; toss well to mix; cover. Chill several hours or overnight.

CORN PIQUANT

Makes about 4 cups

1 teaspoon sugar
½ teaspoon salt
¼ teaspoon paprika
¾ cup salad oil
¼ cup cider vinegar
1 tablespoon prepared horseradish
1½ teaspoons Worcestershire sauce
2 drops red-pepper seasoning
2 cans (12 or 16 ounces each) whole-
    kernel corn, drained

1. Combine all ingredients, except corn, in a jar with tight-fitting lid; shake well to mix.
2. Pour over corn; toss lightly to mix; cover. Chill several hours or overnight.

Sandwich "twists" to fix in the kitchen

OPEN-FACE HEROES

Makes 8 servings

1 large onion, chopped (1 cup)
3 tablespoons salad oil
2 pounds ground beef
2 cans (8 ounces each) tomato sauce with mushrooms
1 teaspoon oregano
1 teaspoon salt
4 hero rolls, split and buttered
1 package (8 ounces) sliced mozzarella or pizza cheese, cut in triangles
8 stuffed green olives, sliced

1. Saute onion in salad oil just until soft in a large frying pan; push to one side.
2. Shape ground beef into a large patty in same pan; brown 5 minutes on each side, then break up into chunks. Stir in tomato sauce, oregano, and salt; simmer 10 minutes.
3. Place split rolls in a single layer in a large shallow baking pan; spoon meat mixture on top; cover with cheese triangles, then olive slices.
4. Broil, 4 to 6 inches from heat, 3 minutes, or just until cheese starts to melt and bubble up.

Cooksaver tip:

When making Mexicali Cheeseburgers, use a biscuit cutter to cut rounds from bread slices. Or simply cut squares from centers with a sharp knife. Set rounds or squares aside to toast for breakfast or turn into crisp croutons for another day

MEXICALI CHEESEBURGERS

Makes 4 servings

½ pound ground beef
½ cup finely chopped celery
1 medium-size onion, finely chopped (½ cup)
1 teaspoon chili powder
½ teaspoon sugar
½ teaspoon salt
⅛ teaspoon pepper
⅛ teaspoon garlic powder
¼ cup tomato paste (from a 6-ounce can)
¼ cup water
12 slices white sandwich bread
4 tablespoons (½ stick) soft butter or margarine
1 package (8 ounces) sliced process American cheese

1. Mix ground beef lightly with celery, onion, chili powder, sugar, salt, pepper, and garlic powder until well-blended; shape into a large patty in a frying pan.
2. Brown 5 minutes on each side, then break up into small chunks; stir in tomato paste and water; simmer 15 minutes.
3. Cut a 3-inch round from the center of each of 4 of the bread slices; spread both sides of remaining 8 slices with butter or margarine.
4. Put each sandwich together this way: Buttered slice of bread, cheese slice, bread slice with center removed, about ⅓ cup meat mixture spooned into center hole, cheese slice, and buttered bread.
5. Saute in a large frying pan, adding more butter or margarine, if needed, 3 to 4 minutes on each side, or until golden and cheese filling melts slightly. Cut each in half diagonally; serve hot.

QUICK CHILIBURGERS

Makes 4 servings

1 pound ground beef
1 can condensed chili-beef soup
1 can (about 9 ounces) cream-style corn
8 split hamburger buns, toasted

1. Shape ground beef into a large patty in a frying pan; brown 5 minutes on each side, then break up into chunks. Stir in soup and corn; simmer, stirring often, 5 minutes to blend flavors.
2. Spoon, sandwich style, into toasted buns. Serve with small sweet pickles, if you wish.

JUMBO JOES

Makes 8 servings

    2 pounds ground beef
    2 eggs
    2 teaspoons salt
  ¼ teaspoon pepper
    2 teaspoons chili powder
    1 medium-size onion, peeled and sliced
    2 tablespoons salad oil
    2 cans (about 1 pound each) barbecue
         beans
  16 slices white bread, toasted and buttered
    1 package (8 ounces) sliced sharp Cheddar
         cheese

1. Mix ground beef lightly with eggs, salt, pepper, and ½ teaspoon of the chili powder until well-blended; shape into 8 large patties about ½ inch thick.
2. Saute onion in salad oil just until soft in a medium-size frying pan; stir in beans and remaining 1½ teaspoons chili powder; cook slowly until thick.
3. Pan-fry meat patties 4 minutes on each side for medium, or until meat is done as you like it.
4. Top half of the toasted bread slices with a meat patty, a spoonful of bean mixture, and a cheese slice. Broil just until cheese melts and bubbles up. Top, sandwich style, with remaining toast.

CHILI MEAT-BALL HEROES

Makes 8 servings

    2 pounds ground beef
  1½ teaspoons chili powder
  ½ teaspoon salt
  ⅛ teaspoon pepper
    1 medium-size onion, chopped (½ cup)
    1 clove garlic, minced
    2 tablespoons butter or margarine
    2 cans (about 11 ounces each) beef gravy
  ¼ cup catsup
    8 split frankfurter rolls, toasted and
         buttered

1. Mix ground beef lightly with ½ teaspoon of the chili powder, salt, and pepper; shape into 32 balls.
2. Brown, all at one time, with onion and garlic in butter or margarine in a large frying pan. Stir in beef gravy, catsup, and remaining 1 teaspoon chili powder. Cook, stirring often, 15 minutes.
3. Spoon 4 meat balls and gravy into each buttered frankfurter roll.

CANYON BURGERS

Makes 6 servings

  1½ pounds ground beef
    1 tablespoon bottled steak sauce
    1 teaspoon salt
  ¼ teaspoon pepper
    6 slices white bread
    6 slices mild onion
    2 tablespoons melted butter or margarine
    2 tablespoons brown sugar
  ¼ cup crumbled blue cheese
    6 slices tomato

1. Mix ground beef lightly with steak sauce, salt, and pepper; shape into 6 patties about 1 inch thick.
2. Broil, 4 inches from heat, 6 minutes; turn.
3. Place bread in a single layer on broiler pan with patties; toast one side; turn. Top each slice with an onion slice; brush all with butter or margarine; sprinkle with brown sugar.
4. Top each meat patty with blue cheese and a tomato slice. Broil 2 to 3 minutes longer, or until onion is glazed and meat is done as you like it.
5. Serve meat patties on top of onion toast.

KING CHEESEBURGER

Makes 6 servings

  1½ pounds ground beef
  ¼ cup chili sauce
    1 clove garlic, minced
  1½ teaspoons salt
  ⅛ teaspoon pepper
    1 loaf long thin French bread
         Prepared mustard
         Mayonnaise or salad dressing
    1 medium-size sweet onion, peeled, sliced,
         and separated in rings
    1 package (8 ounces) sliced process
         American cheese, cut in strips

1. Mix ground beef lightly with chili sauce, garlic, salt, and pepper.
2. Split French bread lengthwise; spread each half lightly with mustard and mayonnaise or salad dressing, then meat mixture.
3. Broil, 6 inches from heat, 10 to 12 minutes, or until meat is done as you like it; top with onion rings and cheese strips. Broil 1 to 2 minutes longer, or just until cheese melts. Slice into thirds for serving.

Land-ho Subs *(recipe at right)* and Texas Tacos *(recipe on page 110)* show two inviting ways ground beef goes on an eating-outing. Both, pictured here with picnic-favorite frankfurters, can be fixed at home and reheated on the grill

LAND-HO SUBS
(Pictured at left)

Makes 8 servings

 1 large onion, chopped (1 cup)
 2 tablespoons salad oil
 2 pounds ground beef
 2 cans (8 ounces each) tomato sauce with
     mushrooms
 2 teaspoons salt
 2 teaspoons barbecue spice seasoning
 2 loaves long thin French bread, split
     lengthwise and buttered
 4 dill pickles, cut lengthwise in thin slices
 4 tomatoes, sliced
 4 slices (from an 8-ounce package) process
     Swiss cheese, each cut in 4 strips
16 green onions, trimmed

1. Saute onion in salad oil just until soft in a kettle or Dutch oven; remove and set aside.
2. Shape ground beef into two large patties. Brown, one at a time, in drippings in same kettle 5 minutes on each side, then break up into chunks.
3. Return all meat and onion to kettle; stir in tomato sauce, salt, and barbecue spice seasoning. Simmer 15 minutes, or until thick.
4. Spoon mixture onto bread halves; top with pickle and tomato slices, then cheese strips.
5. Broil, 4 to 6 inches from heat, 3 minutes, or just until cheese bubbles up.
6. Stick 4 green onions, sail fashion, in top of each half; cut each long loaf in half for serving.

CHUBBIES

Makes 8 servings

1½ pounds ground beef
 1 jar (1 pound) meatless spaghetti sauce
 ½ cup (1 stick) butter or margarine
 1 tablespoon grated onion
 1 teaspoon thyme
 8 club rolls, split
 ½ cup grated Romano cheese

1. Shape ground beef into a large patty in a frying pan; brown 5 minutes on each side, then break up into chunks.
2. Stir in spaghetti sauce; heat to boiling; simmer 5 minutes to blend flavors.
3. Melt butter or margarine with onion and thyme; brush over cut surfaces of rolls; sprinkle with half of the cheese. Toast in broiler 2 to 3 minutes, or until golden.
4. Spoon hot meat mixture over bottom halves of rolls; sprinkle with remaining cheese; top with remaining rolls.

MEAT-LOAF DIVIDEND

Bake at 400° for 20 minutes.
Makes 8 servings

 ½ cup (1 stick) butter or margarine
 2 tablespoons horseradish-mustard
 1 loaf long French bread, split lengthwise
16 thin slices baked meat loaf
 2 medium-size tomatoes, sliced
 1 package (8 ounces) sliced caraway cheese

1. Mix butter or margarine with horseradish-mustard; spread on bread.
2. Layer half of the meat loaf on bottom half of bread. (You'll find many meat-loaf choices in Chapter 3.) Top with layers of tomato, remaining meat loaf, and cheese slices; cover with remaining bread; wrap loaf in foil.
3. Bake in hot oven (400°) 20 minutes, or until cheese is melted and loaf is heated through.
4. Cut into 8 serving-size sandwiches.

MEXICAN ROLLUPS

Makes 6 servings

 2 pounds meat-loaf mixture (ground beef,
     pork, and veal)
 1 large onion, chopped (1 cup)
 1 tablespoon chili powder
 2 tablespoons flour
 1 can (8 ounces) tomatoes
 ½ cup water
 2 teaspoons salt
 2 teaspoons sugar
 1 teaspoon cumin
 1 can (11 ounces) tortillas
 4 tablespoons (½ stick) butter or
     margarine
   Crisp shredded lettuce
   Diced green pepper
   Grated Cheddar cheese

1. Shape meat-loaf mixture into a large patty in a frying pan; brown 5 minutes on each side, then break up into chunks. Stir in onion and chili powder; cook 5 minutes longer.
2. Sprinkle flour over meat mixture, then stir in with tomatoes, water, salt, sugar, and cumin. Heat to boiling; simmer, stirring several times, 15 minutes, or until very thick.
3. Saute tortillas, a few at a time, and adding butter or margarine as needed, 1 minute, or just until soft; remove and drain; keep warm.
4. When ready to serve, spoon about ¼ cup of the meat mixture onto each tortilla; sprinkle with shredded lettuce, green pepper, or grated cheese; roll up to eat like a sandwich.

PICCOLO PIZZAS

Bake at 400° for 8 minutes.
Makes about 18 servings, 2 rounds each

   3 pounds ground beef
   2 large cloves garlic
   1 teaspoon salt
   2 cans (3 or 4 ounces each) chopped
        mushrooms
   2 teaspoons oregano
   3 cans condensed tomato soup
  ¼ pound salami, diced
   2 loaves sliced white bread
   2 cups grated Cheddar cheese (8 ounces)
   2 cups grated mozzarella cheese (8 ounces)

1. Shape ground beef lightly into two large patties.
   Brown, one at a time, in a kettle or Dutch oven
   5 minutes on each side, then break up into small
   chunks.
2. Mash garlic with salt; stir into kettle with mushrooms and liquid, oregano, and tomato soup;
   cover.
3. Simmer, stirring often, 20 minutes, or until
   thick; stir in salami.
4. Toast bread lightly; arrange slices in a single
   layer on large cooky sheets or in large shallow
   baking pans.
5. Mix Cheddar and mozzarella cheeses. Spoon hot
   meat mixture onto each slice of toast; sprinkle
   with cheeses.
6. Bake in hot oven (400°) 8 minutes, or just until
   cheeses melt.

CRISPY BURGERS

Makes 8 servings

   2 pounds ground beef
   1 medium-size onion, grated
  ½ cup mixed vegetable juices
 1½ teaspoons salt
   1 teaspoon bottled steak sauce
   4 slices (half an 8-ounce package) process
        American cheese, halved
   8 split hamburger buns, toasted and
        buttered

1. Mix ground beef lightly with onion, mixed vegetable juices, salt, and steak sauce until well-
   blended; shape into 16 very thin patties.
2. Pan-fry quickly just until brown on both sides.
   (Edges will get crisp and lacelike.) Top 8 patties
   with halved slices of cheese; let melt in slightly,
   then top each with a plain patty.
3. Put together, sandwich style, with buttered buns.
   Serve plain or with catsup or thinly sliced sweet-
   onion rings, if you wish.

FIESTA CHEESEBURGERS

Makes 8 servings

   2 pounds ground beef
   1 cup soft bread crumbs (2 slices)
  ½ cup evaporated milk
   2 teaspoons salt
  ¼ teaspoon pepper
   8 split hamburger buns
   4 tablespoons (½ stick) butter or
        margarine
   1 tablespoon prepared mustard
   1 jar (5 ounces) relish-cheese spread

1. Mix ground beef lightly with bread crumbs,
   evaporated milk, salt, and pepper; shape into 8
   patties about 1 inch thick.
2. Broil, 4 inches from heat, 6 minutes on each side
   for medium, or until meat is done as you like it.
3. While meat cooks, spread bottom halves of buns
   with butter or margarine and mustard; spread
   top halves with cheese.
4. Broil along with meat patties 2 to 3 minutes, or
   just until toppings bubble up. Put together, sandwich style, with meat patties.

BACON ROLLUPS

Makes 12 servings

  12 slices bacon (½ pound)
   2 pounds ground beef
   1 small onion, grated
   1 cup crushed potato chips
   1 egg
  ¼ cup catsup
   2 tablespoons Worcestershire sauce
        Dash of thyme
  ½ teaspoon salt
  ¼ teaspoon pepper
   1 can (about 11 ounces) mushroom gravy
  12 split hamburger buns, toasted and
        buttered

1. Broil bacon just until fat starts to cook out; remove and drain on paper toweling.
2. Mix ground beef lightly with onion, potato chips,
   egg, catsup, and seasonings until well-blended;
   shape into 12 patties about 1¼ inches thick.
   Wrap a bacon slice around each; fasten with
   moistened wooden picks. (Dampening picks first
   keeps them from charring.)
3. Broil, 4 inches from heat, 7 minutes on each side
   for medium, or until meat is done as you like it.
4. While patties cook, heat mushroom gravy to boiling. Remove picks from patties; place each patty
   on a bun half on a serving plate; spoon mushroom gravy over; top with remaining bun halves.

PARTY PIZZA

Bake at 400° for 20 minutes.
Makes 2 fourteen-inch pizzas

 2 sweet Italian sausages
 1 pound ground beef
 1 can (about 1 pound) tomatoes
 1 can (6 ounces) tomato paste
 1 clove garlic, minced
 2 teaspoons oregano
 1 teaspoon sugar
 1 teaspoon salt
 ¼ teaspoon pepper
 1 can (3 or 4 ounces) sliced mushrooms
 1 package hot-roll mix
 2 tablespoons salad oil
 1 package (8 ounces) sliced mozzarella or
   pizza cheese, cut up

1. Squeeze sausage meat from casings; mix lightly with ground beef. Shape into a patty in a large frying pan; brown 5 minutes on each side, then break up into small chunks.
2. Stir in tomatoes, tomato paste, garlic, oregano, sugar, salt, pepper, and mushrooms and liquid. Heat to boiling, then simmer 45 minutes, or until as thick as chili sauce.
3. Prepare hot-roll mix, following label directions for pizza dough. (No need to let dough rise.) Divide in half; roll each to an about-15-inch round; fit into an ungreased 14-inch pizza pan; flute edge, if you wish. Brush with salad oil. (Or roll each half to a 14-inch round on an ungreased cooky sheet or heavy foil; turn up dough to make a narrow edge so filling won't bubble out, then brush with salad oil.)
4. Spoon meat sauce into shells, dividing and spreading evenly; top with cheese.
5. Bake in hot oven (400°) 20 minutes, or until sauce bubbles and crust is golden. Cut each pizza in 6 or 8 wedges.

Cooksaver tip:

To step up pizza-making, call on one of the versatile canned sauces. Besides tomato sauce, there's spaghetti sauce— plain or with mushrooms, meat, or tiny meat balls. Or choose spaghetti-sauce mix in a foil envelope. A good rule of thumb is to allow 1½ cups sauce for a 14-inch pizza

MONTE CARLO BURGERS

Makes 8 servings

16 slices French bread
   Butter or margarine
   Garlic salt
 2 pounds ground beef
 ½ cup catsup
 1 medium-size onion, grated
 2 teaspoons salt
 ¼ teaspoon pepper
 1 teaspoon basil
 ½ teaspoon oregano
 1 package (8 ounces) sliced mozzarella or
   pizza cheese, halved

1. Toast bread on one side in broiler; spread untoasted sides with butter or margarine; sprinkle lightly with garlic salt. Remove and set aside.
2. Mix ground beef lightly with catsup, onion, salt, pepper, basil, and oregano until well-blended; shape into 16 patties about ½ inch thick, the same size as toast slices.
3. Broil, 3 inches from heat, 4 minutes on each side.
4. Place on untoasted sides of bread slices; top each with a halved slice of cheese. Broil 1 to 2 minutes longer, or just until cheese melts.

BURGER MILE-HIGHS

Makes 8 servings

 2 pounds ground beef
 2 teaspoons salt
 ¼ teaspoon pepper
 2 packages (8 ounces each) sliced process
   American cheese
 8 split frankfurter rolls, buttered
   Prepared sandwich spread
   Finely shredded iceberg lettuce
 4 tomatoes, sliced thin
   Bread-and-butter pickles

1. Mix ground beef lightly with salt and pepper; shape into 24 patties about ½ inch thick.
2. Pan-fry over medium heat, using two or three large frying pans, 4 minutes on each side for medium, or until meat is done as you like it.
3. Cut cheese slices into 3 strips each; crisscross 2 over each patty; cover. Turn off heat and let stand 1 minute to melt cheese.
4. Spread each roll with sandwich spread; top with 3 meat patties, shredded lettuce, tomato slices, and pickles.

SPANISH MEAT-BALL KEBABS

Makes 6 servings

- 2 pounds ground beef
- 2 eggs
- ¼ cup bottled hamburger relish
- ½ cup flour
- 2 teaspoons salt
- 1 bottle small stuffed green olives, drained
  Shortening for frying
- 1 cup bottled barbecue sauce
- ½ cup tomato juice
- ⅛ teaspoon pepper
- 6 split frankfurter rolls, toasted

1. Mix ground beef lightly with eggs, hamburger relish, flour, and salt until well-blended. Shape, a generous tablespoonful at a time, around a stuffed olive to make 36 small balls.
2. Thread 3 meat balls through the stuffed-olive center onto each of 12 metal skewers.
3. Brown, half at a time, in just enough shortening to keep them from sticking, about 5 minutes in a large frying pan. Return all kebabs to pan.
4. While meat browns, mix barbecue sauce, tomato juice, and pepper in a 2-cup measure; spoon part over kebabs. Continue cooking and spooning on remaining sauce, 2 to 3 minutes longer, or until richly glazed.
5. Remove meat balls from skewers; put together, sandwich style, with toasted rolls.

MEAT-LOAF REUBENS

Makes 4 servings

- 1 can (about 1 pound) sauerkraut
- 1 tablespoon brown sugar
- ¼ cup mayonnaise or salad dressing
- ¼ cup bottled pickle relish
- 4 large poppy-seed rolls, split
- 8 slices baked meat loaf, cut ¼ inch thick
- 2 teaspoons butter or margarine
- 4 slices Swiss cheese (from an 8-ounce package)

1. Mix sauerkraut with brown sugar in a small saucepan; cook 10 minutes, or just until liquid is absorbed.
2. Mix mayonnaise or salad dressing with pickle relish; spread on rolls.
3. Heat meat-loaf slices, turning once, in butter or margarine in a large frying pan. (You'll find many meat-loaf choices in Chapter 3.)
4. Put rolls together, sandwich style, with hot meat loaf, cheese slices, and hot sauerkraut mixture.

RIVIERAS

Makes 8 servings

- 2 eggs
- ½ teaspoon salt
- ⅔ cup milk
- 8 slices French bread
- 1 pound ground beef
- 2 tablespoons butter or margarine
- ¼ cup pizza sauce (from an about-11-ounce can)
- 1 can (about 5 ounces) chopped ripe olives
- 4 slices mozzarella or pizza cheese (from an 8-ounce package), halved

1. Beat eggs with salt and milk in a small bowl. Arrange bread slices in a single layer in a shallow pan; pour egg mixture over; turn to coat well. Let stand about 5 minutes, or until all liquid is absorbed.
2. Shape ground beef lightly into 8 patties about ½ inch thick. Pan-fry 3 minutes on each side for medium, or until meat is done as you like it; keep hot.
3. Saute bread slices in butter or margarine, turning once, just until golden in a second frying pan; place on a cooky sheet. Spread with pizza sauce, then sprinkle with olives; top with a meat patty and a halved cheese slice.
4. Broil, 4 to 6 inches from heat, 3 minutes, or until cheese melts and bubbles up.

MEAT-LOAF CLUBS

Makes 4 servings

- 12 slices white bread, toasted
- ½ cup mayonnaise or salad dressing
- 8 slices cold baked meat loaf, cut ¼ inch thick
- ¼ cup sweet-pickle relish
  Lettuce
- 2 medium-size tomatoes, sliced
- 8 slices crisp bacon
- 16 stuffed green olives

1. Spread toast with mayonnaise or salad dressing and meat-loaf slices with pickle relish. (You'll find many meat-loaf choices in Chapter 3.)
2. Put each sandwich together this way: Slice of toast, spread side up; meat loaf; toast, spread side up; lettuce; tomato slice; crisp bacon; toast, spread side down.
3. Hold sandwiches in place with wooden picks; top each pick with an olive. Cut sandwiches diagonally into quarters.

BEEF-MUSHROOM WAFFLES SUPREME

Makes 6 servings

 1 medium-size onion, chopped (½ cup)
 1 tablespoon butter or margarine
1½ pounds ground beef
 1 can (3 or 4 ounces) sliced or chopped
      mushrooms
 1 envelope mushroom-gravy mix
 1 teaspoon Worcestershire sauce
 ½ cup cream
 6 frozen waffles, toasted

1. Saute onion lightly in butter or margarine; push to one side of pan.
2. Shape ground beef lightly into a large patty in same pan; brown 5 minutes on each side, then break up into chunks.
3. Drain liquid from mushrooms into a 1-cup measure; add water to make 1 cup. Stir into ground-beef mixture with mushrooms, mushroom-gravy mix, and Worcestershire sauce. Heat to boiling, then simmer, stirring often, 5 minutes. Stir in cream; simmer, stirring several times, 3 minutes longer to blend flavors.
4. Spoon over toasted waffles; sprinkle with chopped parsley, if you wish.

Cooksaver tip:

Here are two easy ways to heat frozen waffles: Simply pop them into a toaster, or if you're fixing lots at once, place in a single layer in a jelly-roll pan or on a cooky sheet and heat in hot oven (400°) for 10 minutes. And do try this undercover tip for keeping home-baked waffles hot if they must stand awhile: Stack them on a plate, cover with a colander turned upside down, and set in a warm place. Colander lets steam out, keeps heat in

PERSIAN SPOONBURGERS

Makes 6 servings

 1 pound ground beef
 1 teaspoon curry powder
 ½ cup wheat pilaf (from a 12-ounce
      package)
 2 tablespoons flour
 2 teaspoons sugar
 1 teaspoon salt
 ½ teaspoon cardamom seeds, crushed
 1 can (about 1 pound) stewed tomatoes
 ½ cup water
 2 teaspoons lemon juice
 ½ cup chopped parsley
 6 split hamburger buns, toasted and
      buttered

1. Shape ground beef lightly into a patty in a large frying pan; brown 5 minutes on each side, then break up into chunks.
2. Stir in curry powder and wheat pilaf; cook 1 minute; blend in flour, then stir in sugar, salt, cardamom seeds, tomatoes, water, and lemon juice; cover.
3. Heat to boiling; simmer, stirring often, 15 minutes, or until pilaf is tender and mixture is thick; stir in parsley.
4. Spoon over bottom halves of buns; top with remaining buns.

DOUBLE BEEFBURGERS

Makes 4 servings

 1 pound ground beef
 ¼ cup sliced green onions
 1 clove garlic, minced
 1 teaspoon paprika
 2 tablespoons flour
 1 can condensed beef broth
 ½ cup dairy sour cream
 4 split hamburger buns, toasted and
      buttered

1. Shape ground beef lightly into a patty in a large frying pan; brown 5 minutes on each side, then break up into chunks.
2. Stir in green onions, garlic, and paprika; cook 2 minutes. Blend in flour, then stir in beef broth. Simmer, stirring often, 10 minutes to blend flavors.
3. Stir about ½ cup of the hot mixture into sour cream, then stir back into remaining mixture in pan. Heat slowly, stirring constantly, until hot.
4. Spoon on top of split hamburger buns to serve open-face style.

Scotch Eggs *(recipe on page 142)* give ground beef a new look,
and they're a wonderful way to make a little meat go far.
Good go-withs: Creamy potatoes in a spinach ring, and carrot salad

CHAPTER 7

BE KNOWN FOR YOUR

SPECIALTIES OF THE HOUSE

Versatile ground beef goes high-fashion here, starting with conversation-piece main dishes for company, then on to dress-up ways with party appetizers, and simple specialties when you want to fuss a bit for the family.

Looking for a good-to-the-budget company classic? Continental Pâté Loaf, Scotch Eggs, East-West Sukiyaki, Matambre Roll—and more—are the choices here.

Planning a buffet? Fill a chafing dish or keep-hot server with miniature meat balls or pass a tray of hot appeteasers. More than a dozen ideas are yours under "Savory Appetizers."

Tired of fixing hamburger the same old way? Surprise the family with a good butter-upper, beginning on page 159. Is it any wonder good cooks everywhere love thrifty, versatile, hearty hamburger?

When company comes, serve these dress-ups

CONTINENTAL PATE LOAF
(Pictured on pages 144-145)

Bake at 350° for 1 hour and 45 minutes.
Makes 6 to 8 servings

- 1 pound ground beef
- 1 pound ground veal
- 2 eggs
- 1 small onion, grated
- 1 tablespoon flour
- 2 teaspoons salt
- ½ teaspoon marjoram
- ¼ teaspoon pepper
- 2 cans condensed beef broth
  Meat-pie Pastry *(recipe follows)*
- 10 small sweet pickles, quartered lengthwise
- 1 envelope unflavored gelatin
  Fluffy Mustard Sauce *(recipe follows)*

1. Combine ground beef and veal in a large bowl. Beat eggs slightly in a cup; measure 2 tablespoons into a second cup and set aside for brushing loaf. Stir remaining into meat mixture with onion, flour, salt, marjoram, pepper, and ½ cup of the broth; mix well.
2. Make MEAT-PIE PASTRY. Roll out ⅔ to a rectangle, 15x10, on a lightly floured pastry cloth or board; fit into a loaf pan, 9x5x3, to line.
3. Spoon one third of the meat mixture in an even layer in bottom of pan; place half of the pickle slices lengthwise in five evenly spaced rows on top. Repeat with another layer of each, then top with remaining meat. Fold edges of pastry over.
4. Roll out remaining pastry to a rectangle; cut out a piece, 9x5, then cut several slits to let steam escape. Place over meat loaf; pinch edges to seal; brush with saved beaten egg.
5. Bake in moderate oven (350°) 1 hour and 45 minutes, or until golden. (During baking, juices from meat may bubble up around edges and through openings in top but will soak back into loaf as it cools.) Place pan on a wire rack to cool while preparing gelatin mixture.
6. Soften gelatin in ½ cup of the remaining broth; heat slowly, stirring constantly, just until gelatin dissolves. Stir in remaining broth.
7. Push a skewer through each of the openings in top of loaf, pushing it carefully to bottom of meat, then spoon in just enough of the warm gelatin mixture to fill holes. Let stand until gelatin mixture soaks into meat. Repeat several more times with remaining gelatin mixture until no more will soak into meat. (If there is any gelatin mixture left, save to add to soup.) Chill loaf several hours, or even overnight.
8. When ready to serve, loosen around edges with a knife; turn out onto a serving plate. Cut in thick slices with a sharp knife. Serve with FLUFFY MUSTARD SAUCE.

Meat-pie Pastry

- 2 cups sifted regular flour
- 1 teaspoon salt
- ⅔ cup shortening
- 4 to 5 tablespoons cold water

Combine flour and salt in a medium-size bowl; cut in shortening with a pastry blender until mixture is crumbly. Sprinkle cold water over, 1 tablespoon at a time, mixing lightly with a fork until pastry holds together and leaves side of bowl clean.

Fluffy Mustard Sauce

Makes about 1 cup

- 3 tablespoons dry mustard
- 2 tablespoons sugar
- 1 tablespoon cornstarch
- 1 teaspoon salt
- 1 egg yolk
- ½ cup water
- 1 tablespoon butter or margarine
- ¼ cup white vinegar
- ¼ cup cream for whipping

1. Mix mustard, sugar, cornstarch, and salt in a small saucepan. Beat egg yolk slightly with water; stir into mustard mixture.
2. Cook, stirring constantly, over low heat until mixture thickens and boils 3 minutes. Remove from heat; stir in butter or margarine and vinegar. Strain into a small bowl; cool.
3. Beat cream until stiff; fold into cooled mustard mixture. Chill until serving time.

PAGODA BURGERS
(Pictured on page 144)

Makes 4 servings

1½ pounds ground beef
1 can (5 ounces) water chestnuts, drained and chopped fine
1 egg, beaten
4 teaspoons soy sauce (for meat)
1 can (about 9 ounces) sliced pineapple, drained
1 large tomato, cut in 4 slices
5 tablespoons butter or margarine
  Salt and pepper
1 tablespoon cornstarch
1 tablespoon molasses
2 tablespoons soy sauce (for sauce)
1 cup water
1 tablespoon lemon juice
½ cup sliced green onions
3 cups cooked hot rice (¾ cup uncooked)
4 slices cucumber

1. Mix ground beef lightly with chopped water chestnuts, egg, and the 4 teaspoons soy sauce until well-blended; divide mixture in half.
2. Shape half into 4 patties about ½ inch thick. Shape two thirds of remaining, then other third, into 4 medium-size and 4 small patties. (Keep all 12 patties evenly thick so they will cook in the same time.) Place, close together, on rack in broiler pan.
3. Broil, 4 inches from heat, 4 minutes; turn. Place pineapple and tomato slices beside meat; dot with 3 tablespoons of the butter or margarine; sprinkle tomatoes with salt and pepper. Broil 4 minutes longer for medium, or until meat is done as you like it.
4. Blend cornstarch, molasses, and the 2 tablespoons soy sauce; stir in water. Cook, stirring constantly, until sauce thickens and boils 3 minutes. Stir in remaining 2 tablespoons butter or margarine, lemon juice, and green onions.
5. Spoon rice onto 4 serving plates; place a pineapple slice on each; top each with a large meat patty, tomato slice, medium-size patty, cucumber slice, and small meat patty. Spoon some of the sauce over each, then serve remaining separately. Garnish each with a kumquat "flower," as pictured, if you wish.

Note—To fix kumquat "flower," make 4 lengthwise cuts in a preserved kumquat from tip almost to stem end; place a tiny sweet pickle in center; thread onto a wooden pick and stick into a meat patty.

STUFFED CREPES AU GRATIN

Bake at 350° for 30 minutes.
Makes 6 servings

Filling
1 package (10 ounces) frozen chopped spinach
1 medium-size onion, peeled and sliced thin
1 tablespoon salad oil
½ pound ground beef
½ teaspoon salt
1 medium-size tomato, peeled and chopped
½ cup grated Cheddar cheese

Crepes
2 eggs
1¼ cups milk
1 cup sifted regular flour
2 tablespoons melted butter or margarine

Sauce
1 tablespoon butter or margarine
1 tablespoon flour
¼ teaspoon salt
1 cup milk
¼ cup grated Parmesan cheese

1. Make filling: Cook spinach, following label directions; drain well. Saute onion lightly in salad oil in a frying pan; push to one side. Shape ground beef into a large patty in same pan; brown 5 minutes on each side, then break up into small chunks. Stir in salt, tomato, cheese, and drained spinach; simmer 5 minutes. Remove from heat.
2. Make crepes: Beat eggs lightly with milk; beat in flour and melted butter or margarine just until smooth. (Batter will be thin.)
3. Heat a 7-inch frying pan slowly; test temperature by sprinkling in a few drops of water. When drops bounce about, temperature is right; grease lightly. Pour batter, a scant ¼ cup for each crepe, into pan; tip pan to cover bottom completely. Bake 2 to 3 minutes, or until top appears dry and underside is golden. (No need to turn.) Repeat with remaining batter, lightly greasing pan before each baking, to make 12 crepes.
4. As each crepe is baked, spoon about ¼ cup meat filling down middle; roll up and place, seam side down, in a greased shallow baking dish, 13x9x2. Keep warm in very slow oven (250°) until all are baked and filled.
5. Make sauce: Melt butter or margarine in a small saucepan; stir in flour, salt, and milk. Cook, stirring constantly, until sauce thickens and boils 1 minute. Pour over pancake rolls; sprinkle with cheese.
6. Bake in moderate oven (350°) 30 minutes, or until golden-brown.

SCOTCH EGGS
(Pictured on page 138)

Makes 6 servings

1½ pounds ground beef
 1 small onion, chopped (¼ cup)
 2 tablespoons bottled steak sauce
1½ teaspoons salt
 ¼ teaspoon pepper
 ¼ cup milk
 6 hard-cooked eggs, shelled
 1 raw egg, slightly beaten
 ⅔ cup corn-flake crumbs (from an about-
     10-ounce package)
    Shortening or salad oil for frying

1. Mix ground beef lightly with onion, steak sauce, salt, pepper, and milk until well-blended.
2. Divide meat mixture evenly into 6 mounds; shape each around a hard-cooked egg to cover completely and make an oval shape.
3. Brush each meat roll with beaten egg, then roll in corn-flake crumbs to coat well.
4. Melt enough shortening or pour in salad oil to make a 2-inch depth in a deep saucepan; heat to 325°.
5. Fry meat rolls, 2 or 3 at a time, turning once or twice, 5 minutes, or until crispy-brown. Lift out with a slotted spoon; drain on paper toweling. Keep hot.
6. When all are cooked, cut each in half lengthwise; place on a heated serving platter. To serve as pictured, spoon creamed potatoes and peas into center of platter and buttered spinach in a ring next to potatoes. Arrange halved meat rolls around edge.

Cooksaver tip:

Versatile ground beef takes easily to all kinds of shapings, and Scotch Eggs are just one example of a new and different twist on this favorite. To fix them, form the meat into patties about one half inch thick (remember to handle meat lightly), then place a shelled hard-cooked egg in the center of each and mold the meat around it

MATAMBRE ROLL
(Pictured on pages 144-145)

Bake at 350° for 1 hour.
Makes 8 servings

 2 pounds ground beef
 1 teaspoon seasoned salt
 ½ teaspoon seasoned pepper
 ¼ cup bottled smoke-flavor barbecue sauce
 ¼ cup catsup
 2 cups shredded pared raw carrots
 1 cup soft bread crumbs (2 slices)
 ½ cup chopped parsley
 1 teaspoon salt
 2 eggs, beaten
 1 cup water
 ¼ cup flour
 1 cup milk

1. Mix ground beef lightly with seasoned salt and pepper; pat into a thin rectangle, 14x12, on waxed paper or foil. (For easy handling, paper should be a few inches longer than meat layer.)
2. Mix barbecue sauce and catsup; brush about half over meat layer.
3. Combine carrots, bread crumbs, parsley, salt, and eggs to make a stuffing mixture; spread evenly over meat. Roll up, jelly-roll fashion, using waxed paper or foil as a guide; lift into a greased large shallow baking pan; remove waxed paper or foil. Brush roll all over with part of remaining sauce mixture.
4. Bake in moderate oven (350°), brushing several times with sauce mixture, 1 hour, or until richly glazed. Remove from pan and keep hot while making gravy.
5. Stir water into drippings in pan, scraping any brown bits from bottom of pan. Blend flour and milk; stir into drippings mixture. Cook, stirring constantly, until gravy thickens and boils 1 minute. Season with salt and pepper, if needed.
6. Slice roll and serve with gravy. To serve as pictured, spoon German-style potato salad in the center of a large serving platter; stand meat slices around edge; garnish salad with red-onion rings.

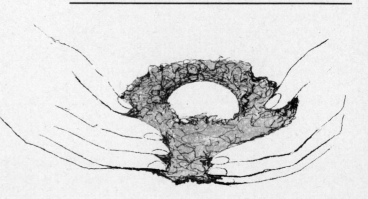

TORTILLA TOWER

Bake at 400° for 30 minutes.
Makes 6 servings

Filling
- 1 large onion, chopped (1 cup)
- 1 clove garlic, minced
- 2 teaspoons chili powder
- 2 tablespoons olive oil or salad oil
- 1 pound ground beef
- 2 cans (about 1 pound each) tomatoes
- 2 cans (about 1 pound each) red kidney beans
- 2 teaspoons sugar
- 2 teaspoons salt

Pancakes
- 1 egg
- 1 cup sifted regular flour
- ½ cup yellow corn meal
- ¼ teaspoon salt
- 1½ cups water

Topping
- 1 small onion, peeled, sliced, and separated into rings
- ½ cup pitted ripe olives, sliced
- 1 cup grated Cheddar cheese (4 ounces)

1. Make filling: Saute onion and garlic with chili powder in olive oil or salad oil just until soft in a large frying pan; push to one side. Shape ground beef into a large patty in same pan; brown 5 minutes on each side, then break up into small chunks.
2. Stir in tomatoes, kidney beans, sugar, and salt; cover. Simmer 15 minutes to blend flavors.
3. Make pancakes: Beat egg well; beat in flour, corn meal, salt, and water until smooth. (Batter will be thin.)
4. Heat a 9-inch heavy frying pan slowly; test temperature by sprinkling in a few drops of water. When drops bounce about, temperature is right; grease lightly. Pour batter, a scant ⅓ cup for each pancake, into pan; bake 3 minutes, or until top appears dry and underside is golden; turn; bake 2 minutes longer. Repeat with remaining batter, lightly greasing pan before each baking, to make 8 pancakes.
5. As each pancake is baked, stack with 1 cup sauce between in a 12-cup round deep baking dish, ending with pancake. (Pancakes take up sauce during baking.)
6. Arrange topping: Place onion rings and sliced olives in a pretty pattern on top of pancakes; sprinkle with cheese.
7. Bake in hot oven (400°) 30 minutes, or until bubbly hot. Cut into wedges.

SCANDINAVIAN BEAN POT

Makes 6 to 8 servings

- ½ pound dried white kidney beans
- 3 cups boiling water
- 3 medium-size carrots, pared and sliced
- 2 medium-size potatoes, pared and sliced
- 2 medium-size apples, pared, quartered, cored, and sliced
- 2 medium-size pears, pared, quartered, cored, and sliced
- ½ pound green beans, cut in 1½-inch pieces
- 1 pound ground beef
- 2 tablespoons salad oil
- 1½ cups water
- 1½ teaspoons salt
- ¼ teaspoon pepper
- Dash of ground cloves
- 4 smoked sausage links (half a 12-ounce package), cut in ½-inch pieces

1. Pick over and rinse kidney beans. Place in a large saucepan; pour the 3 cups boiling water over; cover. Let stand 1 hour, then heat to boiling; lower heat and simmer 1 hour; drain well and set aside.
2. While kidney beans cook, combine carrots, potatoes, apples, pears, and green beans in a large bowl.
3. Shape ground beef into a patty in a large frying pan; brown in salad oil 5 minutes on each side, then break up into chunks. Stir in the 1½ cups water, salt, pepper, and cloves; heat to boiling; remove from heat.
4. Combine drained kidney beans, meat mixture, sausages, and vegetable-fruit mixture in a large kettle; cover.
5. Simmer 40 minutes, or until vegetables are tender. Sprinkle with chopped parsley, if you wish.

Cooksaver tip:

Here's an easy but important touch: Give curry or chili powder a good "burn" by sauteing either of these husky seasoners well in butter, margarine, salad oil, or drippings. This is a gourmet chef's trick, and — like cooking onion lightly before adding it to ground beef or sauce — it brings out the full richness and gives your dish a long-simmered mellowness

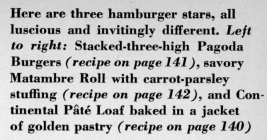

Here are three hamburger stars, all luscious and invitingly different. *Left to right:* Stacked-three-high Pagoda Burgers *(recipe on page 141)*, savory Matambre Roll with carrot-parsley stuffing *(recipe on page 142)*, and Continental Pâté Loaf baked in a jacket of golden pastry *(recipe on page 140)*

ROYAL EGGPLANT FONDUE

Bake at 350° for 45 minutes.
Makes 6 servings

- 1 large eggplant (about 1½ pounds)
- ½ pound ground beef
- 1 small onion, grated
- 1½ cups soft bread crumbs (3 slices)
- ½ teaspoon salt
- ½ teaspoon basil
- ⅛ teaspoon nutmeg
- ½ cup tomato sauce (from an 8-ounce can)
- 4 eggs, separated

1. Halve eggplant; pare, then dice pulp. (There should be about 8 cups.) Cook, covered, in a small amount of boiling salted water 10 to 15 minutes, or until soft; drain well. (Pulp should now measure 1½ cups.)
2. Shape ground beef into a large patty in a medium-size frying pan; brown 5 minutes on each side, then break up into small chunks.
3. Stir in drained eggplant, onion, 1 cup of the bread crumbs, salt, basil, nutmeg, and tomato sauce; remove from heat; let cool while beating eggs.
4. Beat egg whites just until they form soft peaks. Beat egg yolks until creamy-thick; blend in cooled eggplant mixture; fold in beaten egg whites until no streaks of white remain. Pour into an ungreased 6-cup souffle or straight-side baking dish. Sprinkle remaining ½ cup bread crumbs on top.
5. Bake in moderate oven (350°) 45 minutes, or until puffy-firm and golden on top. Serve at once.

Cooksaver tip:

Whether you're planning for company or you just want to make a delicious main dish for the family, you'll find it's hard to beat a baked sandwich-custard dish — often called Strata. Our Swiss Sandwich Puff version uses simple on-hand foods, and it's best prepared the night before and chilled. Then when you bake it — with hardly any watching needed — it puffs up into a handsomely golden treat

BEEF-CORN FRITTER PUFFS

Makes 24 puffs

- 4 eggs, separated
- ½ pound ground beef
- 1 can (7 ounces) whole-kernel corn, drained
- ¼ cup flour
- 1 teaspoon salt
- ½ teaspoon baking powder
- ⅛ teaspoon pepper
- ⅛ teaspoon thyme
- Salad oil

1. Beat egg whites until they stand in firm peaks. Beat egg yolks until creamy-thick; stir in ground beef, corn, flour, salt, baking powder, pepper, and thyme; fold in beaten egg whites.
2. Drop by tablespoonfuls into about 2 tablespoons hot salad oil in a frying pan; cook until puffed and brown around edges; turn; brown other side. Repeat with remaining batter, adding more salad oil as needed.
3. Serve hot with applesauce or spiced apple rings, if you wish.

SWISS SANDWICH PUFF

Bake at 325° for 50 minutes.
Makes 6 servings

- ½ pound ground beef
- 1 teaspoon salt
- ½ teaspoon paprika
- ½ cup chili sauce
- 2 cups grated Swiss cheese (8 ounces)
- 1 teaspoon prepared mustard
- 12 slices white bread, toasted
- 6 eggs
- 2½ cups milk

1. Mix ground beef lightly with ½ teaspoon of the salt and paprika; shape into a large patty in a frying pan. Brown 5 minutes on each side, then break up into small chunks. Remove from heat; stir in chili sauce, cheese, and mustard.
2. Spread thickly on 6 of the toast slices; put together with remaining toast to make 6 sandwiches. Cut each diagonally into quarters; stand, crust edge down, in a buttered baking dish, 13x9x2.
3. Beat eggs slightly with milk and remaining ½ teaspoon salt; pour over sandwiches; cover. Chill at least 4 hours. (Overnight is even better.)
4. Bake in slow oven (325°) 40 minutes; uncover. Bake 10 minutes longer, or until custard is set.
5. Let stand about 5 minutes, then cut between sandwiches, allowing 4 triangles for each serving.

BALI BEEF DINNER

Makes 6 servings

½ cup flaked coconut (from a 3½-ounce
    can)
1 tablespoon curry powder
2 teaspoons cornstarch
1 cup water
1 pound ground beef
1 teaspoon monosodium glutamate (MSG)
1 teaspoon salt
⅛ teaspoon ground ginger
1 large onion, chopped (1 cup)
1 package (10 ounces) frozen peas
1 can (4 ounces) pimiento, drained and cut
    in 1-inch squares
4 cups hot cooked rice

1. Combine coconut, curry powder, cornstarch, and water in a 2-cup measure; set aside.
2. Mix ground beef lightly with MSG, salt, and ginger; shape into a large patty in a frying pan; brown 5 minutes on each side, then break up into chunks. Stir in onion; saute 5 minutes, or just until soft, then stir in coconut mixture.
3. Cook, stirring constantly, until sauce thickens and boils 3 minutes. Sprinkle peas and pimiento on top; cover. Simmer 10 minutes, or just until peas are tender.
4. Spoon hot cooked rice in a ring on a heated serving plate; spoon beef mixture into center.

QUICK SPANISH BAKE

Bake at 350° for 1 hour.
Makes 8 servings

2 pounds ground beef
1 teaspoon salt
2 tablespoons butter or margarine
2 packages (6 ounces each) Spanish Rice
    mix with tomatoes
5 cups boiling water
1 tablespoon chopped parsley

1. Mix ground beef with salt and shape into 32 balls; saute in butter or margarine until lightly browned. Place in a 10-cup baking dish.
2. Add contents of both packages of rice; stir in boiling water until flavor buds (from packages) dissolve; cover.
3. Bake in moderate oven (350°) 45 minutes; uncover; bake 15 minutes longer, or until all liquid is absorbed.
4. Fluff up meat balls and rice with a fork; sprinkle with chopped parsley.

Cooksaver tip:

Look to the Orient for inspiration and cook deliciously different sukiyaki at your table, where all can watch. Arrange the rich red ground beef and carefully cut vegetables in rows on a tray. Then use an electric skillet or a big frying pan set on a frame over canned heat, and saute meat first, vegetables next, for in true Japanese style, vegetables should have a crisply inviting fresh look

EAST-WEST SUKIYAKI
(Pictured on page 156)

Makes 4 servings

1 pound ground beef
1 Bermuda onion, peeled and sliced thin
1 tablespoon salad oil
3 stalks celery, sliced thin
6 large fresh mushrooms, trimmed and
    sliced thin
¼ pound green beans, sliced lengthwise
1 can (about 5 ounces) bamboo shoots,
    well-drained
1 tablespoon sugar
⅓ cup soy sauce
1 envelope instant chicken broth
    OR: 1 chicken-bouillon cube
½ cup water
1 package (10 ounces) spinach, washed
    and stemmed
Seasoned hot cooked rice

1. Shape ground beef into a large patty in a large frying pan; brown 5 minutes on each side, then break up into chunks. Push to one side.
2. Add onion and salad oil; saute just until onion starts to soften. Stir in celery, mushrooms, green beans, drained bamboo shoots, sugar, soy sauce, instant chicken broth or bouillon cube, and water; heat to boiling, crushing cube, if using, with a spoon; cover.
3. Simmer 10 minutes. Lay spinach on top of meat and vegetables; cover. Simmer 5 minutes longer, or just until spinach wilts and vegetables are crisply tender.
4. Serve with seasoned rice.

147

STUFFED CABBAGE CROWN
(Pictured on page 151)

Makes 4 servings

- 1 pound ground beef
- 1/3 cup flour (for meat)
- 1½ teaspoons salt
- 1/4 teaspoon pepper
- 1 egg
- 1 cup milk
- 1 small onion, grated
- 1 large head cabbage (about 3 pounds)
- 2 tablespoons butter or margarine
- 2 tablespoons flour (for gravy)

1. Combine ground beef, the 1/3 cup flour, salt, pepper, and egg in the large bowl of electric mixer; beat until blended, then gradually beat in milk, 1 tablespoon at a time, until smooth and paste-like; stir in onion.
2. Trim off outside leaves of cabbage. Cut off a slice about an inch thick from core end; set aside for next step. Cut core from cabbage with a sharp knife, then hollow out cabbage to make a shell about ½ inch thick. (Chop cut-out pieces coarsely and cook separately to serve along with stuffed cabbage, as pictured, or save to cook as a vegetable for another day.)
3. Spoon meat mixture into shell; fit cut slice back into place; tie tightly with string.
4. Place stuffed cabbage, core end down, in a kettle; pour in boiling water to cover about 3/4 of the way; cover.
5. Simmer 1½ hours, or until cabbage is tender. Lift from water with two large spoons; keep hot while making gravy. Pour 1½ cups of the liquid into a 2-cup measure; discard any remaining liquid.
6. Heat butter or margarine just until it foams up and turns golden in a small saucepan; blend in the 2 tablespoons flour; cook, stirring constantly, just until bubbly.
7. Stir in the 1½ cups saved liquid; continue cooking and stirring until gravy thickens and boils 1 minute. Season to taste with salt and pepper; darken with a few drops bottled gravy coloring, if you wish.
8. Place stuffed cabbage on a heated serving platter; remove string. Pour gravy into a separate bowl; garnish each with parsley, if you wish. Cut cabbage into wedges; spoon gravy over.

Note: Any left over can be reheated easily. Use a frying pan, lay wedges on their side in gravy, cover, and heat slowly.

Cooksaver tip:

When hollowing out cabbage for Stuffed Cabbage Crown, remember to start from the core end. Capped, the filled shell will be firm enough to tie securely, as shown

MEAT ROLLS CORONADO

Bake at 375° for 45 minutes.
Makes 4 servings

- 1 pound ground beef
- 1 egg
- 1/4 cup corn-flake crumbs (from an about-10-ounce package)
- 1/4 cup evaporated milk
- 1 teaspoon grated orange rind
- 1 teaspoon salt
- 1/8 teaspoon pepper
- 8 thin slices boiled ham (about 1 pound)
- 1/4 cup orange juice
- 1/4 cup light corn syrup
- 1/4 cup firmly packed brown sugar
- 1 teaspoon lemon juice
- 1 teaspoon dry mustard

1. Mix ground beef lightly with egg, corn-flake crumbs, evaporated milk, orange rind, salt, and pepper until well-blended; shape into 8 sausage-like rolls, the width of a ham slice.
2. Lay each roll across one end of a ham slice and roll up; place, seam side down, in a greased shallow baking dish, 10x6x2.
3. Blend orange juice with corn syrup, brown sugar, lemon juice, and mustard; pour over rolls.
4. Bake in moderate oven (375°), basting several times, 45 minutes, or until richly glazed. Serve with hot buttered rice or hominy grits.

TAORMINA BAKE

Bake at 350° for 1 hour.
Makes 8 servings

- 1 medium-size eggplant, pared and sliced ¼ inch thick
- ½ cup salad oil
- 4 medium-size onions, peeled and sliced
- 1 clove garlic, minced
- 1 pound ground beef
- 1 can (8 ounces) tomato sauce
- 1½ teaspoons salt
- 1 teaspoon oregano
- 2 tablespoons butter or margarine
- 2 tablespoons flour
- ⅛ teaspoon nutmeg
- 1½ cups milk
- ½ cup soft bread crumbs (1 slice)
- 2 eggs, separated

1. Brown eggplant slices, a few at a time, in salad oil in a medium-size frying pan, adding oil as needed. Drain well on paper toweling; set aside.
2. Saute onions and garlic just until onions are soft in same pan, adding more oil if needed; push to one side. Shape ground beef into a large patty in same pan; brown 5 minutes on each side, then break up into small chunks.
3. Stir in tomato sauce, 1 teaspoon of the salt, and oregano; cover.
4. Simmer 30 minutes; remove from heat; let cool while making sauce-topping.
5. Melt butter or margarine in a small saucepan. Stir in flour, remaining ½ teaspoon salt, and nutmeg; cook, stirring constantly, just until bubbly. Stir in milk; continue cooking and stirring until sauce thickens and boils 1 minute.
6. Stir bread crumbs and unbeaten egg whites into *cooled* meat mixture. Beat egg yolks slightly in a small bowl; stir in a generous ½ cup of the hot sauce; stir back into remaining sauce in pan. Cook, stirring constantly over medium heat 3 minutes, or until thick.
7. Make 2 layers each of eggplant slices and meat mixture in a greased 8-cup baking dish; pour sauce over.
8. Bake in moderate oven (350°) 1 hour, or until topping is a rich golden-brown.

DOUBLE-GOOD MANICOTTI

Bake at 350° for 40 minutes.
Makes 8 servings

- 1 large onion, chopped (1 cup)
- 1 clove garlic, minced
- 2 tablespoons butter or margarine
- 1 tablespoon Italian seasoning
- 2½ teaspoons salt
- 1 teaspoon sugar
- 4 cans (8 ounces each) tomato sauce
- 1 can (1 pound) Italian tomatoes
- 1 package (12 ounces) manicotti noodles
- 1 pound ground beef
- ½ cup chopped walnuts
- 2 eggs
- 1 package (9 ounces) frozen chopped spinach, thawed and drained
- 1½ cups cream-style cottage cheese
- 1 package (3 or 4 ounces) cream cheese, softened
- 1 package (8 ounces) sliced mozzarella or pizza cheese, cut in triangles

1. Saute onion and garlic in butter or margarine just until onion is soft in a medium-size saucepan; stir in Italian seasoning, 1 teaspoon of the salt, sugar, tomato sauce, and tomatoes. Simmer, stirring several times, 15 minutes; keep hot.
2. Cook manicotti noodles, a few at a time, in a large amount of boiling salted water, following label directions; lift out carefully with a slotted spoon so as not to break them; place in a pan of cold water until ready to fill.
3. Shape ground beef into a large patty in a large frying pan. Brown 5 minutes on each side, then break up into small chunks; remove from heat; cool. Stir in 1 teaspoon of the remaining salt, walnuts, 1 of the eggs, and half of the spinach.
4. Blend cottage cheese with cream cheese, remaining ½ teaspoon salt, egg, and spinach in a medium-size bowl.
5. Lift manicotti noodles, 1 at a time, from water; drain well. Fill half with meat mixture and half with cheese mixture, using a long-handle teaspoon.
6. Spoon 2 cups of the hot tomato sauce into a buttered baking pan, 13x9x2; arrange filled noodles on top; spoon remaining sauce over; cover.
7. Bake in moderate oven (350°) 30 minutes; uncover. Arrange mozzarella cheese triangles, overlapping, on top. Bake 10 minutes longer, or until cheese melts.

ORIENTAL PEPPER POT

Bake at 350° for 1 hour.
Makes 6 servings

 1 pound ground beef
 ½ cup thinly sliced green onions
 1 clove garlic, minced
 1½ teaspoons sugar
 ¼ cup soy sauce
 2 pounds fresh haddock fillets, cut in
     2-inch pieces
 1 large onion, chopped (1 cup)
 6 large mushrooms, trimmed and sliced
 4 medium-size carrots, pared and cut in
     2-inch-long sticks
 ½ cup sliced celery
 1½ teaspoons salt
 1 teaspoon pepper
 ¼ teaspoon ground ginger
 ¾ cup water
 1 egg
 1 tablespoon butter or margarine

1. Mix ground beef with green onions, garlic, sugar, and 2 tablespoons of the soy sauce until well-blended in a medium-size bowl.
2. Spread half of the meat mixture evenly in a 12-cup baking dish; top with half each of the haddock, chopped onion, mushrooms, carrots, and celery.
3. Mix salt, pepper, and ginger; sprinkle half over layers in dish. Repeat with remaining ground-beef mixture, haddock, vegetables, and seasoning mixture to make another layer of each.
4. Combine remaining 2 tablespoons soy sauce and water; pour over layers; cover tightly.
5. Bake in moderate oven (350°) 1 hour, or until haddock flakes easily with a fork and all vegetables are tender.
6. Just before serving, beat egg well in a small bowl; cook in butter or margarine, turning once, just until firm in a small frying pan. Remove and place on a cutting board. Slice in thin strips; mound in a petal design in center of baking dish.
7. Serve in soup plates or shallow bowls for it's eat-with-a-spoon food.

Cooksaver tip:

When seasoning with dried herbs, be miserly, for the herb should enhance—not take over—the flavor of the dish. And crushing the herb first gives a more even flavor

ITALIAN HERB PIE

Bake at 400° for 35 minutes.
Makes 8 servings

 1½ pounds ground beef
 2 tablespoons butter or margarine
 1 small onion, chopped (¼ cup)
 4 tablespoons flour
 1 can (about 1 pound) tomatoes
 1 can (8 ounces) tomato sauce
 3 tablespoons grated Parmesan cheese
 1 tablespoon sugar
 1 teaspoon basil
 ½ teaspoon salt
 ½ teaspoon garlic salt
 ½ teaspoon oregano
 ⅛ teaspoon pepper
     Herb Pastry (recipe follows)
 4 slices (half an 8-ounce package)
     Cheddar cheese

1. Shape ground beef into a patty in a large frying pan; brown in butter or margarine 5 minutes on each side, then break up into chunks; remove and set aside.
2. Saute onion just until soft in same pan; blend in flour, tomatoes, tomato sauce, Parmesan cheese, and seasonings. Heat, stirring constantly, until mixture thickens slightly, then simmer 10 minutes to blend flavors. Stir in browned ground beef.
3. While filling simmers, make HERB PASTRY. Roll out ⅔ of dough to a 12-inch round on a lightly floured pastry cloth or board; fit into a 9-inch pie plate. Trim overhang to ½ inch; turn under, flush with rim; flute to make a stand-up edge. Spoon meat mixture into prepared shell; arrange cheese slices on top. Roll out remaining pastry to ⅛-inch thickness; cut into rounds with a 2-inch cutter; place on top of cheese.
4. Bake in hot oven (400°) 35 minutes, or until pastry is golden and filling is bubbly hot.
5. Cool 5 minutes on a wire rack; cut into wedge-shape servings.

HERB PASTRY—Mix 1½ cups sifted regular flour, ½ cup grated Parmesan cheese, 1 teaspoon garlic salt, and 1 teaspoon oregano in a medium-size bowl. Cut in ½ cup (1 stick) butter or margarine until mixture is crumbly. Sprinkle 4 to 5 tablespoons cold water over, 1 tablespoon at a time, mixing lightly with a fork until pastry holds together and leaves side of bowl clean.

This new-look way with ground beef is Danish-inspired Stuffed Cabbage Crown *(recipe on page 148)*. Beef is seasoned and stuffed into a hollowed-out jumbo cabbage, then steamed. Cut in wedges for serving, and top with gravy

Win fame for your savory appetizers

BEEF TARTLETS

Bake at 425° for 15 minutes.
Makes 36 tarts

½ package piecrust mix
½ pound ground beef
1 small onion, grated
¼ cup flour
1 teaspoon Worcestershire sauce
½ teaspoon salt
Dash of pepper
1 egg
½ cup milk
2 small dill pickles, sliced thin

1. Prepare piecrust mix, following label directions, or make pastry from your own favorite one-crust recipe. Roll out, half at a time, ⅛ inch thick; cut into 18 two-inch rounds. Fit into shallow 1¾-inch tart pans or tiny muffin-pan cups.
2. Combine ground beef, onion, flour, Worcestershire sauce, salt, pepper, and egg in the large bowl of electric mixer; beat until blended, then gradually beat in milk, 1 tablespoon at a time, until mixture is smooth and pastelike. Place 1 teaspoonful in each tart shell.
3. Bake in hot oven (425°) 15 minutes, or until pastry is golden-brown. Top each with a thin slice of dill pickle. Serve hot.

Variations:

PARMESAN PUFFS — Prepare BEEF TARTLETS, following recipe above, and bake 10 minutes. While tarts bake, blend ¼ cup mayonnaise or salad dressing with ¼ cup grated Parmesan cheese and a drop of red-pepper seasoning; spoon a dollop on top of each tart; return to oven. Bake 5 minutes longer, or until puffy-golden.

CHIPPIES — Prepare BEEF TARTLETS, following recipe at left, and add ¼ cup finely chopped walnuts or toasted almonds to the meat mixture; spoon into tart shells. Top each with a walnut or almond half before baking.

OLIVE TARTLETS — Prepare BEEF TARTLETS, following recipe at left, and add ¼ cup chili sauce or catsup to the meat mixture; spoon into tart shells. Bake, then garnish with thinly sliced stuffed green olives.

CHEESE SAVORIES — Prepare BEEF TARTLETS, following recipe at left, and add ¼ cup chopped dill pickle or pickle relish to the meat mixture; spoon into tart shells. Press a tiny cube of Cheddar cheese into meat in each before baking.

Note—For a big party, bake only one panful at a time to keep them coming piping-hot. And for variety, top with different garnishes. A few suggestions: Thin slices of pitted ripe olives, cherry tomatoes, or water chestnuts (from a 5-ounce can); tiny mounds of hard-cooked egg yolk put through a fine sieve; sprigs of parsley or fresh dill weed.

RELISH MEAT BALLS

Makes 4 dozen

1 pound ground beef
½ cup chopped walnuts
1 tablespoon lemon juice
1 teaspoon salt
⅛ teaspoon pepper
1 egg
½ cup soft bread crumbs (1 slice)
2 tablespoons salad oil
1 can (1 pound) jellied cranberry sauce
¼ cup bottled steak sauce
2 tablespoons brown sugar

1. Mix ground beef lightly with walnuts, lemon juice, salt, pepper, egg, and bread crumbs; shape into 48 small balls.
2. Brown, part at a time, in salad oil, then return all meat to pan. Beat cranberry sauce with steak sauce and brown sugar; pour over meat balls; cover.
3. Simmer, stirring often, 10 minutes, or until meat balls are cooked through.

Note—Meat balls may be browned ahead, if you wish, then chilled. Just before serving, top with cranberry-sauce mixture and simmer. For flavor variety another time, use half each ground beef and veal.

BURGER BITES

Bake at 375° for 12 to 15 minutes.
Makes 5 dozen

1 package (3 or 4 ounces) cream cheese
   with chives
1 tablespoon bottled hamburger relish
1 teaspoon Worcestershire sauce
½ teaspoon salt
¼ teaspoon garlic salt
½ pound ground beef
2 packages refrigerated plain or buttermilk
   biscuits

1. Blend cheese with hamburger relish, Worcestershire sauce, salt, and garlic salt; stir in ground beef to make a soft mixture. Shape into 60 tiny balls.
2. Roll each biscuit to a 3-inch round; cut each into 3 strips. Place a meat ball on each strip; fold ends, overlapping, over meat; moisten with water and press to seal. Place, seam side down, in a large shallow baking pan.
3. Bake in moderate oven (375°) 12 to 15 minutes, or until golden-brown. Serve hot.

Note—If you wish, prepare filled rolls several hours ahead and chill in their baking pan, then bake just before serving.

PIQUANT PATTY-BALLS

Bake at 425° for 15 minutes.
Makes 4 dozen

¼ pound liverwurst
1 pound ground beef
½ cup soft bread crumbs (1 slice)
1 egg
½ cup milk
1 teaspoon salt
⅛ teaspoon pepper
24 small stuffed olives, halved
3 tablespoons butter or margarine

1. Mash liverwurst; mix in ground beef, bread crumbs, egg, milk, salt, and pepper lightly until well-blended; shape around olive halves to make 48 balls.
2. Melt butter or margarine in a large shallow baking pan; add meat balls, tossing lightly to give them a buttery coating.
3. Bake in hot oven (425°), turning once, 15 minutes, or until crispy brown. Serve hot.

Note—If you wish, mix and shape meat balls several hours ahead and chill, then bake just before serving.

DANISH APPETEASERS

Makes 4 dozen

1 pound meat-loaf mixture (ground beef
   and pork)
1 small onion, grated
½ cup fine dry bread crumbs
2 eggs
½ cup milk
1 teaspoon salt
¼ teaspoon pepper
⅛ teaspoon nutmeg
⅛ teaspoon marjoram
3 tablespoons shortening
1 can condensed consomme
2 tablespoons flour
¼ cup cold water
2 tablespoons pickle relish

1. Mix meat-loaf mixture lightly with onion, bread crumbs, eggs, milk, and seasonings until well-blended; shape into 48 balls.
2. Brown, half at a time, in shortening in a large frying pan; drain off all drippings. Return all meat to pan; stir in consomme; cover.
3. Simmer, stirring often, 15 minutes, or until meat balls are cooked through. Remove with a slotted spoon; keep hot while making sauce.
4. Pour all liquid into a 1-cup measure; add water, if needed, to make 1 cup. Return to pan; heat to boiling. Stir flour into cold water, then into hot liquid. Cook, stirring constantly, until sauce thickens and boils 1 minute; stir in pickle relish.
5. Pile meat balls into a chafing dish or heated serving bowl; pour hot sauce over.

Note—These appetizer meat balls may be made ahead, if you wish, and chilled. At serving time, reheat slowly in their sauce.

Cooksaver tip:

Some of the recipes in this appetizer group call for their own sauce-gravy; others are served plain. If you would like to add your own dip choice, set out small bowls of bottled cocktail sauce or savory sauce, or make your own Horseradish-almond Sauce, Javanese Peanut Sauce, or, for an extra-special treat, gourmet-fancy Mock Bearnaise Sauce *(all recipes on pages 128-129)*

Easy-to-make, good-to-eat vegetable trims

Radish pompon

Slice a trimmed radish one way, then crosswise, almost through to stem. Chill in ice and water until opened into a puffy flowerlike ball

Pickle fan

Slice small pickles into 5 or 6 strips, starting at tip end and cutting almost to stem. Spread slices to form open fans

Cucumber accordion

Cut 3-inch lengths of split pared cucumber; slice thin almost to flat side. Poke thin radish slices into cuts

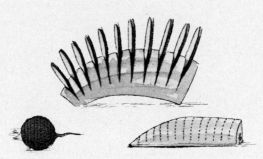

Fancy capers with carrots

In making carrot curls, your vegetable parer is your handiest helper. Just shave paper-thin strips from a pared carrot, roll them up, fasten with wooden picks, and chill in a bowl of ice and water. Or for zigzags, thread the strips, accordion style, onto picks. Want a pretty posy for the center of a sandwich tray? Trim strips to an about-5-inch length, rounding ends slightly, and thread 7 or 8 through the middle onto a pick. Spread ends, flower-petal fashion, and, as before, chill until curled

Lemon cartwheel

How easy it is to fix this pretty! Just cut small notches all around the rim of lemon slices with a knife or scissors

Celery flute

Slit 2-inch lengths of celery into narrow strips, cutting from ends toward the middle. Chill in ice and water until strips curl

Onion ruffle

Trim root and tip from a green onion, then shred the top down about three inches. Place in a bowl of ice and water to curl

Olive dumbbell and bundle

So simple! Just place a pitted ripe olive on each end of a thick carrot stick, or thread several sticks through the olive

Turn hard-cooked eggs into flower fancies

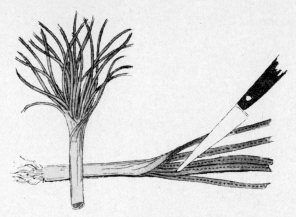

Fun to "grow," they add a bright note to a casserole after baking. To fix these, overlap slices around an olive; or cut wedges for petals and arrange with parsley between. For a "tulip" cup, make saw-tooth cuts around middle of egg; separate. Sieve yolk, mix with mayonnaise, and refill whites

Flavor secrets of this delicious East-West Sukiyaki *(recipe on page 147)* are light handling, short cooking, and a generous dash of soy sauce. Orientals use chopsticks to toss the meat and vegetables just until vegetables are crisply tender

PATE BURGERS

Makes about 6 dozen

    1 pound ground beef
    1 small onion, grated
    1 teaspoon salt
    ⅛ teaspoon pepper
    ¼ cup flour
    ½ cup milk
    ½ cup cream for whipping
       Salad oil
       Bottled cocktail sauce

1. Mix ground beef with onion, salt, pepper, and flour in the large bowl of an electric mixer. Beat until blended, then beat in milk and cream, a tablespoon at a time, until mixture is smooth and pastelike. Cover and chill well. (Two to three hours is best.)
2. Drop meat mixture, a teaspoonful at a time, into hot salad oil in a large frying pan, adding more salad oil, as needed. Cook quickly just until brown; drain on paper toweling.
3. Spear with wooden picks; serve hot with cocktail sauce.

Note—Brown burgers just before serving time; place in a large shallow baking pan; cover loosely with foil and keep hot in slow oven (325°).

BANANA-BURGER WRAPUPS

Bake at 425° for 15 minutes.
Makes 4 dozen

    1½ pounds ground beef
    ½   teaspoon grated lemon rind
    1   tablespoon lemon juice
    1   teaspoon salt
    ⅛   teaspoon nutmeg
        Dash of cayenne
    2   large bananas
    24 slices bacon, halved (1 pound)

1. Mix ground beef lightly with lemon rind and juice, salt, nutmeg, and cayenne until well-blended.
2. Peel bananas; halve lengthwise, then cut each half into 12 slices.
3. Shape meat mixture around each banana slice to make 48 balls. Wrap a half slice of bacon around each; fasten with a moistened wooden pick. Place balls on a rack in a large shallow baking pan.
4. Bake in hot oven (425°) 15 minutes, or until bacon is crisp. Serve hot.

Note—If you wish, prepare meat balls several hours ahead and chill on rack in baking pan, then bake just before serving.

CAPER MEAT BALLS

Makes 6 dozen

    1   pound ground beef
    1   pound ground pork
    2   eggs
    1   cup soft bread crumbs (2 slices)
    1   medium-size onion, grated
    1½   teaspoons salt
    ⅛   teaspoon pepper
    1   bottle capers, drained (⅓ cup)
    ¼   cup flour
    2   tablespoons salad oil
    1   can condensed beef broth
    ¼   cup water
    1   tablespoon lemon juice

1. Mix ground beef and pork lightly with eggs, bread crumbs, onion, salt, pepper, and half of the capers until well-blended; shape into 72 balls; roll each in flour to coat well.
2. Brown, a third at a time, in salad oil in a large frying pan; pour off all drippings. Return meat balls to pan; stir in beef broth, water, and lemon juice; cover.
3. Simmer, stirring often, 15 minutes, or until meat balls are cooked through. Stir in remaining capers.

Note—These appetizer meat balls may be made ahead, if you wish, and chilled. At serving time, reheat slowly in their sauce.

Cooksaver tip:

It's fun to make colorful, good-to-eat kebabs to decorate party foods. Just spear small or cut raw vegetables, pickles, or olives onto plain or fancy picks. Here we chose a pickled pepper, cherry tomato, and cucumber slice

MEAT-BALL MINIATURES

Makes 25 servings

- 2 pounds ground beef
- 2 pounds ground veal
- ½ cup flour
- ½ teaspoon ground ginger
- 1 cup light or table cream
- ¼ cup soy sauce
- 4 tablespoons (½ stick) butter or margarine
  Ginger Soy Sauce (recipe follows)
- 2 medium-size green peppers
- 1 can (5 ounces) water chestnuts

1. Mix ground beef and veal with flour and ginger in the large bowl of an electric mixer. Beat until blended, then beat in cream and soy sauce, 1 tablespoon at a time, until mixture is smooth and pastelike.
2. Divide meat mixture into quarters; shape each into about 45 marble-size balls. (Recipe will make as many as 180 balls.)
3. Saute, a single layer at a time, in part of the butter or margarine until browned and cooked through in a large frying pan. Keep hot while cooking remaining meat balls and making GINGER SOY SAUCE.
4. Quarter green peppers; remove seeds; cut peppers in small cubes. Drain water chestnuts; cut in thin slices.
5. Pour GINGER SOY SAUCE into a chafing dish or keep-hot server. Spoon meat balls on top; tuck in green peppers and water chestnuts. Serve with wooden picks for spearing meat balls.

GINGER SOY SAUCE—After all meat balls are cooked, tip pan so fat will rise to top; pour off all fat, leaving brown drippings in pan. Measure ¼ cup fat and return to pan; blend in ¼ cup flour and ¼ teaspoon ground ginger; cook, stirring constantly, just until bubbly. Stir in 2 cups water and 3 tablespoons soy sauce; continue cooking and stirring, scraping baked-on bits from bottom and side of pan, until sauce thickens and boils 1 minute. Makes about 2 cups.

Note—Meat balls can be shaped ahead and chilled until about an hour before partytime, then use two or three frying pans to speed cooking. To keep them hot for serving, spoon into a large shallow baking pan; cover lightly with foil and place in a very slow oven (250°).

GLAZED PATE LOAF

Bake at 350° for 1½ hours.
Makes 12 servings

- 1 pound ground beef
- ⅓ cup flour
- 1 teaspoon seasoned salt
- ¼ teaspoon seasoned pepper
- 1 envelope unflavored gelatin
- 1 can condensed beef broth
- 1 can (4½ ounces) deviled ham
- ½ cup chopped walnuts
- ½ cup chopped ripe olives
- 2 tablespoons grated onion
- 2 tablespoons prepared mustard
- ¼ cup water
- 2 tablespoons lemon juice
- 1 pimiento
- 4 whole pitted ripe olives

1. Combine ground beef, flour, seasoned salt and pepper in the large bowl of an electric mixer; beat until very smooth.
2. Soften gelatin in beef broth in a 2-cup measure. Measure out ⅔ cup and beat, 1 tablespoon at a time, into meat mixture until smooth and pastelike. Set remaining broth-gelatin mixture aside.
3. Blend deviled ham, walnuts, chopped ripe olives, onion, and mustard into beef mixture. Pack into a loaf pan, 8x4x2. Cover pan with a double thickness of foil.
4. Set in a shallow baking pan; place on oven shelf; pour boiling water into pan to a depth of about 1 inch.
5. Bake in moderate oven (350°) 1½ hours, or until no red juices bubble up. Remove at once from pan of water.
6. Uncover; let meat cool in pan about 2 hours, or until all juices are absorbed. Unmold and chill.
7. Stir water and lemon juice into remaining broth-gelatin mixture in a small saucepan; heat, stirring constantly, just until gelatin dissolves. Remove from heat. Chill until as thick as unbeaten egg white.
8. Cut pimiento into thin strips; cut whole ripe olives into thin wedges; arrange each, alternately, in rows across top of loaf. Spoon broth-gelatin mixture over carefully to cover completely; brush remaining around sides. Chill several hours, or until glaze is firm. (Overnight is best.)
9. Place loaf on a serving plate; cut into thin slices. Serve with your favorite crisp crackers.

Note—Pâté can be served warm without glaze, if you wish. For a garnish, top with sauteed mushroom caps.

Delight the family with these specials

PASTA E FAGIOLI

Makes 8 servings

½ pound pork sausage links
1½ pounds ground beef
½ teaspoon seasoned salt
¼ teaspoon seasoned pepper
¼ teaspoon oregano
¼ teaspoon basil
1 envelope onion-soup mix
6 cups boiling water
1 can (8 ounces) tomato sauce
1 cup sliced celery
1 can (12 or 16 ounces) whole-kernel corn
1 can (about 1 pound) red kidney beans
1 cup (about half an 8-ounce package) small macaroni shells

1. Brown sausages in a kettle or Dutch oven; remove; cut each in thirds and set aside. Pour off all drippings.
2. Shape ground beef into a large patty in kettle; brown 5 minutes on each side, then break up into chunks. Stir in seasonings, onion-soup mix, water, and tomato sauce; cover.
3. Simmer, stirring several times, 15 minutes. Stir in sausages, celery, corn and beans and liquids, and uncooked macaroni; cover.
4. Simmer, stirring several times, 20 minutes longer, or until macaroni is tender.
5. Ladle into heated soup bowls.

Cooksaver tip:

Perfect go-withs for this hearty main-course soup are a green salad and thick slices of crusty Italian bread or buttered, toasted, split hard rolls

DENVER PANCAKES

Makes 12 pancakes

½ pound ground beef
1 small onion, minced
2 tablespoons minced green pepper
2 tablespoons butter or margarine
1 can (8 ounces) cream-style corn
½ teaspoon salt
1 cup pancake mix
1 egg
1 cup milk

1. Mix ground beef lightly with onion and green pepper; shape into a large patty in a frying pan. Brown in butter or margarine 5 minutes on each side, then break up into small chunks. Remove from heat; stir in corn and salt.
2. Mix pancake mix, egg, and milk, following label directions; fold in meat mixture.
3. Drop by tablespoonfuls onto a hot greased griddle; bake, turning once, 5 minutes, or until well-browned.
4. Serve with catsup or chili sauce, if you wish.

HAMBURGER STROGONOFF

Makes 4 servings

1 large onion, chopped (1 cup)
1 tablespoon butter or margarine
1 pound ground beef
1 tablespoon flour
1 can (6 ounces) sliced mushrooms
2 tablespoons chili sauce
1 teaspoon salt
1 cup (8-ounce carton) dairy sour cream

1. Saute onion in butter or margarine until richly browned in a large frying pan; remove with a slotted spoon and set aside.
2. Shape ground beef into a large patty in same pan; brown 5 minutes on each side, then break up into chunks.
3. Sprinkle flour over meat and blend in, then stir in browned onion, mushrooms and liquid, chili sauce, and salt. Cook, stirring constantly and scraping brown bits from bottom of pan, until mixture thickens and boils 1 minute. Remove from heat.
4. Stir about ½ cup of the hot meat mixture into sour cream, then stir back into remaining mixture in pan. Heat over *very low* heat just until hot. (Do not let it boil, for sour cream may curdle.) Stir in a few drops of bottled gravy coloring to darken, if you wish.
5. Spoon over buttered toast, fluffy rice, mashed potatoes, or buttered noodles, if you wish.

TUREEN TREAT

Makes 4 servings

½ pound ground beef
2 medium-size onions, peeled and sliced
3 tablespoons salad oil
4 small zucchini, trimmed and sliced
    ¼ inch thick
1 teaspoon salt
¼ teaspoon garlic salt
⅛ teaspoon pepper
1 can condensed beef broth
1 soup can of water
4 slices French bread, toasted
¼ cup grated Parmesan cheese

1. Shape ground beef into a patty in a large saucepan; brown with onions in salad oil 5 minutes on each side, then break up into small chunks. Push to one side.
2. Add zucchini and saute, stirring lightly, 2 to 3 minutes. Stir in seasonings, beef broth, and water; cover.
3. Simmer 15 minutes, or just until zucchini is tender.
4. Place a toasted bread slice in each of 4 heated soup plates; top with soup; sprinkle with cheese.

WENATCHEE VALLEY BEEF BALLS

Makes 8 servings

2 pounds ground beef
2 teaspoons salt
¼ teaspoon pepper
1 large onion, chopped (1 cup)
1 clove garlic, minced
2 teaspoons curry powder
½ teaspoon ground allspice
1 jar (about 8 ounces) junior prunes
1 jar (about 8 ounces) junior apples-and-
    apricots
1 cup water
¼ cup lemon juice

1. Mix ground beef lightly with 1½ teaspoons of the salt and pepper; shape into 48 small balls.
2. Brown, half at a time, in a large frying pan; remove and set aside.
3. Stir onion, garlic, curry powder, allspice, and remaining ½ teaspoon salt into drippings in pan; saute, stirring often, until onion is soft.
4. Stir in fruits, water, and lemon juice; heat to boiling; return meat balls to pan; cover.
5. Simmer, stirring once or twice, 30 minutes, or until sauce thickens slightly.

YORKSHIRE BEEF BAKE

Bake at 375° for 1 hour.
Makes 6 servings

1½ pounds ground beef
 ½ cup unsalted cracker crumbs
 1 tall can evaporated milk
 2 teaspoons salt
 ¼ teaspoon pepper
 2 tablespoons butter or margarine
 3 eggs
 1 cup sifted regular flour
 1 teaspoon mixed salad herbs
 1 cup milk
   Cream Gravy (*recipe follows*)

1. Mix ground beef lightly with cracker crumbs, ½ cup of the evaporated milk, 1½ teaspoons of the salt, and pepper until well-blended; shape into 30 small balls. (Set remaining evaporated milk aside for gravy and salt for popover batter.)
2. Brown meat balls in butter or margarine in a large frying pan; keep hot.
3. Place a shallow 8-cup baking dish in oven to heat while making batter. Beat eggs slightly in a medium-size bowl; add flour, salad herbs, remaining ½ teaspoon salt, and milk. Beat briskly ½ minute; scrape down side of bowl; beat 1½ minutes longer.
4. Place browned meat balls in heated baking dish; pour batter over top.
5. Bake in moderate oven (375°) 1 hour, or until batter is puffed and golden-brown. Serve with CREAM GRAVY.

CREAM GRAVY—Pour all fat from frying pan, leaving brown drippings in pan; measure 4 tablespoonfuls fat and return to pan. Blend in 4 tablespoons flour and 1 teaspoon salt; cook, stirring constantly, just until bubbly. Stir in remaining evaporated milk and 1 cup water; continue cooking and stirring, scraping cooked-on juices from bottom and side of pan, until gravy thickens and boils 1 minute. Stir in a little gravy coloring to darken, if you wish. Makes about 2 cups.

Cooksaver tip:

For the best results and to prevent spillovers in your oven, be sure to use the exact-size baking dish suggested in your recipe. Yorkshire Beef Bake also calls for a shallow dish so the popover batter will puff up around the meat balls

CHEESE-BISCUIT PIE

Bake at 350° for 45 minutes, then at
425° for 12 minutes.
Makes 8 servings

2 pounds ground beef
1 egg
2 teaspoons salt
1/8 teaspoon pepper
1/2 cup milk
2 tablespoons salad oil
6 tablespoons flour
3 cups water
1 envelope instant beef broth
  OR: 1 beef-flavor bouillon cube
1 bay leaf
8 small white onions, peeled
2 cups cubed pared potatoes
1 package (9 ounces) frozen Italian
  green beans, slightly thawed
  Cheese Biscuits (recipe follows)

1. Mix ground beef lightly with egg, 1 teaspoon
of the salt, pepper, and milk until well-blended;
shape into 24 balls.
2. Brown in salad oil in a large frying pan; place
in a shallow baking dish, 13x9x2.
3. Pour all drippings from pan, then measure 6
tablespoonfuls and return to pan. (Add more
salad oil, if needed, to make this measure.) Blend
in flour, then stir in water, instant beef broth or
bouillon cube, bay leaf, and remaining 1 teaspoon salt. Cook, stirring constantly and crushing
bouillon cube, if using, with a spoon, until gravy
thickens and boils 1 minute.
4. Combine onions, potatoes, and green beans with
meat balls in baking dish; pour hot gravy over;
cover.
5. Bake in moderate oven (350°) 45 minutes; raise
heat to hot (425°).
6. While meat mixture cooks, make CHEESE BIS-
CUITS; arrange on top of meat and vegetables in
dish.
7. Bake in hot oven (425°) 12 minutes, or until
biscuits are puffed and golden.
CHEESE BISCUITS—Sift 3 cups sifted regular flour,
4 1/2 teaspoons baking powder, 1 1/2 teaspoons sugar,
and 3/4 teaspoon salt into a large bowl; stir in 3/4
cup grated Cheddar cheese. Cut in 3 tablespoons
shortening with a pastry blender until mixture is
crumbly; add 1 cup milk all at once; stir just until
mixture is moist. Turn dough out onto a lightly
floured pastry cloth or board. Pat out to a rectangle
about 1 inch thick; cut into rounds with a 2-inch
cutter. Makes about 16 biscuits.

POLENTA-CHILI BAKE

Bake at 400° for 40 minutes.
Makes 6 servings

1 cup yellow corn meal
1/2 pound sweet Italian sausages
1/2 pound ground beef
1 medium-size onion, chopped (1/2 cup)
1/2 medium-size green pepper, chopped
1 envelope spaghetti-sauce mix without
  tomato
2 teaspoons chili powder
1 can (about 1 pound) tomatoes
1 can (7 ounces) pitted ripe olives,
  drained and halved
3/4 cup grated Cheddar cheese

1. Stir corn meal slowly into 4 cups boiling water;
cook until thick; about 30 minutes. Spread about
half in an even layer in a greased shallow 8-cup
baking dish. Pour remaining into a greased pan,
9x5x3; chill layer in pan.
2. Peel casings from sausages; mix meat with
ground beef; shape into a large patty in a frying
pan. Brown 5 minutes on each side, then break
up into chunks; push to one side.
3. Stir onion and green pepper into drippings in
pan; saute just until onion is soft. Stir in spaghetti-sauce mix, chili powder, and tomatoes;
heat, stirring constantly, to boiling; remove from
heat.
4. Set aside 12 olive halves for garnish, then stir
remaining with 1/4 cup of the cheese into hot
sauce; pour over corn-meal layer in baking dish.
5. Remove chilled corn-meal layer from pan by
turning upside down onto a cutting board; cut
into 6 even-size pieces, then halve each diagonally
to make 12 wedges. Arrange on top of meat mixture in baking dish; sprinkle with remaining 1/2
cup cheese.
6. Bake in hot oven (400°) 40 minutes, or until
bubbly hot. Garnish with remaining olive halves.

Cooksaver tip:

Looking for a make-ahead dish?
Polenta-chili Bake is a fine choice.
Put everything together in its baker
and chill. When ready to bake, place
dish in a cold oven, set heat regulator
to hot (400°), and bake as above,
allowing 10 minutes' extra cooking time

MEAT-LOAF ROLLUPS

Bake at 425° for 50 minutes.
Makes 8 servings

2 pounds ground beef
1 can condensed cream of celery soup
1 cup grated pared raw carrots (about 3 medium-size)
1 small onion, grated
1 egg
1 teaspoon salt
½ teaspoon Italian seasoning
¼ teaspoon pepper
1 package piecrust mix
   Milk Pan Gravy (recipe follows)

1. Mix ground beef lightly with soup, carrots, onion, egg, salt, Italian seasoning, and pepper until well-blended.
2. Prepare piecrust mix, following label directions, or make pastry from your own favorite two-crust recipe. Roll out, half at a time, to a 12-inch square; cut each into quarters.
3. Divide meat mixture into eighths and spoon onto middle of each square, then shape each into a small loaf. Fold pastry up over meat; pinch edges to seal, but leave ends open. Place on a rack in a shallow baking pan.
4. Bake in hot oven (425°) 50 minutes, or until pastry is golden. Remove loaves to a heated serving platter; keep hot while making MILK PAN GRAVY.
MILK PAN GRAVY—Remove rack from baking pan. Measure fat in pan and add butter or margarine, if needed, to make 4 tablespoons; return to pan. Blend in 4 tablespoons flour; cook, stirring constantly, just until bubbly. Stir in 1 cup water and 1 cup milk; continue cooking and stirring, scraping baked-on juices from bottom of pan, until gravy thickens and boils 1 minute. Season to taste with salt and pepper. Makes 2 cups.

Cooksaver tip:

If water chestnuts are new to you, do try this Oriental treat. Packed in 5-ounce cans, each marble-size chestnut is snowy and crisp with a celerylike flavor. Slice or chop them to add to meat balls, as called for in the recipe at right, or stir into hamburgers or their sauce or gravy toppers. After the can has been opened, cover any leftover nuts with cold water and keep chilled

HAMBURGER JUMBLE

Bake at 350° for 40 minutes.
Makes 6 servings

1 pound ground beef
2 cups uncooked regular noodles
1 can (about 1 pound) tomatoes
2 cups shredded cabbage
1 cup sliced pared raw carrots
1 can condensed cream of celery soup
1 cup water
1 teaspoon instant minced onion
½ teaspoon salt

1. Shape ground beef into a large patty in a large frying pan; brown 5 minutes on each side, then break up into small chunks.
2. Stir in remaining ingredients; spoon into an 8-cup baking dish; cover.
3. Bake in moderate oven (350°) 40 minutes, or until noodles and vegetables are tender.

GLAZED POLYNESIAN MEAT BALLS

Makes 4 servings

1 pound ground beef
1 cup soft bread crumbs (2 slices)
1 egg
½ cup chopped water chestnuts (from a 5-ounce can)
½ cup water (for meat balls)
2 tablespoons prepared horseradish
½ teaspoon salt
¼ cup flour
2 tablespoons peanut oil or salad oil
¾ cup orange marmalade
¼ cup cream-style peanut butter
1 clove garlic, minced
3 tablespoons soy sauce
2 tablespoons lemon juice
3 tablespoons water (for sauce)

1. Mix ground beef lightly with bread crumbs, egg, water chestnuts, the ½ cup water, horseradish, and salt until well-blended; shape into 24 balls; roll in flour to coat well.
2. Brown in peanut oil or salad oil in a large frying pan; pour off all drippings.
3. While meat balls brown, combine orange marmalade, peanut butter, garlic, soy sauce, lemon juice, and 3 tablespoons water; beat until well-blended; stir into frying pan.
4. Heat, stirring constantly, over low heat 2 to 3 minutes, or until sauce is bubbly and meat balls are richly glazed.

COLCANNON

Bake at 350° for 45 minutes.
Makes 8 servings

 4 or 5 large potatoes, pared and quartered
 1 medium-size yellow turnip, pared and
        cubed
 6 tablespoons (¾ stick) butter or
        margarine
    Salt and pepper
 1 tablespoon brown sugar
    Dash of nutmeg
 2 slices bacon, cut in 1-inch pieces
 1 pound ground beef
 ½ pound ground pork
 1 medium-size onion, chopped (½ cup)
 1 envelope brown gravy mix
 1 small head cabbage, shredded

1. Cook potatoes and turnip in boiling salted water in separate medium-size saucepans 15 minutes, or just until tender; drain well.
2. Mash potatoes with 2 tablespoons of the butter or margarine; season with salt and pepper. (There should be about 5 cups.) Mash turnip with 2 tablespoons of the butter or margarine, brown sugar, and nutmeg. (There should be about 3 cups.) Set both aside.
3. Saute bacon until crisp in a large frying pan; remove with a slotted spoon and set aside.
4. Mix ground beef and pork; shape into a large patty in same pan; brown 5 minutes on each side, then break up into chunks; push to one side.
5. Stir onion into pan and saute just until soft; stir into meat mixture.
6. Prepare brown gravy mix, following label directions; stir into meat mixture.
7. Spread mashed potatoes evenly over bottom and sides of a buttered shallow 8-cup baking dish to make a shell; spread mashed turnips next to potatoes to make a double shell; spoon meat mixture into center.
8. Bake in moderate oven (350°) 45 minutes, or until bubbly hot.
9. While meat bakes, cook cabbage in a small amount of boiling salted water 10 minutes, or just until tender; drain well. Toss with remaining 2 tablespoons butter or margarine. Spread over hot meat and vegetables in baking dish; sprinkle with crisp bacon.

BEEF PATTIES FRICASSEE

Bake at 425° for 30 minutes.
Makes 8 servings

 1 medium-size onion, chopped (½ cup)
 4 tablespoons (½ stick) butter or
        margarine
 2 pounds ground beef
 1 egg
 ¼ cup chopped parsley
 ½ cup soft bread crumbs (1 slice)
 1 teaspoon salt
 1 package (10 ounces) frozen peas,
        partly thawed
 1 can condensed cream of celery soup
 1 can (about 8 ounces) cream-style corn
 ½ cup milk
 1 cup (8-ounce carton) dairy sour cream
    Herb Biscuits (recipe follows)

1. Saute onion in 2 tablespoons of the butter or margarine just until soft in a large frying pan; mix lightly with ground beef, egg, parsley, bread crumbs, and salt until well-blended. Shape into 24 balls, then flatten.
2. Saute in remaining 2 tablespoons butter or margarine 2 minutes on each side, or just until brown. Place in a single layer in a shallow baking dish, 13x9x2; sprinkle with peas.
3. Stir soup, corn, and milk into drippings in frying pan; heat, stirring constantly and scraping browned bits from bottom of pan, just to boiling. Stir about ½ cup hot sauce into sour cream, then stir back into remaining sauce in pan; pour over meat and peas in baking dish.
4. Bake in hot oven (425°) 15 minutes.
5. While meat mixture cooks, make HERB BISCUITS; arrange on top of hot meat mixture.
6. Bake 15 minutes longer, or until biscuits are golden-brown.
HERB BISCUITS—Combine 2 cups biscuit mix and 2 teaspoons mixed salad herbs in a medium-size bowl; add ⅔ cup milk all at once; stir with a fork until evenly moist. Drop by tablespoonfuls into 3 tablespoons melted butter or margarine in a pie plate; roll to coat all over, then roll in 1 cup soft bread crumbs (2 slices). Makes 8 biscuits.

Cooksaver tip:

Most frozen whole vegetables break up easily if you tap the package firmly on the counter top, so there's no need to thaw them before adding to a top-of-the-range or casserole dish

INDEX OF RECIPES AND HOW-TO'S